Habermas and Modernity

Edited with an Introduction by
Richard J. Bernstein

The MIT Press
Cambridge, Massachusetts

First MIT Press edition, 1985

Library of Congress Cataloging in Publication Data

Habermas and modernity.

   (Studies in contemporary German social thought)
   "All the essays . . . were published in Praxis
international"—Acknowledgments.
   Bibliography: p.
   Includes index.
   1. Habermas, Jürgen—Addresses, essays, lectures.
I. Bernstein, Richard J.   II. Praxis international.
III. Series.
B3258.H324H3 1985   193   85-7227
ISBN 0-262-02227-3
ISBN 0-262-52102-4 pbk

Typeset by DMB (Typesetting), Oxford
Printed in Great Britain by Billing and Sons Ltd, Worcester

To Our Yugoslav Praxis Colleagues

Contents

Acknowledgements

All the essays in this volume were published in *Praxis International*. Habermas's talk, "Psychic Thermidor and the Rebirth of Rebellious Subjectivity" was originally published in the *Berkeley Journal of Sociology*, 1980. The English translation of Habermas's essay, "Neoconservative Culture Criticism in the United States and West Germany: An Intellectual Movement in Two Political Cultures" first appeared in *Telos*, 56 (1983). It was translated by Russell A. Berman. The essays by Martin Jay, Joel Whitebook, Richard Rorty, and Thomas McCarthy appeared in a symposium on Habermas in Volume 4 of *Praxis International*. Habermas's reply to these four critics, "Questions and Counterquestions" also appeared in Volume 4 of *Praxis International*. James Bohman translated Habermas's "Questions and Counterquestions." I want to thank Julie Herman who edited the manuscript and Shirley Averill who typed the Introduction.

Richard J. Bernstein

Introduction

RICHARD J. BERNSTEIN

I

In 1969 George Lichtheim, one of the most perceptive commentators on European cultural life, wrote the following about Jürgen Habermas:

> It is not altogether easy to assess the work of a scholar whose professional competence extends from the logic of science to the sociology of knowledge, by way of Marx, Hegel and the more recondite sources of the European metaphysical tradition . . . [At] an age when most of his colleagues have painfully established control over one corner of the field, he has made himself master of the whole, in depth and breadth alike. There is no corner-cutting, no facile evasion of difficulties or spurious enunciation of conclusions unsupported by research: whether he is refuting Popper, dissecting the pragmatism of Charles Peirce, delving into the medieval antecedents of Schelling's metaphysics, or bringing Marxist sociology up to date, there is always the same uncanny mastery of the sources, joined to an enviable talent for clarifying intricate logical puzzles. He seems to have been born with a faculty for digesting the toughest kind of material and then refashioning it into orderly wholes.[1]

Habermas, who was then forty years of age, was already recognized as a leading younger social theorist in postwar Germany. To appreciate the thrust of Habermas's intellectual project – even in its most theoretical dimensions – one needs to recollect and recover the situation and mood of young German intellectuals during the period immediately following the collapse of Nazi Germany. Habermas, a teenager when the Second World War ended, was shocked by the discovery of the horrors of the Nazi regime. This experience has had a lasting effect on him and has always been central for his work.

> At the age of 15 or 16, I sat before the radio and experienced what was being discussed before the Nuremberg Tribunal; when others, instead of being struck silent by the ghastliness, began to dispute the justice of the trial, procedural questions, and questions of jurisdiction, there was that first rupture, which still gapes. Certainly it is only because I was still sensitive and easily offended that I did not close myself to the fact of a collectively realized inhumanity in the same measure as the majority of my elders.[2]

"Rupture" and a break with the immediate past were the primary disorienting experiences of Habermas during his student days. How could one explain why a culture that had given rise to the tradition of Kant through to Marx – where the themes of critical emancipatory reason and the concrete realization of freedom were so dominant – provided such fertile soil for the rise of Hitler and the Nazis? Why hadn't Germans resisted this monstrous pathology more forcefully? Habermas became increasingly concerned with rethinking and appropriating the tradition of German thought that was left in shambles. Reason, freedom, and justice were not only theoretical issues to be explored, but practical tasks to be achieved – practical tasks that demanded passionate commitment.

Habermas tells us that as a student he lived "theoretically" in the 1920s. He read Lukács's *History and Class Consciousness* "both with fascination and regret that it belonged to the past."[3] His studies led him back to Marx, the young Hegelians, Hegel, Schelling, Fichte, and Kant. It is as if the trauma of the Nazi period required a reimmersion in the German classics of the nineteenth and early twentieth centuries in order to reestablish a thread of continuity – in order to secure a grounding and orientation.

Even before Habermas became fully aware of the Critical Theory of the 1930s (written in exile from Europe) he was recreating the experience and pathways followed by Horkheimer, Adorno, Marcuse – and other members of "the Frankfurt School." Recalling these intellectually formative years, Habermas has written: "In retrospect, I sometimes have the impression that a student can recreate a segment of the critical theory of the 1930s, if he systematically works his way from Kant through Hegel, including Schelling, and then approaches Marx via Lukács."[4]

The sense of rupture that Habermas experienced as a student had further dramatic consequences. It opened him to a serious encounter with other intellectual traditions and movements. The insularity, even the provincialism, of German cultural life was broken. Haber- mas was deeply influenced by the American pragmatic thinkers, especially Peirce, Mead, and Dewey. He felt a strong affinity with the pragmatists' vision and understanding of radical participatory democracy. In the centrality of the idea of a fallibilistic critical community, and in the probing of the dynamics of intersubjectivity, he discovered the kernal of what he was to later call "communicative action"– action oriented to mutual understanding. Later he avidly read the writings of analytic philosophers, including Wittgenstein, J. L. Austin, and John Searle. No field of inquiry that was relevant to the reconstruction of social theory was beyond his grasp – including the "new" linguistics stimulated by the contributions of Chomsky and the theories of psychological and moral development elaborated by Freud, Piaget, and Kohlberg. And always, as Lichtheim notes, he exhibited an uncanny ability "for digesting the toughest kind of material and then refashioning it into orderly wholes."

He sought not only to learn from the major trends of contem- porary philosophy, but to grapple with the sociological tradition and the different areas of sociology and social science. He has returned again and again to a critical encounter with Marx, Weber, Durkheim, Mead, and Parsons. He has explored the intricacies of structural-functionalism, systems theory, ethnomethodology, as well as the varieties of hermeneutical and phenomenological social science.

The most striking and impressive feature of Habermas's approach to the range and complexities of human inquiry is the way in which he weaves whatever he analyzes into a coherent whole. There is a unity of vision that informs his work. A systematic impulse is evi- dent in his earliest writings. Through the various pathways he has followed, he has sought to develop a powerful, comprehensive, critical understanding of social and cultural modernity, which clarifies our history, present horizon, and future prospects.

A significant impetus to Habermas's development was the return of the Institute for Social Research to Frankfurt after the Second World War. Here was a tangible connection with the very tradition that so excited the imagination of Habermas. Even before Haber- mas became an assistant to Adorno in 1956 – a mentor who had the profoundest influence on Habermas (despite or even because of his sharp temperamental and intellectual differences with Adorno) – he had read Horkheimer's and Adorno's *Dialectic of Enlightenment*.

That gave me the courage to read Marx systematically and not simply historically. Critical Theory, a Frankfurt School – there was no such

thing at the time. Reading Adorno had given me the courage to take
up systematically what Lukács and Korsch represented historically:
the theory of reification as a theory of rationalization, in Max
Weber's sense. Already at that time, my problem was a theory of
modernity, a theory of the pathology of modernity from the viewpoint of the realization – the deformed realization – of reason in
history.[5]

The above statement epitomizes the questions that are at the heart
of Habermas's intellectual project. A "theory of rationalization"
requires not only the elaboration of categories and concepts for
a systematic examination of the character and different modes of
rationality, but an explanation of how they are concretely
embodied in social and cultural life. Such a theory must be both
synchronic and diachronic. To speak of "the pathology of modernity" and "the deformed realization of reason in history" presupposes a normative standard for judging what is pathological and
deformed. Can we still, in our time, provide a rational justification
for universal normative standards? Or are we faced with relativism,
decisionism, or emotivism which hold that ultimate norms are arbitrary and beyond rational warrantability? These became primary
questions for Habermas. The fate – indeed, the very possibility, of
a critical theory of society with the practical intent of furthering
human emancipation – depends on giving an affirmative answer to
the first question and a negative answer to the second.

Although one can detect Habermas's systematic intent in his
earliest writings, this has become more focused and explicit in the
course of his development. In the preface to *Knowledge and
Human Interests* (published in 1968 and translated into English in
1971) Habermas announced:

I am undertaking a historically oriented attempt to reconstruct the
prehistory of modern positivism with the systematic intention of
analyzing the connections of knowledge and human interests. In
following the process of the dissolution of epistemology which has
left the philosophy of science in its place, one makes one's way over
abandoned stages of reflection. Retreading this path from a perspective that looks back towards the point of departure may help to
recover the forgotten experience of reflection. That we disavow
reflection *is* positivism.[6]

By 1968 the positivist tradition, which had its origins in the nineteenth century and was revitalized and refined by the logical positivists, was already under severe attack. But one cannot underestimate
the extent to which the positivistic *temper* pervaded and dominated

intellectual and cultural life. Habermas, in this context, is speaking of "positivism" in a broad encompassing manner. He wants to identify that tendency, to which many independent movements have contributed, that narrows and restricts the scope of rationality. Reason, from this perspective, can enable us scientifically to explain the natural and even the social world. It can discern nomological regularities, predict, and grasp the empirical consequences of different courses of action. It can evaluate rational decision procedures and assess the cost of competing means to achieve specified ends. But it is beyond the scope of reason to justify ends or warrant universal norms. If we accept this characterization of reason, then we disavow the type of critical reflection where, through a depth explanation and understanding of social processes, we can further human emancipation from hidden forms of domination and repression.

The stance that Habermas was challenging is most poignantly and even tragically represented by Max Weber. For all of Weber's rationalist proclivities, he despaired about the possibility of rationally grounding the ultimate norms that guide our lives; we must *choose* the "gods or demons" we *decide* to pursue. With the disenchantment of the world that results from the ineluctable processes of modernization which destroys the foundations of traditional world-views, we are left with a void. Weber bequeathed to us unresolved tensions and *aporias*. Habermas saw clearly that the logic of Weber's unstable resolutions leads to the relativism and decisionism so characteristic of our times. From Habermas's earliest to his most recent writings, this is the very tendency that he has combatted.

The primary issue here is not merely philosophical or theoretical. Weber's methodological skepticism is itself an echo and expression of his sociological analyses. Weber argued that the hope and expectation of the Enlightenment thinkers was a bitter and ironic illusion. They maintained a strong necessary linkage between the growth of science, rationality, and universal human freedom. But when unmasked and understood, the legacy of the Enlightenment was the triumph of *Zweckrationalität* – purposive – instrumental rationality. This form of rationality affects and infects the entire range of social and cultural life encompassing economic structures, law, bureaucratic administration, and even the arts. The growth of *Zweckrationalität* does not lead to the concrete realization of universal freedom but to the creation of an "iron cage" of bureaucratic rationality from which there is no escape. Weber's chilling and sobering warning still hovers over us and may well be the epigraph of modernity.

No one knows who will live in this cage in the future, or whether at the end of this tremendous development entirely new prophets will arise, or there will be a great rebirth of old ideas and ideals, or if neither, mechanized petrification, embellished with a sort of convulsive self-importance. For of the last stage of this cultural development, it might well be truly said: "Specialists without spirit, sensualists without heart; this nullity imagines that it has attained a level of civilization never before achieved."[7]

Ironically, for all the explicit opposition to Weber's thesis about the triumph of *Zweckrationalität*, Lukács, Horkheimer, and Adorno not only appropriated and refined it, they generalized it. Weber's thesis was interwoven with Marx's analysis of alienation and with Lukács's Hegelian–Marxist theory of reification. The "hidden" logic of this form of rationalization is a logic of increased domination and repression. The domination of nature turns into the domination of human beings over other human beings, and ultimately into the nightmare of self-domination. There are still suggestions in Weber of other historical possibilities, other forms of rationalization processes. Weber never gives in to the temptation of believing that there is a historical *necessity*, but Horkheimer and Adorno, in their late writings, come remarkably close to maintaining such an historical inevitability. They argue that the seeds of the triumph of *Zweckrationalität* are already contained in the origins of western rationality – in what they called "identity logic." There is another irony here. Horkheimer, and especially Adorno, were steadfast opponents of Heidegger. Yet there is a striking affinity in their analyses of the fate of western rationality. There is a thin line that separates Horkheimer's and Adorno's analysis of instrumental rationality and Heidegger's analysis of calculative thinking, *Gestell* (Enframing) – "the essence of technology" which he takes to be the concealed essence of western metaphysics.

It was characteristic of the older generation of Frankfurt thinkers to oppose instrumental rationality with the idea of a dynamic emancipatory Reason that Hegel called *Vernunft* (even when they, and in particular, Adorno, were deconstructing this concept of Reason). But the appeal to *Vernunft*, to Reason dynamically actualizing itself through history, became less and less convincing in light of the catastrophic events of the twentieth century. Adorno, in his late writings, wavers between a despairing cultural pessimism where a critical theory with an emancipatory intent is no longer a real historical possibility, and a hope that there may still be a new aesthetics of reconciliation. Art appears as a "prefigurative cipher of redemption" – the last vestige of *Vernunft* in a thoroughly "rationalized" world.

Habermas was acutely aware of the ways in which the "conclusions" of Horkheimer and Adorno could be interpreted as deepening the Weberian thesis of the disenchantment of the world, the triumph of *Zweckrationalität*, and the portrait of the contemporary age as an iron cage. To resolve the *aporias* of the *Dialectic of Enlightenment*, to meet the challenge of Weber, to justify the possibility of a viable critical theory of society, nothing less was required than rethinking the question of rationality and rationalization processes.

There was another closely related feature of the older generation of Frankfurt thinkers that troubled Habermas. Critical Theory identified itself with the Marxist legacy. The very idea of critique as *via media* between philosophy and positivistic science was itself traced back to its Marxist origins. Marx had sought to forge a new dialectical synthesis of philosophy and the scientific understanding of society. This is manifest in his own progression from the critique of religion and philosophy to the critique of political economy and the specific scientific critique of nineteenth century capitalism. Marx's heritage was reaffirmed in the early days of the founding of the Frankfurt Institute for Social Research. The program of the Institute called for a new integration of theory and empirical scientific research. But the vicissitudes of Critical Theory from the 1920s through the 1960s moved in a direction which was very different from Marx's development. There was less and less concern with working out a substantive critique of political economy; and a turn to a more generalized critique of instrumental rationality – culminating in Adorno's "negative dialectics." In part this was due to a growing skepticism about the historical possibility of anything resembling the proletarian revolution that Marx envisioned; the rise of fascism; the resistance of twentieth-century capitalism to radical transformation; and the perversion of Marxism in the Soviet Union. From Habermas's perspective, the turn away from developing a critical *social science* to a "negative dialectics" threatened the explanatory–diagnostic function of Critical Theory. Critical Theory had distinguished itself from "traditional" social theory by virtue of its ability to specify those real potentialities in a concrete historical situation which could further the processes of human emancipation and overcome domination and repression. If this promise was to be fulfilled then one could not avoid the task of a scientific understanding of the dynamics of contemporary society. In this respect, Habermas clearly saw the need to return to the *spirit* of what Marx sought to achieve, a project which was reaffirmed in the early days of the Institute for Social Research. One had to root out, honestly and ruthlessly, the errors in the Marxist legacy and show why Marx's analysis of nineteenth-century capitalist societies was no longer adequate to explain twentieth-century industrial societies. For Horkheimer and Adorno – from their perspective of a generalized critique of instrumental rationality – the character and fate of the social sciences were part of the "problem" of modernity, not a way of "solving" this problem. But for Habermas, the task was to appropriate the most promising developments in the social sciences and integrate them into a critical social science. A Critical Theory without empirical content could too easily degenerate into an empty rhetorical gesture. There was a real danger that Critical Theory might "regress" to the type of "critical criticism" that Marx so ruthlessly attacked when he turned away from the young Hegelians to a more empirical account of political economy.

II

In *Knowledge and Human Interests* the outlines of Habermas's *first* systematic synthesis began to become clear. His major theses were succinctly summarized in the inaugural address he gave at Frankfurt University (published as an appendix to the book). He distinguished three non-reducible "quasi-transcendental" cognitive interests: the technical, the practical, and the emancipatory. These knowledge-constitutive interests served as the basis for three different forms of knowledge and three different types of discipline – each with its own distinctive methodological approach, object domain, and aims. Each of these cognitive interests is itself rooted in a dimension of human social existence: work, symbolic interaction, and power. "The approach to the empirical–analytic sciences incorporates a *technical* cognitive interest; that of the historical-hermeneutic sciences incorporates a *practical* one; and the approach of critically oriented sciences incorporates the *emancipatory* cognitive interest."[8]

By a technical cognitive interest, Habermas did *not* mean to suggest that the empirical–analytic sciences are to be understood as technical applied disciplines. Rather he stressed the *form* of these inquiries which require the isolation (constitution) of objects and events into dependent and independent variables, and the investigation of nomological regularities. This type of inquiry is based upon a model of negative feedback where prediction plays a central

role, and where there are established procedures for the confirmation and falsification of empirical hypotheses and theories. It is
because empirical–analytic science has this form that it lends itself
to powerful technical application. There is a sense in which the pursuit of such science can be pure and disinterested. But the character
of this disinterested pursuit of pure scientific research is itself determined by a "quasi-transcendental" technical cognitive interest.
This is the type of scientific knowledge that logical positivists,
logical empiricists, and philosophers of science in the analytic tradition were primarily interested in analyzing. Habermas was not
denigrating or criticizing this form of knowledge. His point is that it
is only *one* type of knowledge; it is not to be taken as the canonical
standard for all forms of knowledge. This is why Habermas challenged positivistically minded philosophers of science who explicitly or implicitly presupposed that the empirical–analytical sciences
provide *the* model for all legitimate knowledge, and dismissed all
other claims to knowledge as pseudo-knowledge. This is also why
Habermas was so sympathetic with philosophers (such as Gadamer)
and social scientists influenced by the hermeneutical tradition of
the *Geisteswissenschaften* who exposed the false "objectivism" and
"scientism" of those who claimed that the empirical–analytic
sciences are the proper measure and standard for all legitimate
scientific inquiry.

The historical–hermeneutic disciplines are governed by a practical interest of furthering understanding (*Verstehen*).

> The *historical–hermeneutic* sciences gain knowledge in a different
> methodological framework. Here the meaning of the validity of pro-
> positions is not constituted in the frame of reference of technical
> control . . . Access to the facts is provided by the understanding of
> meaning . . . The verification of lawlike hypotheses in the empirical-
> analytic sciences has its counterpart in the interpretation of texts.
> Thus the rules of hermeneutics determine the possible meaning of the
> validity of statements of the cultural sciences.[9]

In using the expressions "technical" and "practical" to identify
the first two cognitive interests, Habermas was self-consciously
drawing upon the insights of the contemporary appropriation of
Aristotle's distinction of *techne* and *praxis* (as in the works of
Gadamer and Arendt). *Techne* names the type of purposive action
exhibited in making or fabricating (*poesis*), while *praxis* – which
for Aristotle is closely associated with *lexis* (speech) – names the
distinctive form of human interaction exhibited in intersubjective
communication.

Although Habermas has appropriated the insights of the hermeneutic tradition, especially insofar as it illuminates the distinctive character of understanding, interpretation, and communicative symbolic interaction, he has been sharply critical of its implicit historicism – its own hidden form of positivism. This hidden positivism becomes evident in hermeneutical and interpretative approaches to social phenomena when it is mistakenly claimed that we can understand and interpret forms of life and *bracket* critical rational evaluation of these forms of life. One of Habermas's most basic and challenging theses is that we cannot even make sense of the concepts of meaning, understanding, and interpretation unless we rationally evaluate the validity claims that are made by participants in these forms of life. We must be able to discriminate what participants themselves count as reasons for their actions, and this requires a performative attitude on our part where we assess what "they" count as good reasons for action with reference to "our" standards of rationality. (See Thomas McCarthy's discussion of this "strong" thesis in chapter 4 of part 2 in this book.) We are always in danger of being ethnocentric, but we never escape the horizon of rationality. It is a fiction to think that we can leap out of such a horizon and bracket all judgments of the validity claims made by participants in a form of life.

So, while Habermas does think that positivistically oriented philosophers of science have enabled us to grasp the important features of the empirical–analytic sciences, and hermeneutically oriented thinkers have illuminated the methodological framework of the historical–hermeneutical disciplines, both camps have been guilty of a false universalism. Implicitly or explicitly they valorize a distinctive form of knowledge as if it were the *only* or the most fundamental type of knowledge.

A critical social science is a dialectical synthesis of the empirical–analytic and the historical–hermeneutical disciplines. It incorporates the study of nomological regularities and the interpretation of the meaning of symbolic interaction. But, at the same time, it goes beyond both of these one-sided approaches. Habermas's synthesis comes into clear focus when we turn to the third type of cognitive interest: the emancipatory interest. This interest is at once derivative and the most fundamental cognitive interest. If we reflect upon the forms of knowledge and the disciplines guided by the technical and practical interests, we realize that they contain an internal demand for open, free, non-coercive communication. The validity of knowledge claims in empirical–analytic sciences and the historical–hermeneutical disciplines always allows of further testing, challenge, and rational reevaluation. This is the "truth" contained in Popper's call for constant and vigilant criticism, and it is paralleled by Gadamer's insistence that ongoing dialogue can never reach *final* closure. We can "derive" the emancipatory interest from what is presupposed by the technical and practical interests. But an emancipatory interest is basic in the sense that the interest of reason is in furthering the conditions for its full development; the demand for non-distorted communication becomes fully explicit. Furthermore, we can begin to grasp the practical implications of disciplines that are governed by an emancipatory interest. Non-distorted, reciprocal communication cannot exist unless we realize and institute the material social conditions that are required for mutual communication.

A critical social science which is at once empirical and interpretive has as its goal (as do the empirical–analytic sciences) the discovery of nomological knowledge. However

> A critical social science will not remain satisfied with this. It is concerned with going beyond this goal to determine when theoretical statements grasp invariant regularities of social action as such and when they express ideologically frozen relations of dependence that can in principle be transformed . . . Thus the level of [non-reflective] consciousness which is one of the initial conditions of such laws, can be transformed. Of course, to this end, a critically mediated knowledge of laws cannot through reflection alone render a law itself inoperative but can render it inapplicable.
>
> The methodological framework that determines the meaning of the validity of critical propositions of this category is established by the concept of *self-reflection*. The latter releases the subject from dependence on hypostatized powers. Self-reflection is determined by an emancipatory cognitive interest.[10]

III

When *Knowledge and Human Interests* was published it immediately attracted an enormous amount of critical attention. Habermas had touched upon fundamental issues that preoccupied thinkers in a variety of fields. He had advanced a provocative interpretation of a movement of thought that encompassed Kant, Fichte, Hegel, Marx, Dilthey, Peirce, Nietzsche, Comte, and Freud. He had integrated his narrative account with a systematic examination of the basic cognitive interests and the different forms of knowledge that they govern; and he explored the relation of these cognitive interests to the dimensions of social existence and action. Against positivists and historicists, he argued for a critical social science that redeems the "forgotten" experience of emancipatory self-reflection. One of the many reasons why Habermas's work attracted so much attention is that he not only argued for the contemporary relevance and validity of a major motif of the German idealistic tradition, but he sought to vindicate and revitalize a theme that has also been central for western philosophy. This theme is exemplified in the Platonic portrait of Socrates. Socrates in his words and deeds embodies the basic conviction that there is a type of self-reflection that can free us from the tyranny and bondage of false opinion (*doxa*). Habermas is also in the Socratic tradition in linking self-reflection with dialogue. For it is only in and through dialogue that one can achieve self-understanding. If dialogue is not to be an empty impotent ideal, then a transformation and reconstruction of the social institutions and practices in which dialogic communication is embedded becomes a practical imperative.

However, Habermas soon came to realize that the systematic program sketched in *Knowledge and Human Interests* was seriously flawed. I want to indicate four major flaws or inadequacies, and how Habermas has addressed these in his writings during the past fifteen years – culminating with the publication of *The Theory of Communicative Action*.[11] In this book, and in the writings leading up to it, one can discern a new systematic synthesis – which preserves Habermas's earlier insights, corrects its inadequacies, and points to new directions for research.

The most glaring flaw, which Habermas himself recognized almost as soon as he completed *Knowledge and Human Interests*, goes to the heart of his analysis. There is a radical ambiguity in the basic concepts of reflection and self-reflection. There are at least two logically distinct concepts of reflection which needed to be carefully distinguished (and which Habermas had fused together). The first concept derives from the Kantian sense of the self-reflection of reason upon the conditions of its employment. This is the core of Kant's own understanding of *Critique* – where reason can self-reflexively come to grasp the universal and necessary conditions for the very possibility of theoretical knowledge, practical reason, and teleological and aesthetic judgment. But the second concept of self-reflection is one that aims at freeing a subject from dependence on hypostatized powers – "from ideological frozen forms of dependence that can in principle be transformed." This is the emphatic emancipatory sense of self-reflection. We can also find this concept in Kant, especially in his understanding of "What is Enlightenment." This concept of emancipatory self-reflection is subtly transformed in Hegel and Marx. Although these two concepts of self-reflection are logically distinct, they are intimately related. Emancipatory self-reflection is dependent on giving a rational reconstruction of the universal conditions for reason. To use the Kantian analogy, only when we understand the nature and limits of theoretical and practical reason does it become intelligible to specify what must be done to achieve autonomy and enlightenment.

Habermas fails not only to make this crucial distinction fully explicit in *Knowledge and Human Interests*, he slides from one pole to the other. Thus when he proposes that Marx's critique of ideology and Freud's therapeutic psychoanalysis are models of critical sciences based upon self-reflection, he emphasizes the second sense of emancipatory self-reflection – without however fully explaining its normative foundations; without adequately elucidating the dialogical character of communicative rationality that is presupposed by them.

The second major flaw is closely related to the first one. When Habermas classified the knowledge-constitutive interests as "quasi-transcendental" he was really identifying a tangled problem, not offering a solution. These cognitive interests are not merely contingent or accidental. They are basic and unavoidable, rooted in what we are as human beings. Consequently, they approximate the epistemological status of transcendental claims. But for Kant – and for the tradition of transcendental philosophy he helped to initiate – transcendental claims are *a priori* and must be distinguished from what is *a posteriori* and empirical. For Kant, we cannot justify the universality and necessity of synthetic *a priori* judgments unless we "purify" them of empirical content.

Habermas has always been sympathetic with the idea that we can identify basic structures, rules, and categories that are presupposed by reason and communicative action. But he has also been extremely skeptical that such an inquiry can be carried out by pure transcendental philosophy. A critical social science, which develops genuine scientific empirical hypotheses, demands a break with this legacy of pure *a priori* transcendental philosophy. But in *Knowledge and Human Interests* Habermas had not yet shown us how we can at once justify the claim that there are unavoidable necessary universal conditions of communicative action and rationality, and maintain that these can be discovered and warranted in a scientific manner.

We can approach the basic issue here from a slightly different perspective. In Habermas's reply to his critics (included in this volume) he begins by sketching two extreme responses to the modern experience of radical pluralism: pure historicism and pure transcendentalism. He indicates the difficulties of both extremes – how they lead us to a "double bind." In *Knowledge and Human Interests* he was already aware of this "double bind," and it was clear he was seeking to escape from it. But he did not adequately show how this is to be accomplished. Yet without showing a "third way," his systematic interplay of philosophy and social science was in danger of foundering.

The third flaw radicalizes the first two difficulties. For Habermas, this is the most basic inadequacy of his first systematic synthesis. It is the key for understanding what has been called his "linguistic turn"– a shift required not because of contemporary fashions but necessitated in order to justify his most fundamental intuitions. The methodological approach in *Knowledge and Human Interests* was oriented by epistemological concerns. But an epistemological orientation is itself dependent of what Habermas now calls "the philosophy of consciousness" and "the philosophy of the subject." It has its modern roots in the Cartesian turn to subjectivity. In German idealism and Husserl's phenomenology, "consciousness" and the "subject" still have primary status. Habermas came to realize that this orientation – even as modified in *Knowledge and Human Interests* – obscures and even blocks the way to grasping the intrinsic intersubjective and dialogical character of communicative action. Even the expression "intersubjectivity" carries the burden of the philosophy of the subject, insofar as it suggests that the main problem is to understand how self-sufficient subjects can be interrelated, rather than focusing attention on how subjects are constituted and formed in and through their social interactions. Habermas became acutely aware of how even in Hegel and Marx (and in his own early writings) there was an unresolved tension between the philosophy of consciousness and the philosophy of the subject on the one hand, and the need to do full justice to the integrity of the intersubjectivity of communicative action which always involves a genuine *plurality* of actors.

The fourth shortcoming in *Knowledge and Human Interests* can be seen as a "promissory note" which had not yet been redeemed. When Habermas adumbrated the physiognomy of a critical social science, he directed his attention primarily to the idea or the possibility (in the Kantian sense) of such a science, not to its *substantive* development. The use he made of Marx's critique of ideology and his interpretation of Freudian psychoanalysis highlighted the methodological character of a critical social science.

Considering the intellectual climate of the time, we can sympathetically understand the rationale for this emphasis. Not only had the legacies of positivism and historicism called into question the very possibility of a critical social science, but as we noted earlier, the older generation of critical theorists were also voicing their skepticism about the real historical possibility of a critical social science. One needed to establish a clearing for, to show the conceptual possibility of, a critical social science in the face of these multifaceted challenges. Here, too, a formal analogy with Kant may be helpful. When Kant began his critical project and took up the question of metaphysics, he realized that one first needed to ask whether such a "science" is possible and how it is possible. So Habermas's first task was to show the viability of a critical social science. But he had promised much more. Even if one were persuaded that such a scientific research program is feasible, one might remain skeptical about its substantive realization. There were suggestions about how such a research program might be developed but he had not yet made much progress in its systematic articulation. *Knowledge and Human Interests* was a prolegomenon to a future critical scientific analysis of society.

IV

Habermas's self-criticism is the mark of a genuine dialectical thinker. When difficulties have been pointed out by his critics, or when he has come to appreciate deficiencies of his analyses, he has confronted them directly. He does this in a spirit of *rejecting* what is no longer defensible, *preserving* what he still deems valid, and *moving beyond* earlier formulations to new frontiers. This is why one can detect continuities and discontinuities throughout his intellectual journey. Habermas's work during the past fifteen years can be viewed from the perspective of addressing the four flaws that I have outlined of his first systematic synthesis. *The Theory of Communicative Action* draws together the many strands of his thinking into a new, more detailed, and much more persuasively argued systematic whole. I want to indicate some of the major aspects of his current position by showing how he meets the difficulties that I have outlined. This will enable a reader to understand the context for the current discussions of Habermas on modernity and postmodernity.

Because the first two problems are so closely intertwined, I will discuss them together. In discriminating the two concepts of self-reflection, I indicated (as does Habermas himself) that emancipatory self-reflection is dependent upon giving a rational reconstruction of the universal conditions of reason. Habermas has argued that the legacy of what is sound in the Kantian project of transcendental philosophy is to be found in what he now calls the "reconstructive sciences." These are sciences that elucidate the depth grammar and rules of "pre-theorectical" knowledge. These reconstructive sciences must be carefully distinguished from empirical–analytic sciences typified by contemporary natural sciences. Chomsky's generative grammar, Piaget's theory of cognitive development, and Kohlberg's theory of moral development are *examples* of reconstructive sciences. In each case – to use Ryle's distinction between "knowing-how" and "knowing-that"– the aim is to provide explicit theoretical knowledge ("knowing-that") of implicit pre-theoretical "knowing-how." These sciences study a symbolically structured social reality. The rational reconstructions advanced by these sciences are directed toward making explicit universal species competences (e.g., the competence to speak and understand a language). Like all scientific disciplines the hypotheses they advance are fallible. But the hypothetical quality of such reconstructive sciences is not incompatible with the aim of discovering the universal conditions presupposed by and required to perform the relevant competence. The most important methodological point, however, is that reconstructive sciences are *empirical* (not disguised forms of transcendental philosophy). They are themselves subject to appropriate canons of confirmation and falsification. They are to be critically evaluated by their empirical success in substantiating their claims to identify species competences and to account for the rules and conditions that these competences presuppose. Unlike the empirical–analytic sciences that seek to *replace* "pretheoretical knowledge" with a more adequate scientific explanation of the world, reconstructive sciences explain and clarify the basic grammar and rules of our "pretheoretical knowledge." The theory of communicative action and rationality is a reconstructive science. But it has a more universal thrust than linguistics and current theories of psychological and moral development. It seeks to isolate, identify, and clarify the conditions required for human communication. This reconstructive science, which Habermas also calls "universal pragmatics," enables us to specify the contributions and limitations of reconstructive sciences that have more restricted domains. All human symbolic competences presuppose the universal species competence of communication.

We can now see how this new methodological analysis of the character of reconstructive sciences addresses the first two flaws described above. Habermas does want to preserve what he takes to be sound in the Kantian program of transcendental philosophy – in the program of reason reflecting on the universal conditions required for its employment. Yet he also wants to break with the notion that such an enquiry is *a priori*. Such an inquiry is hypothetical, fallible, empirical – in short, it is scientific and must satisfy the procedures for the acceptance and rejection of scientific hypotheses. The reconstructive science of a universal pragmatics enables us to understand the foundation or ground for emancipatory critique (the second concept of self-reflection). For it shows that emancipatory critique does not rest upon arbitrary norms which we "choose"; rather it is grounded in the very structures of intersubjective communicative competences. One reason why many critics, even sympathetic critics, of Habermas have been perplexed by his "linguistic turn" is because during the past fifteen years he has been more concerned with elaborating, justifying, and working out the details of this ambitious research program of a theory of communicative action or universal pragmatics than with engaging in the practice of emancipatory critique. But the rationale for this emphasis should now be clear. The very intelligibility of emancipatory critique – if it is to escape the charge of being arbitrary and relativistic – requires a clarification and justification of its normative foundations. This is what the theory of communicative action seeks to establish.

Habermas no longer speaks of "quasi-transcendental" cognitive interests. This has led some to think that he has simply abandoned the major systematic theses of *Knowledge and Human Interests*. It is true he has sought to purge his thinking of the vestiges of the philosophy of consciousness and the philosophy of the subject. But the insights contained in his original trichotomy of human interests are conceptually transformed in a new register within the context of his theory of communicative action. The distinction between the technical interest on the one hand, and the practical and the emancipatory interests on the other hand, is itself based upon a categorial distinction of purposive–rational action and communicative (symbolic) action. This distinction is not abandoned in Habermas's universal pragmatics. On the contrary, it is refined and developed in far more detail than in his earlier work. Furthermore, from the perspective of the theory of communicative action, we gain a clearer understanding of the conceptual space and foundations for what Habermas called the practical and emancipatory cognitive interests.

I have already anticipated how Habermas meets the third difficulty. The theory of communicative action is no longer wedded to the philosophy of consciousness and the philosophy of a self-sufficient subject. Its primary source of inspiration is the philosophy of language, specifically speech act theory (which Habermas significantly modifies and refines). Habermas fully realizes that the range of communicative interactions is broader than that of explicit speech acts. Nevertheless, by approaching communication from the perspective of speech we can gain an understanding of the distinctive features of communication. One primary reason – perhaps *the* primary reason – for "the linguistic turn" is that it no longer entraps us in the *monological* perspective of the philosophy of the subject. Communicative action is intrinsically *dialogical*. The starting point for an analysis of the pragmatics of speech is the situation of a speaker *and* a hearer who are oriented to *mutual* reciprocal understanding; a speaker and a hearer who have the capacity to take an affirmative or negative stance when a validity claim is challenged.

Although the details of Habermas's theory of communicative action are subtle, complex, and controversial, we can sketch some of its leading ideas. (Most of the articles included in this volume touch on various aspects of it.) Communicative action is a distinctive type of social interaction – the type of action oriented to mutual understanding. It must be distinguished from other types of social action and non-social action which are oriented to "success," to the efficient achievement of ends. These latter action-types exhibit the form of purposive–rational action where we seek to achieve an end or goal by appropriate means.

However "the goal of coming to an understanding [*Verständigung*] is to bring about an agreement [*Einverständis*] that terminates in the intersubjective mutuality of reciprocal understanding, shared knowledge, mutual trust, and accord with one another. Agreement is based on recognition of the corresponding validity claims of comprehensibility, truth, truthfulness and rightness."[12] All communicative action takes place against a background consensus. But this consensus can break down or be challenged by one of the participants in the communicative context. Habermas argues that anyone acting communicatively *must*, in performing a speech action, raise universal validity claims and suppose that such claims can be vindicated or redeemed. As indicated in the above quotation there are four types of validity claims: comprehensibility, truth, truthfulness (sincerity), and normative rightness. These are not always thematic but they are implicit in every speech act. In most empirical situations we resolve our conflicts and disagreements by a variety of strategies and techniques. But to resolve a breakdown in

communication, we can move to a level of *discourse* and argumentation where we explicitly seek to warrant the validity claims that
have been called into question. Ideally, the only force that should
prevail in such a discourse is the "force of the better argument."
Habermas, of course, is aware that he is describing an "ideal type,"
that in many empirical contexts we do not engage in such uncoerced
argumentation. We break off communication, or seek strategically
to manipulate others. But his major point is that however we in fact
resolve disputes and breakdowns in communication, universal validity claims "are set in the general structures of possible communication," in "the intersubjective structures of social reproduction."
This is true not only in our everyday "pretheoretical" communicative interactions, but also in our theoretical, practical, and
aesthetic discourses.

The point that Habermas is making has long been recognized in
the realm of scientific discourse. When there are serious conflicts
between competing scientific theories and hypotheses, research
programs, or paradigms, we are committed to resolving such differences through nonmanipulative and noncoercive argumentation.
As Habermas interprets recent work in the philosophy of science,
he does not believe that it significantly challenges this ideal. Rather
it teaches us that there may be no algorithms for resolving scientific
disputes, that even what constitutes "the better argument" may
itself be open to rational dispute. The novel feature of his theory of
communicative action is that he claims that the same appeal to
redeeming validity claims through appropriate types of argumentation is implicit in practical (moral and legal) disputes as well as in
disputes about aesthetic judgments. In this sense, Habermas defends
a strong "cognitivist" thesis. No dispute about a validity claim is
beyond rational argumentation by the participants involved. But
what is most fundamental for Habermas – the basic intuition which
he seeks to develop systematically – is that this anticipation and
presupposition of noncoercive and nondistortive argumentation is
"built into" our everyday, pretheoretical communicative interactions.

There is a danger that, with a social theorist whose thought is as
complex and as textured as is Habermas's, we can lose sight of his
overall vision when pursuing details. Habermas has been extremely
eloquent in expressing the vision that informs his detailed analyses.
Speaking of practical discourse, he tells us:

> In practical discourse we thematize one of the validity claims that
> underlie speech as its *validity basis*. In action oriented to reaching

understanding validity claims are "always already" implicitly raised. These universal claims (to the comprehensibility of the symbolic expression, the truth of the propositional content, the truthfulness of the intentional expression, and the rightness of the speech act with respect to existing norms and values) are set in the general structures of possible communication. In these validity claims communication theory can locate a gentle, but obstinate, a never silent although seldom redeemed claim to reason, a claim that must be recognized de facto whenever and wherever there is to be consensual action.[13]

In a similar spirit, he writes:

> Again and again this claim [to reason] is silenced, and yet in fantasies and deeds it develops a stubbornly transcending power, because it is renewed with each act of unconstrained understanding, with each moment of living together in solidarity, of successful individuation, and of saving emancipation.[14]

These passages point to what I earlier called the diachronic dimension of communicative rationality. Thus far I have concentrated on the synchronic dimension of the theory of communicative action and rationality, on what is presupposed and anticipated in communication, on what is "always already" implicit in this type of interaction. But the theory would be radically incomplete if we did not grasp how different types of action and rationality are embedded in historical social institutions and practices, how they change and develop in historical time. This is what Habermas calls "rationalization" processes. The expression in English can be misleading because we frequently think of "rationalization" as an activity that disguises or conceals underlying motives and intentions. This common use of "rationalization" has been influenced by the legacy of the "hermeneutics of suspicion." But by "rationalization" Habermas means increasing the rationality or reasonableness of a form of social action. Nevertheless the meanings of the rationalization of purposive-rational actions and communicative actions are categorically distinct.

> *Purposive–rational actions* can be regarded under two different aspects – the empirical efficiency of technical means and the consistency of choice between suitable means. Actions and action systems can be rationalized in both respects. The rationality of means requires technically utilizable, empirical knowledge. The rationality of decisions requires the explication and inner consistency of value systems and decision maxims, as well as the correct derivation of acts of choice.[15]

These rationalization processes closely approximate what Weber meant by *Zweckrationalität* – the form of rationalization process which he took to be basic to modernization. In the twentieth century the advance of the empirical–analytic sciences and the explosive development of decision and game theory have increased our understanding of this form of rationalization.

But the rationalization of communicative action is radically and categorically different.

> Rationalization here means extirpating those relations of force that are inconspicuously set in the very structures of communication and that prevent conscious settlement of conflicts, and consensual regulation of conflicts by means of interpsychic as well as interpersonal communication. Rationalization means overcoming such systematically distorted communication in which the action-supporting consensus concerning the reciprocally raised validity claims – especially consensus concerning the truthfulness of intentional expressions and the rightness of underlying norms – can be sustained in appearance only, that is counterfactually.[16]

When we grasp the import of Habermas's theory of communicative action, and especially the way in which he categorically distinguishes the two different types of rationalization processes, we can discern how he rectifies the fourth deficiency, how he substantively develops a research program for a critical social science. Here too the details are enormously complex, but I want to indicate briefly some of the major strands that he weaves together.

At the most fundamental level, Habermas argues that a theory of communicative action and an adequate sociological theory that can explain the dynamics of social processes are *not* two independent endeavors. They are conceptually and inextricably related to each other. One of the major goals of *The Theory of Communicative Action* is to explain and demonstrate this. The "rationality debates" that have so preoccupied contemporary philosophers lead us to develop a sociological theory where we can discriminate the different forms of rationalization processes. And no adequate sociological theory can escape confronting the question of rationality. Once again, but in a far more detailed and penetrating manner than previously, Habermas argues against the bias that we can "simply" describe, explain, and understand social forms of life without explicitly or implicitly evaluating the rationality of social action and action systems.

This dialectical mediation reflects Habermas's long-standing conviction that critical theory must fuse together both philosophical and scientific–empirical dimensions of analysis. In *The Theory of Communicative Action* he supports this basic thesis by showing how Marx, Weber, Durkheim, Mead, Lukács, Horkheimer, Adorno, and Parsons can all be seen as making contributions to (or are blinded from aspects of) a comprehensive sociological theory grounded in a full understanding of rationality and rationalization processes.

Given this basic approach, Habermas explores the concepts of system and life-world. Retrospectively we can see how much of the sociological tradition has gravitated to these two competing orientations. There have always been social scientists who have argued that the proper study of society is one that studies society as a complex system, where there are underlying interacting structures, systematic imperatives, and dynamic forms of systemic integration and/or breakdown. In its extreme form a systems theory approach diminishes the significance of the role of social actors. They are seen as "place-holders" within a total system. But the other pole in sociological analyses gives primacy to the creative role of social actors, and the ways in which they construct, negotiate, and reconstruct the social meanings of their world. In its extreme form, advocates of this orientation claim that the very concepts of system and structure are reified fictions.

In *The Theory of Communicative Action* Habermas forges a dialectical synthesis of these "competing" orientations. He wants to do justice to the integrity of the life-world and social systems, and to show how each presupposes the other. We cannot understand the character of the life-world unless we understand the social systems that shape it, and we cannot understand social systems unless we see how they arise out of activities of social agents. The synthesis of system and life-world orientations is integrated with Habermas's delineation of different forms of rationality and rationalization: systems rationality is a type of purposive–rational rationality, life-world rationality is communicative rationality. Furthermore, Habermas's diagnosis of the dominating trends in the recent history of industrialized societies enables him to formulate what Wellmer calls "the paradox of rationalization" in a new way. As Wellmer succinctly phrases it:

> The *paradox* of rationalization [is] that a rationalization of the life-world [is] the *precondition* and the *starting point* for a process of systemic rationalization and differentiation, which then [becomes] more and more autonomous vis-à-vis the normative constraints embodied in the life-world, until in the end the systematic imperatives begin to instrumentalize the life-world and threaten to destroy it (see p. 56).

In Habermas's telling phrase, we are threatened today by the "colonization of the life-world" by systemic rationalization processes.

This brings us to the real "pay off" of Habermas's careful and elaborate reconstruction of a sociological orientation grounded in a theory of rationality. Strictly speaking, "the paradox of rationalization" is *not* a paradox. There is no logical, conceptual, or historical *necessity* that systemic imperatives *must* destroy the life-world. The dialectic of Enlightenment *does* highlight what is characteristic of contemporary industrialized societies – the real threats they pose to the communicative integrity of the life-world. What has happened in modern society (and continues to happen at an alarming rate) is a *selective* process of rationalization – where purposive–rational rationalization prevails, encroaches upon, and deforms the life-world of everyday life. As Wellmer tells us:

> Against Weber and Horkheimer/Adorno . . . Habermas objects that this paradox of rationalization does *not* express an internal *logic* (or dialectic) of modern rationalization processes; it is strictly speaking, not a paradox of *rationalization*, if we use this term in the broad sense of a post-traditional conception of rationality which, as Habermas shows, we have to substitute for Weber's restricted conception of rationality. From the perspective of an action theory in Weber's sense, then, there would neither be a paradox of rationalization nor a "dialectic of enlightenment"; rather it would be more adequate to speak of a "selective" process of rationalization, where the selective character of this process may be *explained* by the peculiar restrictions put upon communicative rationalization by the boundary conditions and the dynamics of a capitalist process of production (p. 56).

This thesis about the *selectivity* of rationalization processes is Habermas's most important substantive sociological claim. To speak of "selectivity" entails that there are alternative possibilities. All of the lines of Habermas's reflections on modernity lead to, and are intended to clarify and support, this thesis. We can appreciate anew Habermas's fusing of the theory of communicative action and rationality and his sociological perspective on modernity. It is only when we grasp the different forms of action and rationality that we can clarify and justify the claim that rationalization processes can take a variety of historical forms. We can see through and critically evaluate claims that there is an *inevitable* logic of modernization. Furthermore we can explain why there has been a "colonization of the life-world" by analyzing the causes and dynamics of systemic rationalization and differentiation. We can not only explain, but also diagnose the "pathologies of modernity."

But what is most crucial is that this explanatory–diagnostic function of Habermas's theoretical perspective also helps to illuminate our future prospects – not in the sense of predicting the future, but rather by conceptually highlighting the need to further the communicative rationality of the life-world and achieving a proper balance between the legitimate demands of systemic rationalization and the communicative rationalization of the life-world.

We can even approach the study of new social movements from this communicative–theoretical perspective: movements such as the ecological, antinuclear, women's, and liberation movements – and even neoconservative movements so dominant today. They can be seen (even when misguided) as defensive reactions to preserve the integrity of the communicative structures of the life-world against the impingements and distortions imposed upon it by the processes of systemic rationalization.

Habermas does think that Weber (building on an insight of Kant) was right in distinguishing the *differentiation* of three cultural spheres: science, morality (including law), and art. He is deeply suspicious of those romantic and neoromantic tendencies which lead us to believe that it is still possible to imagine a "new" organic wholeness where all differentiations are overcome (*Aufgehoben*), where human beings are not only reconciled with each other, but also with nature. But he also seeks to root out the bias that cultural differentiation *must* inevitably result in unresolved alienation and reification. There is a logic to social evolution *in the sense* that once social learning processes are achieved we cannot forget them unless we consciously or unconsciously repress them. For Habermas it is an achievement of modernity to differentiate the cultural spheres or worlds of science, morality, and art. But we can accept this differentiation and still seek new ways to integrate and harmonize our everyday lives. We can still seek to restore a proper balance between the legitimate demands of social systems and the life-world. The prospect of furthering the communicative rationalization of our everyday life-world is still a real historical possibility.

Habermas categorically rejects a utopianism that tempts us to think there is a dialectical necessity which inevitably leads to the "good society." He also rejects the mirror image of this conception which calls for a total break with history, or which "places" utopian aspirations in a Never Never Land of fantasy. The utopian aspirations of Marxism and critical theory are transformed. There are rational grounds for social hope. This has nothing to do with either optimism or pessimism about our future prospects. There is no guarantee that what is still possible will be actualized. But against all the varieties of "totalizing critique" which seduce us into despair and defeatism, Habermas takes seriously the role of the philosopher as a "guardian of reason." He is a strong and powerful voice reminding us that the practical need to embody and nurture communicative rationality in our everyday social practices has "a stubbornly transcending power, because it is renewed with each act of unconstrained understanding, with each moment of living together in solidarity, of successful individuation, and of saving emancipation." As he tells us, "Communicative reason operates in history as an avenging force."[17]

V

Habermas is a thinker who at once stands against many of the intellectual currents and self-images of our time and speaks to our deepest aspirations and hopes. For we live in an era when there is a suspicion of reason, and of the very idea of universal validity claims that can be justified through argument. There is a rage against humanism and the Enlightenment legacy. We hear of "postmodernity," "postindustrialism," "poststructuralism," etc., but no one seems to be able to fill in the content of these "posts." From all sides, we hear of "the end of philosophy," "the end of the individual," and even "the end of Western civilization," but there are not only wide divergences about what these "ends" mean, there is also an enormous amount of confusion about what is supposed to happen after these "ends." Any attempt to gain a comprehensive understanding of modernity and its discontents is immediately condemned as a "metanarrative." Postmodernity presumably eschews all metanarratives. The spirit of our times is one of deconstruction rather than reconstruction. Even the hermeneutics of suspicion is turned inside out. We have become masters of the suspicion of the hermeneutics of suspicion. Habermas is aware of this present mood. No one can accuse him of naiveté. Yet he constantly and persistently argues against the facile (and sophisticated) attempts to dismiss the legacy of Western rationality. One reason why Habermas's work has received so much critical attention is because – despite present fashions – he addresses himself to what many of us still believe, or want to believe: that it is possible to confront honestly the challenges, critiques, the unmasking of illusions; to work through these, and still responsibly reconstruct an informed comprehensive perspective on modernity and its pathologies. Given the scope and ambitiousness of Habermas's intellectual project it invites, indeed it demands, rigorous criticism. Habermas in his communicative–theoretical orientation not only gives primacy to argumentation, this has been his own *practice*. The essays in this volume illustrate the richness and challenging quality of Habermas's work. In his reply to the questions and objections posed by his critics, Habermas attempts to meet these objections, clarify his claims, and refine his analyses. Depending on the reader's interests, the essays can be read in any order. But I would like to indicate several themes that run through these essays.

In sketching the course of Habermas's intellectual development I have shown how, from his earliest to his most recent writings, he has engaged in a critical appropriation of the traditions with which he identifies himself. But we need to stand back and ask about Habermas's continuities and discontinuities with these traditions. Has he correctly identified the weaknesses and inadequacies of these traditions? Do the revisions and strategies that he proposes stand up to close scrutiny? This is not simply a question of the historical placing of Habermas. Rather it is a way of fine tuning our understanding of his systematic contribution. For we want to know what are the gains (and perhaps losses) in the directions in which Habermas has developed a critical theory of society.

Wellmer's opening essay is an excellent overview of Habermas's relation to Hegel, Marx, Weber, and Critical Theory. He outlines what he takes to be the central weakness in Marxism and Critical Theory – the failure to establish an intelligible link between their analyses of modern society, rationality, and the utopian horizons of their theories. Wellmer ascribes this failure to the commitment to a categorial framework which does not allow for the necessary differentiations to account for the contradictory and ambiguous character of modern rationalization processes. Wellmer argues that the great merit of Habermas is that he proposes conceptual revisions within Critical Theory which "make it possible to avoid the theoretical impasses of Marxism and Critical Theory." Habermas's conceptual strategy, which categorially differentiates purposive–rational and communicative rationality, enables him to redeem the utopian promise of Marxism and Critical Theory, by showing the centrality of the need for "an adequate 'objectification' of communicative rationality in new social and political *institutions*; by institutions, i.e., which, on the one hand, would represent the normative anchoring of the system in the life-world, and on the other, would protect the communicative structures of the life-world themselves, and secure a rational and democratic control of the system by the life-world" (see p. 58). Consequently Wellmer's essay allows us to see clearly the import and rationale of Habermas's communicative-theoritical orientation.

Jay and Whitebook also approach Habermas's work by first locating tensions within Critical Theory and then asking whether Habermas has adequately resolved or mediated them. Their essays complement Wellmer's although they focus on Habermas's specific claims about art and aesthetic experience (Jay), and Freud and psychoanalysis (Whitebook). There is an affinity not only in the way in which they approach Habermas, but also in their primary concern – one which has troubled many sympathetic critics of Habermas. Jay begins his essay by identifying a fundamental, albeit often subterranean, tension in the Frankfurt School's work between "aesthetic experience as a prefigurative cipher of redemption and rational self-reflection as a critical tool in the struggle to achieve that utopian state" (see p. 125). This tension has a parallel in Whitebook's analysis of the role that Freud's theory of drives played for Adorno and Marcuse, and Habermas's moderating of the idea of an unmediated instinctual life. What concerns both of them is whether Habermas's emphasis on rational self-reflection and the rationalization processes of communication weakens and even suppresses the radical, "explosive" revolutionary motifs of Critical Theory; whether Habermas's "conceptual revisions" of Critical Theory lead to a bland reformism that no longer has a legitimate place for the type of redemptive experience and "promise of happiness" that was so vital for Critical Theory. This is also echoed in Giddens's question whether Habermas's theoretical perspective leads to Reason *without* Revolution. Furthermore, both Jay and Whitebook question the meaning of the new form of social integration that Habermas proposes; they wonder how systemic differentiation and rationalization are to be "balanced" with the communicative rationalization of the life-world; and what role science, morality, and art play in this process.

One theme that surfaces in most of the essays included in this volume is Habermas's understanding of art and aesthetic experience. There are several reasons for this. Art and aesthetic experience has always been central for Critical Theory, and became even more prominent in the late writings of Adorno and Marcuse. It is at the heart of Lowenthal's and Benjamin's work. Increasingly, Adorno and Marcuse came to believe that it is only in art that the radical utopian impulses of Critical Theory find their expression in a thoroughly "rationalized" society. Furthermore, insofar as Habermas has sought to develop a comprehensive understanding of modernity, he cannot avoid coming to grips with "cultural modernity." One of the primary contexts for the discussion of modernity and postmodernity has been the analysis of contemporary culture and the role of the art in everyday life. Yet at first glance, Habermas appears to have slighted the complex issues involved in understanding art and aesthetic experience in contemporary culture. The problems become even stickier and more perplexing because from his communicative–theoretical orientation Habermas speaks of "aesthetic rationality" and "learning processes" involved in artistic experience. But what precisely does this mean? Habermas distinguishes the three cultural spheres of modern life as science, morality, and art. He has had a great deal to say about the first two spheres, but far less about the "third" cultural sphere. Yet if the idea of a new integration of the communicative infrastructure of the life-world is to become plausible, then we need to understand precisely the contribution of art and aesthetic experience. In short, figuring out and assessing Habermas's understanding of art and aesthetic experience is a means of testing and evaluating general claims about modernity and postmodernity.

Jay shows us how Habermas has addressed the relevant issues. But he also locates a number of significant unresolved tensions. These are further explored by Wellmer, McCarthy, and Rorty. In Habermas's reply to his critics we find one of his clearest and most succinct statements of his present understanding of art and aesthetic experience, especially how they are viewed from his communicative–theoretical perspective, and what role they may yet play in an integration of the life-world. He also frankly acknowledges the problems and questions that still need detailed examination.

I have claimed that *The Theory of Communicative Action* represents a new systematic synthesis. Although published in 1981, it is already being recognized as a major – perhaps the major – development in sociological theory in our time. Considering its ambitiousness, complexity, and detailed analyses, it requires careful examination – a process which has already begun; even though only the first volume has been translated into English. Anthony Giddens, who himself has dealt with many of the issues central for Habermas, approaching them from a very different orientation, provides an overview of this work. He raises many of the key questions that need to be asked if we are properly to evaluate Habermas's major claims.

Thomas McCarthy asks further questions but he concentrates on what I have referred to as the primary substantive thesis of Habermas's analysis of modernity – the thesis concerning the *selectivity* of rationalization processes in the modern age. This thesis not only presupposes the adequacy of Habermas's analysis of the different types of rationality (and the ways in which they are interrelated), but also his sociological claims about modernization and rationalization processes. In his reply to McCarthy's questions about rationality and rationalization processes Habermas clarifies some of the central systematic claims of *The Theory of Communicative Action*.

Habermas's own contributions to this volume enable the reader to witness the way in which he deals with other thinkers and movements. His essay on Marcuse, originally given as an informal talk at a symposium held in honor of Marcuse at the University of California, San Diego, is as revealing for what Habermas has to say about Marcuse (and the older generation of Frankfurt thinkers) as it is about Habermas himself. This is especially true in the way in which Habermas explains the "affirmative feature" of Marcuse's thought and singles out Marcuse's sense of "the obligation to give theoretical explanations and thereby to ground action in reason."

In his analysis of social and cultural modernity Habermas has insisted on the important achievement of differentiation. He has resisted what he takes to be seductive attempts to blur crucial differences and to seek totalities within which these differentiations are obscured. This is not only a cardinal tenet of his theoretical work, but is a principle which he himself has practiced. One of the sources of confusion about Habermas has been the failure to appreciate the way in which he differentiates his own activities as a theorist, teacher, and commentator on social and political movements. In the interview from which I earlier cited remarks about his intellectual development, Habermas declares "What annoys me terribly . . . is the aggressivity of people who do not see the role differentiation in me."[18] Pragmatically, what Habermas means is that his efforts to make contributions to social scientific theory must be judged by the appropriate canons for validity of *theoretical* discourse. Theory is not to be confused with specific political interventions or engagements in emancipatory critique. But *differentiation* is compatible with *integration*. This is important not only for understanding and evaluating Habermas's many different theoretical and practical activities, but for appreciating the context of his essay on neoconservatism. He tells us that the occasion and motive for beginning to write *The Theory of Communicative Action* in 1977 was "to understand how the critique of reification, the critique of rationalization, could be reformulated in a way that would offer a theoretical explanation of the crumbling of the welfare-state compromise and of the potential for the critique of growth in new movements without surrendering the project of modernity or descending into post- or anti-modernism, 'tough' new conservatism or 'wild' young conservatism."[19]

For Habermas "neoconservatism" is one of the most virulent and dangerous intellectual movements of our time. Neoconservatism has taken different forms in different cultural contexts. In Germany neoconservatives have frequently claimed that leftist intellectuals are primarily responsible for the ills of modern society. A responsible critique of neoconservatism requires a theoretical understanding of this movement – one which pinpoints its inherent contradictions and shows how it confuses symptoms with causes.

Many of the issues which arise in clarifying what is at stake in the discussion of modernity and postmodernity come into sharp relief in Rorty's essay. Although he presents himself as mediating between Lyotard and Habermas, as "splitting the difference" between them, Rorty in this essay (as well as in his other writings) raises some of the most skeptical criticisms of Habermas's entire theoretical approach. Rorty not only thinks that Habermas's interpretation of modernity – especially the important role of the categorial differentiation of the cultural spheres science, morality, and art – is mistaken, he questions the need for a *theory* of communicative action. This is why Habermas begins his reply by directly meeting and answering Rorty's challenge.

In forging his systematic position Habermas has "taken on" and forcefully argued with his critics. We can even mark the stages of his development by the types of public debate in which he has been engaged. In the early 1960s there was the famous "Positivist Dispute" centering about the confrontation between Popper and Adorno. In the late 1960s, beginning with Habermas's critical review of Gadamer's *Truth and Method*, a debate was begun (which has taken many turns and still continues) between critical theory and hermeneutics. Still later, Habermas and Niklas Luhmann disputed the merits and limitation of sociological systems theory. What has been shaping up most recently is a confrontation between Habermas and the type of poststructuralism and deconstructionism that has emanated from Paris, and which has become so fashionable among literary theorists in the U.S. In *The Postmodern Condition* Jean-François Lyotard directly attacks Habermas. He sees Habermas as still operating within a framework of implicit assumptions that are characteristic of modernity, as offering us only one more "metanarrative." From Lyotard's perspective, Habermas fails to appreciate the radical epistemological break that postmodernity – a skeptical and incredulous attitude to all metanarratives – has made with modernity. In the Paris lectures of Habermas that Rorty discusses (which Habermas will incorporate in a book on modernity and postmodernity), Habermas reviews the entire problematic of modernity and postmodernity, tracing its origins back to Hegel and Nietzsche, and pursuing its variations through Heidegger, Derrida, Deleuze, Bataille, and Foucault. Habermas has already been attacked for his suggestion that there are subterranean affinities between the attack on modernity by French poststructuralists (many of whom think of themselves as radicals) and some varieties of conservative rejections of the Enlightenment legacy.

A great deal is at stake in this confrontation. One might epitomize Habermas's entire intellectual project and his fundamental stance as writing a *new* Dialectic of Enlightenment – one which does full justice to the dark side of the Enlightenment legacy, explains its causes but nevertheless redeems and justifies the hope of freedom, justice, and happiness which still stubbornly speaks to us. The project of modernity, the hope of Enlightenment thinkers, is not a bitter illusion, not a naive ideology that turns into violence and terror, but a practical task which has *not yet* been realized and which can still orient and guide our actions.

VI

All of the essays in this volume have been published in *Praxis International*. In this concluding section, I want to indicate briefly Habermas's relation to the Yugoslav *Praxis* group. The Yugoslav *Praxis* group consists of philosophers and social scientists, some of whom were partisans and were leaders of the Yugoslav revolution. After the Second World War they became leading spokespersons for Marxist humanism and democratic socialism. They strongly opposed Stalinism and Stalinist tendencies in Eastern Europe. In 1964 they founded the Yugoslav journal *Praxis*, and published an international edition. They also started the summer school at the island of Korčula. From the very beginning the *Praxis* group had an international orientation. The journal and the Korčula summer school became a meeting ground for progressive left intellectuals and students from Eastern and Western Europe as well as from English-speaking countries. Bloch, Marcuse, and Habermas actively participated in the discussions in Korčula, and published in *Praxis*.

The Praxis group considers themselves loyal and committed members of Yugoslav society working in the tradition of Marxist humanism. They are strong advocates of the principle of self-management and participatory democracy at *all* levels of society. But they have been attacked by authorities and "hard liners." In 1975, *Praxis* was no longer allowed to be published, the Korčula summer school was closed, and eight professors of the Praxis group from Belgrade University in Serbia were suspended.

During the early 1970s a new international institution was founded in Dubrovnik – the Inter-University Postgraduate Centre. It is formally constituted by member universities and academic institutions from all over the world. Through the initiative of Gajo Petrović, a leading member of the Praxis group in Zagreb (professors from Zagreb were attacked in the press but were not suspended from their teaching positions), a new course "Philosophy and Social Science" was started at the Inter-University Postgraduate Centre. Petrović asked Jürgen Habermas to join him as a co-director of the course. The course was intended to continue the spirit of the Korčula summer school under new and very different historical circumstances. From the beginning, members of the Belgrade Praxis group who had been suspended from teaching were invited to participate. Consequently, from 1976 through 1982 when the Belgrade Praxis members were partially reinstated at a new research center at Belgrade University, the only place in Yugoslavia where they could formally teach and participate in open discussions with colleagues was at the Inter-University Centre in Dubrovnik.

In the context of these lively meetings, discussions began about establishing a new successor journal to *Praxis* with an international board of editors. Habermas was a leading participant in these discussions and has been an active member of the editorial board of *Praxis International*. The first issue of *Praxis International*, edited by Mihailo Marković and Richard J. Bernstein, and published by Basil Blackwell, appeared in April, 1981. The opening editorial declared the double task of *Praxis International*: "it will do all that a journal can do to protect the integrity and dignity of intellectual work and to develop a critical consciousness as an international endeavor. It will dedicate itself to furthering the type of theoretical understanding that is a necessary condition for a relevant, forceful, imaginative praxis." Habermas epitomizes the ideals of *Praxis International*. Consequently, the journal has served as a vehicle for the expression and critique of his views. In the spirit of international solidarity, this volume is dedicated to our Yugoslav Praxis colleagues who have been so courageous in fostering the ideals of democratic socialism by their words and deeds. They are living proof that the claim to reason develops a "stubbornly transcending power, because it is renewed with each act of unconstrained understanding," and with "each moment of living together in solidarity . . ."

Part 1

1

Reason, Utopia, and the
Dialectic of Enlightenment

ALBRECHT WELLMER

I

At the time when Karl Marx developed his theory of capitalist society, socialist and anarchist ideas about a future liberated society were already widely current among oppositional workers and intellectuals of his time. Socialist and anarchists usually held ideal conceptions of a future state of society without exploitation and without domination of human beings over human beings. Marx, who had learned his lesson from Hegel, was deeply convinced of the futility of opposing ideal, utopian counterimages to the bad reality of an existing society. At the same time, however, he shared the radical impulses of socialists and anarchists, and considered Hegel's attempt to justify the existing modern state as a manifestation of Reason as deeply wrong. Marx was much more clearly aware than Hegel was of the catastrophic, dehumanizing, and alienating aspects of the emerging capitalist societies of his day. Consequently, he considered what Hegel has seen as the major achievement of the modern state – the reconciliation of the Universal and the Particular, the restoration of a substantive "ethical life" under conditions of a generally emancipated subjectivity, i.e., the establishment of a polis without slaves – not as being *realized* but as a historical *task* for humankind which was still to be brought about in a communist revolution. Hegel's vindication of the modern state as the highest manifestation of Reason therefore was for Marx only the ideological formulation of a *problem*; the reconciliation of opposites in Hegel's theory was for Marx only a reconciliation in *thought*, while in fact it had still to be brought about practically.

If the "negative" sides of modern societies – the loss of "ethical life" in the sphere of civil society, the catastrophic dynamics of capitalist economy, the dehumanization of work and the misery of the working class – were to be *practically* "negated" instead of being only alleged to be already negated in the concrete ethical life of the state, and if this practical negation was to be conceived of in a realistic way – as a historical *possibility* – and not in the way utopian socialists and anarchists conceived of it, then Marx had to show how the emancipated society was already prefigured in the dynamics, the crisis, and the logic of development of capitalist societies. Marx, in other words, had to transform socialism from a utopia into a science, as Engels later put it.

Marx's theory of capitalist society consequently is an attempt to show how this society – through the universalization of capitalist exchange relationships, the unlimited growth of the productive forces, the ensuing intensification of economic crises, and the production of a revolutionary proletarian class – carries the seed of its own negation within it. The end of capitalism, however, i.e., the abolition of private property, will according to Marx result in the establishment of a classless, communist society. In different ways, Marx again and again tried to show that the objective and subjective conditions of the communist society were already forming themselves within the womb of capitalist society; to show, in other words, that communism was not a mere ideal but would be the necessary result of the dialectical negation of capitalist commodity production. By this attempt to construe the future emancipation of humankind in terms of a historical dialectics, Marx tries to overcome the impotence and arbitrariness of utopian thinking without giving up the radical political impulses of socialism and anarchism. However, trying to theoretically eliminate all the contingencies which might be thought to stand between the present state of capitalist society and the future of a communist society, Marx in fact is led back to the impasses of utopian thinking – only now they reappear in a disguised form. For Marx cannot really show that the planned economy which he predicts for the time after capitalism will take the form of a communist society; consequently the idea of communism remains as much a utopian ideal in his theory as it was for earlier socialists and anarchists.

For Marx the idea of communism refers to a society in which the associated individuals would have brought their metabolism with nature under their conscious and rational control. In this society, bourgeois forms of law, morality, and politics would have lost their function, since they only express the antagonistic relationship of

capitalist class society: bourgeois politics as the agency of an illusory reconciliation of individual interests with a common good;
bourgeois law as, on the one hand, the expression of capitalist commodity production and capitalist exchange relationships, and on
the other hand, the juridical expression of the domination of one
class over the other; bourgeois morality, finally, as a form of moral
consciousness which functions in the interest of the stabilization of
capitalist class-relations. These ideological forms of an illusory
reconciliation between the Universal and the Particular become
superfluous in a classless society, since in this society everybody's
needs can be satisfied and sources of conflict and competition
between individuals have disappeared. The only limitation of
freedom in this society is defined by the continuing necessity to produce a living; since, however, production will be organized according to a rational plan by the associated individuals, it can be
expected that all individuals will equally and voluntarily accept the
restriction of their personal freedom which is unavoidable insofar as
there still exists a realm of necessity. Concerning this realm of
necessity, the freedom of the individuals consists in their voluntary
acceptance of the constraints implied in their participation in the
production process. Beyond this realm of necessity, however, i.e.,
in the realm of freedom, the individuals will live in a community in
which the "free development of each will be the condition for the
free development of all," in which the individuals will develop into
"total" individuals, in which work will have been transformed into
self-affirmation and in which the interaction between the individuals (which so far has been only a "conditioned" interaction) will
have been transformed into an interaction between the individuals
as such. This means, however, that except for the – somehow
trivialized – problem of the administrative regulation of the production process, there will be no need for an institutional objectification of social relationships, i.e., the reconciliation between the
Universal and the Particular will no longer need to be mediated by
a complex system of social and political institutions. As far as
"institutions" are necessary in a classless society, from Marx's
perspective they appear only as instruments of a common will, the
essential unity of which is already guaranteed by the disappearance
of class division. Under conditions of exploitation, class rule, and
scarcity, the common will could have only an illusory existence in
the social, juridical, and political institutions of the modern state.
With the abolition of capitalism, people will no longer be forced to
"externalize" their social powers into institutions which then confront the individuals with an independent existence and with a logic

and power of their own. With the background of such assumptions, Engels has spoken about the transformation of the domination of humans over humans into the administration of things, and Lenin has predicted the "withering away of the state" in the coming communist society.

Freedom in communist society is consequently conceived of as the removal of all obstacles to the unimpeded development of all, the only limitation coming from the continuing necessity of society's metabolism with nature. But since as a consequence of technological progress, the working day will be reduced to a small fraction of what it was under capitalist conditions, even this limitation will hardly be felt, and, what is more important, it will be freely accepted *as* a necessary limitation of freedom by all individuals in society. As far as the coordination of social interaction and the formation of a common will is concerned, however, Marx, in contrast to Hegel, does not develop the categories which would allow him to articulate the idea of a free association of individuals – given the conditions of modern, industrialized societies – beyond its most abstract formulation. Consequently this idea is abstractly opposed to the system of class domination which was the object of Marx's analysis. Since, however, it plays at the same time the "theoretical" role of signifying the type of postcapitalist social formation which, according to Marx, is already immanent in capitalist society, this idea of a free association could be only understood via a built-in category-mistake, as it were, as also spelling out the *organizational* principle of a communist society. But if it is understood as an organizational principle, it implies the denial that there is any *problem* of an institutionalization of freedom after capitalism has been abolished. The idea of a free association of the producers is then turned into the utopian perspective of a collective life process, the unity and harmony of which would spontaneously emerge from the institutionally unmediated interaction of emancipated individuals. Whatever the value of such a utopian perspective is, however, it is obvious that Marx never showed – nor could he have shown – that this is the historical perspective immanent in the crisis mechanisms and the developmental tendencies of capitalist societies. As far as the Hegelian problem of the institutionalization of freedom under conditions of modernity is concerned, one could rather say that Marx, having criticized the Hegelian solution with strong arguments, through his theoretical strategy *buries* the Hegelian problem instead of *solving* it. And generations of Marxists followed him in this respect.

As one might expect there is a reciprocal relationship between what is missing in Marx's articulation of the idea of a classless society, on the one hand, and what is deficient in his critical analysis of capitalist society, on the other. Using modern terminology one could say that Marx had criticized Hegel for justifying the functional differentiation in the modern state, the emergence of relatively autonomous subsystems of economy, politics, administration, jurisdiction or culture, as well as the "loss of ethical life" in civil society, as being in accordance with a fuller conception of reason. Hegel's thesis was that under conditions of modernity, i.e., under conditions of an emancipated subjectivity, of universal human rights, the substantive ethical life of the Greek polis could only be recovered as the reconciliation of opposites on a higher level. The immediate and all-pervasive identification of the individual with the polis was not possible in a polis without slaves and oracles, i.e., in a polis where the rights of individuals qua human beings were universally recognized and where the right to use one's own reason was not limited by tradition, authority or religion. Marx, in contrast, thought that with his critique of the ideological justifications of capitalist property he had found the clue for an *alternative* explanation of all the phenomena of "alienation" in modern societies, and therefore felt entitled to tear down the whole edifice of Hegel's political thought. In his explanation, however, Marx lumped together two different kinds of phenomena which at least *we* ought to keep separate: exploitation, pauperization and degradation of the working class, the dehumanization of work and the lack of democratic control of the economy, on the one hand, and the emergence of formal law based on universalist principles of human right, together with the functional and systemic differentiation of modern societies, on the other. Because in his critique of alienation, Marx lumped together these two different types of phenomena, he could believe that the abolition of capitalist property was sufficient to clear the road not only for an abolition of the dehumanizing features of modern industrial societies, but also for an abolition of all the functional differentiations and the systemic complexities which had come with it – and therefore for the recovery of an immediate unity and solidarity among human beings in a communist society.

The progress of history itself together with a growing awareness of the problems to be faced by industrial societies has made the historical dialectics construed by Marx increasingly implausible, even for Marxists. Neomarxist philosophers in our century, like Lukács and the philosophers of the Frankfurt school, have learned from another great social scientist, namely Max Weber, in whose reconstruction of the modernization process one can find traces of an alternative historical dialectics: a negative dialectics of progress and enlightenment.

II

Max Weber has tried to interpret the world-historical process of modernization as a process of progressive "rationalization." Since "rationalization" signifies an increase in rationality, Weber is in some important sense still the heir of an Enlightenment tradition, for which history appeared as a progress toward Reason. This progress toward reason, however, has assumed for Weber a highly ambiguous meaning; or perhaps I should say rather that the concept of reason – Weber rather speaks of "rationality" – has assumed a highly ambiguous meaning for Weber.

One could distinguish three different aspects in Weber's conception of rationality: purposive, formal, and discursive rationality. In its narrowest sense, rationality for Weber means *Zweckrationalität*, purposive rationality, i.e., the type of rationality exhibited in the choice of the most efficient means for realizing predefined goals; "rationalization" in this sense is therefore tied up with the increase of economic or administrative efficiency. In an extended sense the concept of rationality signifies the imposition of a coherent and systematic order upon the chaotic manifold of different situations, beliefs, experiences, alternatives of actions, etc. In this sense the concept of rationalization is tied up with the formalization and universalization of law in modern bourgeois society, with the extension of bureaucratic forms of organization and even with the systematic reorganization of something like musical material: it signifies an increase in coherence, systematic order, calculability, control, and systematic planning. With respect to modes of action and interaction "rationalization" signifies a transition from "communal" to "associative" forms of social action. While communal social action is oriented toward traditional norms and personal characteristics, associative social action is oriented toward impersonal, enacted, and general norms, and dominated by instrumental or strategic considerations – either in the context of bureaucratic organizations or in the context of market relationships. In its extended sense the notion of rationality assumes connotations of a "practical" rationality in a more traditional sense: for it also signifies the coherence imposed upon the chaotic manifold of impulses, evaluations and possible choices of the individual (the rational life plan of the puritan) as well as the coherence imposed upon a symbolic material (e.g., theology) and the corresponding discursive attitudes. Finally "rationality" is conceptually related to the authenticity of an attitude free from illusions and self-deceptions; it therefore also signifies the "disenchantment" brought about by the de-sacralization of the natural and social world; it signifies scientific rationality and the new ethos of scientific objectivity.

Weber, in a way, continues the tradition of his nineteenth-century predecessors when he analyzes the transition to modernity as a process of rationalization, a process of rationalization, moreover, in which the social sciences are bound to play an increasing role. However, through his analysis of the institutional correlates of progressive rationalization – capitalist economy, bureaucracy, and professionalized empirical science – he shows at the same time that the "rationalization" of society does not carry any utopian perspective, but is rather likely to lead to an increasing imprisonment of modern man in dehumanized systems of a new kind – to an increasing "reification," as Weber's disciple Lukács later on would call it. The paradox, that "rationalization" connotes both emancipation and reification at the same time, remains unresolved in Weber's theory; it is this paradox which Adorno and Horkheimer later tried to resolve through their conception of a "dialectic of Enlightenment."

This paradox, of course, can arise only because for Weber "rationality" and "rationalization" are not only analytical or descriptive categories by which he analyzes the structures and genesis of modern societies, but because they have an irreducible normative connotation which links them up with a more emphatic and comprehensive idea of reason – an idea of reason as it was still alive in the philosophy of the Enlightenment. "Rationalization," therefore, on the one hand, signifies for Weber a set of interrelated tendencies operating on various levels (or in various subsystems) and pointing toward increasing formalization, instrumentalization, and bureaucratization according to an internal systemic "logic" or necessity. These tendencies point toward a state of society in which the European ideal of the autonomous individual becomes more and more of an anachornism and in which the symbolic structures which once supported the formation of "autonomous individuals" and the leading of a meaningful life have disintegrated into a pluralism of privatized value choices; a state of society, therefore, in which the autonomous individual, this creation and discovery of modern European history, is likely to disappear – the "Egyptianization" of society – or to merely survive at the fringes of depersonalized systems. On the other hand, the notion of "rationalization" has for Weber still a normative connotation. The concept of rationalization, in the way he uses it, is still determined by a European tradition in which being rational signifies a basic condition and a task of human beings *qua* human beings. The basic reason why Weber cannot really disconnect his formal conception of rationality and his analysis of the modern European process of rationalization from a more emphatic Enlightenment conception of reason is that for him the emergence of modern science and modern law as well as the emergence of secularized systems of instrumental or strategic action and the destruction of "objective" meaning systems (like religious world-views) is *internally* related to what he has called the "disenchantment of the world." Not only is this disenchantment of the world, historically and conceptually, a necessary precondition for rationalization processes of that type which for Weber are specific to modern European history, it rather *also* signifies for Weber a cognitive achievement of a substantive kind, through which the boundaries of what may be called "rational" are defined in a new way. As Weber uses the term "disenchantment of the world," it also signifies the normative core of his own epistemological and moral position; this comes out most clearly in his methodological reflections. Weber's distinction between matters of fact and matters of value, his notion of an ethics of responsibility, his quasi-existentialist understanding of ultimate value choices – all these elements of Weber's self-understanding, which undisputably have a direct bearing on the way in which he develops the basic categories of his theory, articulate the world-view of someone for whom it is a matter of moral authenticity and intellectual honesty to no longer look for objective meaning or ultimate values in the domain of empirical facts. That the world, objectively speaking, is devoid of meaning and of values, can only be claimed by somebody for whom the process of disenchantment is a process of disillusionment, i.e., a process of enlightenment. This process of enlightenment is a process of rationalization in a peculiar sense: for first it amounts, as Habermas has shown in his recent *Theorie des kommunikativen Handelns*, to a differentiation of categories of knowledge and spheres of validity from each other – the factual, the normative, and the expressive – which in traditional societies are not yet clearly separated from each other, and secondly, on the basis of this process of differentiation, it brings to awareness the sphere of symbolically mediated human praxis as the only possible source of meaning and validity, and therefore as the only possible frame of reference for intersubjective validity claims. Without external guarantees for meaning or validity, every belief becomes a potential validity *claim* for which no intersubjective redemption is possible except through arguments. The disenchantment of the world consequently is the historical process through which those cognitive structures have emerged which could support a specifically modern conception of rationality and which provided the basis for the emergence of modern science, the rationalization of law on the basis of a dissociation of "legality" from "morality," and the emancipation of art from contexts of religious and practical concerns. Now precisely insofar as it is a matter of intellectual honesty that as modern human beings we have to face the world as a disenchanted one, there still exists for Weber an internal relationship between rationalization and enlightenment, or between a formal conception of rationality and rationality as a normative idea, signifying an authentic mode of life. It is for this reason alone that we can speak of a "paradox" of rationalization in Weber's theory: Once the cognitive structures of a disenchanted consciousness are institutionalized as secularized systems of cultural discourse and social interaction, a process of rationalization – now in the specifically Weberian sense – is set into motion which tends to undermine the social basis for the existence of autonomous and rational individuals. For this reason there is a profoundly pessimistic philosophy of history implicit in Weber's theory of modern rationalization. Humanity's becoming rational – i.e., reason's coming of age (which, after all, is humanity's task and destiny) – by an internal logic triggers historical processes which tend to depersonalize social relationships, to desiccate symbolic communication, and to subject human life to the impersonal logic of rationalized, anonymous administrative systems – historical processes, in short, which tend to make human life mechanized, unfree, and meaningless. Given these tendencies, Weber, as is well known, did not consider a socialist society to be a viable alternative to the capitalist societies of his day. Socialism, so he predicted, could only be the ultimate triumph of bureaucracy – a prediction which, one must say, at least for the time being has been rather drastically confirmed by the history of socialist revolutions in our century.

III

Neomarxist philosophers have tried to integrate some of Weber's insights into a revised Marxian framework. Simplifying, one could describe the basic strategy of the philosophers of the "Frankfurt school" (Horkheimer, Adorno, and Marcuse in particular) as follows: they adopted the negative dialectics of progress from Weber and, at the same time, criticized his notion of formal and instrumental rationality as a "truncated" conception of rationality which did not allow him even to conceive of the *possibility* of a rational organization of society which would be in accord with an emphatic conception of reason. This emphatic conception of reason would comprise the ideas of freedom, justice, and happiness, and therefore would provide a vantage point from which the rationalized societies of the twentieth century could be criticized as "irrational," as fundamentally violating the idea of rationality in their internal organization. This is a way of thinking which for Weber would indeed have been impossible. For Weber, in a disenchanted world, no rational justification of norms, values, or forms of social organization was possible; consequently the idea of a rational organization of society as a whole would not have made sense to him. The Frankfurt philosophers, on the other hand, did acknowledge that Weber's "truncated" conception of rationality corresponded to the reality of advanced industrial societies; for them this notion of rationality was not only adequate for describing the actual route which the process of modernization had taken in European history, it rather also expressed the ideological deformation of consciousness and the reification of social relationships which had been brought about by the development of capitalism. For this reason they also could agree with Weber – against Marx – that the *immanent* logic of the capitalist modernization process pointed *not* to the emergence of a classless society but rather to the emergence of a closed system of instrumental and administrative rationality, rooted in the reified consciousness of individuals who were increasingly subsumed under the capitalist production process. For the Frankfurt philosophers, Weber's conception of rationality represented the truth about modern society, its internal logic of development, and its basic ideology. However, holding – against Weber – to the Marxian perspective of a liberated, rationally organized, classless society, they had to rethink the historical dialectics of progress and revolution; or rather they had to disconnect the dialectics of progress from the perspective of a revolutionary transformation of society. The dialectics of progress becomes a negative one, aiming at the destruction rather than the realization of reason. Consequently the liberated society can no longer be conceived of as the natural or logical result of the unfolding of the contradictions of capitalism; its realization has rather to be thought of as a break through the bad continuum of progress, as a leap from the pre-history of compulsive progress into the realm of freedom. A radical revolution thus would be the free historical act by which humankind would finally liberate itself from the negative dialectics of progress.

My sketch of the position of the so-called "Critical Theory" rests on an oversimplification, disregarding in particular much of the work which was done during the early years of the Frankfurt school. However, it comes close to the position which was developed by Horkheimer and Adorno, partly under the influence of Benjamin, during the late thirties and the early forties, notably in the *Dialectic of Enlightenment.* Since it is this version of Critical Theory which has had the greatest impact on postwar critical thought in Germany, and since even the later Marcuse was still rather close to positions developed in the *Dialectic of Enlightenment* (although he tried to recover at least some of the "immanentism" of traditional Marxist thought), I want to focus here mainly on that form of Critical Theory as it was developed around the *Dialectic of Enlightenment* as its seminal text. About this form of Critical Theory one can say that it no longer tries to identify the "objective" historical and social tendencies and mechanisms which point toward the emergence of a liberated postcapitalist society. Thereby it avoids the bad "immanentism" (objectivism) of Marx's theory. However, by stressing the radical *discontinuity* rather than the historical *continuity* between the history of class society and the liberated society, it obviously risks ending up with a new form of utopianism, which would be but the back side of its radical negativism – a form of utopianism, i.e., in which the future would be related to the present only by a radical but abstract negation. Whether the replacement of Marx's positive dialectic of liberation by Weber's negative dialectic of reification – i.e., the reversal of signs, as it were, in Marx's philosophy of history – is compatible with maintaining the Marxian perspective of a liberated, rationally organized society, seems to depend not so much on whether these two aspects of Critical Theory are intelligibly linked to each other by a conception of reason which can be used for a critical analysis of modern societies, but upon opening the perspective of a historical alternative.

The conception of reason, as it has been articulated in the works of critical theorists, clearly reflects the Hegelian–Marxist heritage of Critical Theory. Basically the idea of reason and of a rational organization of society are expressed in terms of a reconciliation between the universal and the particular, where the particular – in contrast to what was done to it in the Hegelian system – is no longer sacrificed to the universal, so that the ideas of freedom, truth, and justice are reconciled with the desire for happiness. Consequently Critical Theory could be said to be based on an idea of reason which comprises the image of a harmonious unity of the collective life process, a situation in which the opposition between *volonté generale* and the individual's will and needs, as well as the opposition between our rational faculties and our sensuous nature would be overcome. Using this idea of reason as a basic, if often only implicit, normative standard for their analysis of contemporary society, the theorists of the Frankfurt school could be said, somewhat simplifying, to make a double claim. First, they claim that the realization of the demands of reason has become historically *possible*, given the technological development of modern industrial societies – if only individuals would grasp this possibility; and secondly they claim that the logic of development of modern societies – of the rationalization process in Weber's sense – points in the opposite direction and tends to lead to the establishment of a closed system of instrumental reason, of reification and repression. Although with the growing threat of barbarism the possibilities of freedom have grown simultaneously, the reverse appears to be more true for Critical Theory: with the growing possibilities of freedom, the threat of barbarism has grown almost to an unlimited degree. This is the critical theorists' version of the old slogan "socialism or barbarism."

Now it seems to be obvious – although somewhat paradoxical – that similar objections, as I have raised them against the utopian perspective of Marx's Theory, can be raised against the utopian perspective of Critical Theory as well. For it is hard to see how any intelligible link between the negative dialectic of progress and the idea of a liberated society could exist, if present societies – as closed systems of instrumental rationality – can be seen *only* as negative counterimages of true reason. The idea of reason must under such conditions appear as the idea of a future state of society *beyond* human history – a human history, i.e., which as a whole appears as hopelessly godforsaken, as "a pile of debris growing skyward," to use a phrase of Benjamin.

i believe that it is not the emphatic idea of reason as such, which the philosophers of the Frankfurt school maintained against Max Weber, which must lead to such desperate consequences. I rather think that it is because of the way in which Horkheimer and Adorno *elaborated* this idea in their reconstruction of the paradox of rationalization, that their attempt to integrate a Weberian perspective into a Marxian framework ultimately took on the tone of an impotent protest against Weber's claim; that in a world without religion or metaphysics, the idea of "objective reason" can have no place. In the *Dialectic of Enlightenment* Horkheimer and Adorno attempt to relate the one-dimensional character of modern processes of rationalization to an internal tendency toward reification and instrumental reason which is inherent in conceptual thinking as such, i.e., in symbolically mediated cognition and action. In the most radical passages of the *Dialectic of Enlightenment*, formal logic, the law of non-contradiction, and the general and "identifying" nature of conceptual thinking appear as the ultimate roots of a process of rationalization, which according to its internal logic terminates in the reduction of reason to formal and instrumental reason, in the establishment of a completely rationalized system of domination, and in the liquidation of the autonomous subject. In the enlightened world there is no longer a place for the idea of reason; in this Horkheimer and Adorno agree with Weber. But the explanation they give is different from Weber's. It is not that the idea of reason has proved untenable, it is rather that the false rationality of the modern world makes the idea of reason *appear* to be a mere illusion. Except for marginal phenomena like advanced art, the idea of reason and the memory of it have been extirpated from the reproduction process of modern societies. For the irresistible tendency of one-dimensional rationality toward the establishment of unity, system, and coherence does not only manifest itself in the rationalization and bureaucratization processes of modernity, it does not only manifest itself in the increasing scientific objectification of the world and in the universalization of the capitalist exchange principle, it rather also expresses itself in a progressive reification of consciousness which in the end makes the idea of reason and therefore the idea of liberation literally unthinkable. Even philosophy, inasmuch as – from Parmenides to Russell – it gives in to the impulse toward systematic thinking, unwillingly executes the laws of a dialectical enlightenment; it is no wonder, then, that humankind as a whole, as contrasted to the monkey in Kafka's *Bericht für eine Akademie*, can no longer remember to which purpose it took upon herself the immense amount of suffering connected with the effort of becoming human; and yet, whether humanization will finally succeed depends alone on whether the spark of memory will be ignited once more.

A philosophical theory with such a dramatic self-interpretation cannot point any more to traces, elements, or tendencies of historical reality itself to substantiate the emphatic idea of reason which it nevertheless opposes to the perverted rationality of existing social reality. Since Horkheimer and Adorno, in ironical agreement with Weber, see conceptual thinking – geared to domination and self-preservation – as the ultimate root of the perversions of modern rationality, they cannot even trust that the idea of an unperverted rationality could be kept alive in the sphere of discursive thinking; only if conceptual thinking is turned against itself and against its own reifying tendencies can there be any hope that the memory of reconciliation is preserved in philosophical thought.

It is Adorno, who in his later writings has worked out the consequences which follow from this desperate position of a Critical Theory which tries to defend an idea of reason which, strictly speaking, it can no longer defend in the medium of discursive thought. For Adorno it is the work of art i.e., the authentic, advanced work of art, which virtually becomes the last residue of reason in a rationalized world. For art represents a type of "logic" and "synthesis" which is markedly different from the repressive type of logic and synthesis characteristic for "identifying" thought. The aesthetic synthesis achieved by the work of art is different from that of conceptual thinking in that it does not do violence to the particular, the suppressed, the nonidentical. It is for this reason that the work of art becomes for Adorno the preeminent medium of a nonreified cognition and, at the same time, the paradigm for a nonrepressive integration of elements into a whole. Both these functions of art are intimately connected with each other: through the configuration of its elements the work of art *reveals* the irrational and false character of existing reality and, at the same time, by way of its aesthetic synthesis, it *prefigures* an order of reconciliation. Correspondingly instrumental (and conceptual) rationality is "sublated" in a twofold sense in the work of art. It owes its specific, aesthetic rationality to the merging of mimetic impulses with elements of rational construction; and it represents a transfiguration of the elements of empirical reality, making reality appear in the light of reconciliation: the work of art as the semblance of reconciliation.

Now it seems that the aesthetic synthesis achieved by the work of art could be understood as prefiguring an order of reconciliation only if the aesthetic integration of elements into a whole could be taken as an analogy, or a model of the dialogical relationships between human individuals in a liberated society. At certain points in his *Aesthetic Theory* Adorno comes close to saying this; but what is perhaps more important is that because of his understanding of the "repressive" character of "identifying" thought, the aesthetic rationality of the work of art became for him the only *possible* model for an alternative form of rationality, in which instrumental rationality would be preserved only as a sublated moment. But then the organization of the work of art *does* become the only possible model for the organization and the rationality of an emancipated society; it is only for this reason that the aesthetic synthesis can prefigure a nonrepressive *social* synthesis.

A peculiar historical dialectic is emerging here. Adorno was Marxist enough to believe in the emancipatory potential of a highly developed technology; correspondingly he believed that a fully developed form of instrumental reason was the precondition for a form of reconciliation, which would not be a relapse into the terror of an archaic age or the repression of traditional societies. But in a closed universe of instrumental rationality the emancipatory potentials of civilization were virtually hidden; they could be unleashed only through a transformation of society, which Adorno could ultimately conceive of only in terms of a sublation of instrumental into aesthetic rationality. However, "instrumental" and "aesthetic" rationality, although they signify different types of orientations, of discourse, of production, of acting, and of thinking, cannot possibly signify alternative forms of social integration. More importantly, the aesthetic synthesis represented by the work of art, even if we concede to Adorno that it contains a *promesse de bonheur*, can hardly be understood as a model of dialogical relationship *between* individuals, who recognize each other in their individuality, as equals and as absolute others both at the same time. If beauty is a promise of happiness, of reconciliation with our internal and with external nature, the work of art would be a *medium* of this transcending experience rather than a *model* of reconciliation itself. For at least the *moral* "synthesis" of a dialogical relationship can only be *mediated*, but not be brought to *appearance* by the aesthetic synthesis of the work of art. Even if, as Adorno stresses, the subject, which comes to speak in the work of art, is a "we" (and not the individual artist), this collective subject speaks with *one* voice, speaking to itself, as it were; i.e., the rules of "synthesis" of this transsubjective speech cannot possibly prefigure the open rules of a dialogue with *many* voices. Aesthetic synthesis is not a possible model for a state of society free from repression. Instead one could also say that the ideas of freedom, of being-oneself in a nonrepressive sense, of justice or of mutual recognition and solidarity, if they are interpreted in terms of the nonrepressive configuration of elements in the work of art, can signify only a transhuman state of affairs, but not a life form of speaking and interacting individuals.

From the vantage point of an idea of reason which ultimately can be explicated only in terms of a transdiscursive aesthetic rationality, the functional, systemic, and cognitive differentiation processes of European modernity can be conceived only as being altogether geared to the process of *instrumental* rationalization. This is the ironical agreement between Critical Theory and Max Weber which I have spoken of before. This ironical agreement with Weber, however, is the reason why Critical Theory could also maintain a quasi-orthodox Marxist perspective on the differentiation processes of modern societies. In particular, the emergence of an economic system with money as a general medium of exchange, the rationalization of law on the basis of a separation of morality from legality, and the emergence of a sphere of autonomous art separated from the material reproduction process of society – these results of capitalist rationalization processes tend to be seen by critical theorists as being *forms* or *symptoms* of *reification* to the same degree as they are forms of *differentiation*. The emancipatory potential of modern rationality, then, can only reside in the advanced work of art inasmuch as it resists being assimilated to the ideological functions which the sphere of art as a whole has assumed in rationalized societies. Under these conditions, however, and without Marx's optimistic evaluation of the logic of modern rationalization processes, the attempt to defend an idea of reason, which would comprise the ideas of truth, justice, and happiness can in the end appear only as an impotent protest against Max Weber's negative verdict about the fate of reason in the modern world.

Both Marx and Critical Theory tried to analyze modern societies in the light of a normatively grounded idea of an emancipated society. Both did not succeed in establishing an intelligible link between their analysis of modern society and the utopian horizon of their theory. Both, so it seems, were committed to a categorial framework which did not allow for the necessary differentiations truly to account for the contradictory and ambiguous character of modern rationalization processes. This categorial framework appears to leave a choice ultimately only between an uncritical affirmation (Marx) and a radical negation (Critical Theory) of instrumental reason. The critical and utopian impulses which both Marx and critical theorists shared could not be articulated adequately within a conceptual framework which was geared to a one-dimensional conception of rationality: *within* such a framework an emancipatory perspective could be only articulated *either* via an uncritical affirmation of the tendencies of formal and technical rationalization (Marx) *or* via an abstract negation of the historically existing forms of rationality (Critical Theory). Of course, these statements should be taken with a grain of salt: I am not talking here about the substantive content of either Marx's theory or Critical Theory as a whole, but about problems of conceptual strategy, about problems of depth-grammar, as it were. However, these metatheoretical problems of conceptual strategy evidently have a bearing on the substantive content of theoretical analysis as well; it is for this reason that sometimes a revision of conceptual strategies appears necessary to save the truth content of great theories.

IV

It is the merit of Jürgen Habermas that he has proposed conceptual revisions within Critical Theory which appear to make it possible to avoid the theoretical impasses of Marxism and of Critical Theory which I have pointed out so far. Over the past twenty years Habermas has worked out his own version of a critical theory of modern society; in his recent *Theorie des kommunikativen Handelns*[1] he has presented his theory in its most elaborated form so far. I cannot attempt to give an outline of Habermas's theory here; rather I want to continue this essay as an essay on conceptual strategy, trying to show the significance of Habermas's conceptual revisions with regard to the problems I have discussed so far.

Basically one could say that Habermas has "translated" the project of a critical theory of society from the conceptual framework of a philosophy of consciousness, geared to a subject–object model of cognition and action, into the conceptual framework of a theory of language and of communicative action. This basic move enabled Habermas to distinguish categorially between types of rationality and of action – in particular between instrumental and communicative rationality and action – which for conceptual reasons neither Marx, nor Weber, nor Adorno and Horkheimer could clearly keep separate from each other. The direct consequences which follow from this conceptual revision with regard to the theories of Marx, Weber, and Adorno/Horkheimer are: (1) Against Marx, Habermas can show that the bourgeois forms of universalist morality and universalist law cannot be understood as being *merely* ideological reflexes of the capitalist mode of production but however closely they may be related genetically to the emergence of capitalism, must be seen *also* as being expressive of an irreversible collective learning process which must be categorially distinguished from learning processes in the dimension of science and technology.

(2) Against Weber, Habermas can show that this emergence of universalist morality and universalist legal conceptions, which has led to a specifically modern conception of democracy and human rights, represents a type of rationalization process which has categorially to be distinguished from rationalization in the sense of formal and bureaucratic rationalization. (3) Against Horkheimer and Adorno, Habermas shows that the idea of a rational organization of society, i.e., an organization of society which would be based on a free agreement among its members, is – in however distorted a form – already embodied and recognized in the democratic institutions, the legitimacy principles and the self-interpretations of modern industrial societies; for this reason alone a critical analysis of modern societies can share a common normative ground with its object of analysis and can assume the form of an *immanent* critique.

To make the basic thrust of Habermas's theoretical approach as contrasted to those of Marx, Weber, and Adorno/Horkheimer a little clearer, I want to say first something about his conception of "communicative rationality." Habermas's claim is that the notion of communicative rationality is implicitly contained in the structure of human speech as such, and that it signifies the basic standard of rationality which competent speakers at least in *modern* societies share. I wish to clarify the notion of communicative rationality by contrasting it to a "minimal" notion of rationality, which according to authors like Steven Lukes would be the only standard of rationality which is universally valid for all cultures: such a notion of rationality can be seen simply as a derivative of the law of non-contradiction and therefore expresses a minimal core of formal logic which we must hold to be valid for all forms of symbolic interaction.

The notion of communicative rationality, in contrast, could be said to express the conception of rationality which a speaker must acknowledge, who understands the internal relationship between the raising of intersubjective validity claims and the commitment to give and be receptive to arguments. Communicative rationality, then, signifies a mode of *dealing with* (raising and accepting) validity claims. However, the formal character of this notion of rationality should not be confused with the formal character of a postulate of logical coherence (Lukes's minimal standard of rationality), even if we understand the latter as demanding coherent relationships between the linguistic utterances, actions, and expressions of an actor. For what cannot be expressed by such a minimal conception of rationality is the internal, normative relationships between the *intersubjectivity* of validity claims, modes of *argumentation*, and the idea of a rational agreement. Through the notion of communicative rationality the law of noncontradiction is, as it were, projected back from the one-dimensional space of logical relationships between propositions (and actions) onto the two-dimensional space of dialogical relationships between different speakers. This means that communicative rationality also signifies a specific (rational) attitude which individuals take towards others and toward themselves as well as a specific relationship of mutual recognition *between* different individuals.

It is obvious that these claims need some more qualifications to make them appear plausible. For one could still argue that the notion of communicative rationality is formal in the sense of *empty*, unless we think it to be operative under specific cultural conditions with specific (substantive) standards of rationality built into them. But then we would not really have gained anything by opposing it to a minimal notion of rationality in the above mentioned sense. The qualification which has yet to be added is, that the notion of communicative rationality is also meant to indicate a conception (and self-conception) of symbolic communication which does not allow for *any* validity claims to be exempt in principle from possible critical examination. This is a reflexive conception of human communication according to which validity claims, because they can only *emerge* from the sphere of communication, can also only be *redeemed* in the sphere of human discourse: there are no possible *external sources of validity*, since the sphere of validity is – conceptually is – identical with the sphere of human speech. This reflexive awareness of human speech as the reference point of all validity claims presupposes, so it seems, that the validity dimensions of objective truth, normative rightness, and subjective sincerity – or, as Habermas has recently put it: the world of objective facts, the world of social norms, and the world of inner experience – have been clearly differentiated from each other. The notion of communicative rationality reflects the cognitive and moral condition of humans in a "disenchanted" world.

It is only for this reason that Habermas can conceive of communicative action not only as a "mechanism of coordination" for the actions of individuals in society, but also as bearing a rationality *potential*, i.e., a potential of communicative rationality, which can become manifest only after the implicit dogmatism of traditional world views has been shattered and validity claims have been recognized as validity claims for which no justification is possible except through arguments. At this point argumentation as a means of restoring intersubjective agreement begins to assume a central role even in those spheres of social reality where in traditional societies the authority of religion or of tradition secured a safe foundation of common beliefs, practices, and orientations. Habermas speaks of *communicative rationalization* (or rationalization of the life-world) wherever forms of communicative action and of argumentation replace other mechanisms of coordination of actions, of social integration, or of "symbolic reproduction."

Before I can point out what we can gain from Habermas's concept of communicative action and his distinction between instrumental and communicative action with regard to the problems I have discussed before, I wish to introduce one further conceptual distinction which is basic for Habermas's theory: the distinction between social integration and systemic integration. Social integration and systemic integration represent for Habermas two different mechanisms of action coordination. While social integration operates through coordinating the action *orientations* of individuals in society, systemic integration operates through "steering media" like money and power *independently* of the action orientations of individual actors. Habermas claims that only in modern societies social and systemic integration are clearly differentiated from each other; his thesis is that the "decoupling" of system and life world from each other – which has occurred with the emergence of economic and administrative systems of action in the early phases of capitalism – became possible only after the "decentering" of world conceptions in early modern history, i.e., after the differentiation of three distinct validity dimensions of discourse from each other and the corresponding differentiation of legality from morality. Or, to put it more simply: the rationalization of law (in the Weberian sense), which was the precondition for the institutionalization of rationalized economic and administrative systems, presupposes the differentiation of a sphere of formal law from the sphere of moral discourse and moral orientations; and this differentiation of legality from morality in turn presupposes what Weber called the "disenchantment of the world" and Habermas the "decentering of world conceptions."

What follows is that systemic rationalization (economic and bureaucratic rationalization) and systemic differentiation, on the one hand, and communicative rationalization, on the other, are *complementary* possibilities of rationalization in the modern world, complementary possibilities which condition and demand each other. Without forms of systemic integration the problems of social integration would become overcomplex in a post-traditional society: communicative action is too fragile a mechanism of action coordination, as it were, to carry the whole load of integration in modern societies. Systemic integration, on the other hand, needs to be institutionalized and thereby anchored in the life-world: it *presupposes* forms of social integration and a legitimation of basic laws and institutions. With these premises Habermas reformulates the *problem* of rationalization (in the Weberian sense) as follows. Given the two complementary trends towards systemic and communicative rationalization in the modern world, there is a range of possible constellations in which "system" and "life-world" can be related to each other: "Either the institutions, through which the steering mechanisms like money or power are anchored in the life-world, are channeling the influence which the life-world exerts upon the formally organized systems of action, or, conversely, they are channeling the influence which the system exerts upon the communicatively structured contexts of action. In the one case, they function as the institutional framework which subjects the maintenance of the system to the normative restrictions of the life-world, in the other case they function as the basis which subjects the life-world to the constraints of material reproduction and thereby mediatizes it" (Habermas (1981), II, 275–6). As far as the internal, logical possibilities are concerned, the process of modernization is an essentially ambiguous one: the balance can shift to one or the other side.

However, what has happened in the actual history of capitalism is that the forces of system rationalization and system differentiation have proved to be superior to those of communicative rationalization. Thus far the counterforces emerging from the life-world in the form of social movements – e.g., the workers' movement in the nineteenth century – have not been able to reverse this trend toward a mediatization of the life-world by an increasingly complex system. Today the structures of the life-world appear to be threatened as such by the logic of systemic differentiation and rationalization – Habermas speaks of a "colonization" of the life-world. Correspondingly there is a shift in the basic themes of new social movements: these new social movements more and more defend the integrity of the life-world as such against the logic of a systemic rationalization process which threatens to push the individuals to the fringes of completely reified systems.

Habermas's diagnosis of dominating trends in the recent history of industrialized societies is not so far apart from what Weber or Horkheimer and Adorno said. However, the paradox of rationalization appears in a new light in Habermas's theory; Habermas reformulates this paradox in terms of his distinction between system and life-world. The *paradox* of rationalization would be that a rationalization of the life-world was the *precondition* and the *starting point* for a process of systemic rationalization and differentiation, which then has become more and more autonomous vis-à-vis the normative constraints embodied in the life-world, until in the end the systemic imperatives begin to instrumentalize the life-world and threaten to destory it (ibid., II, 232–3).

Against Weber and Horkheimer/Adorno, however, Habermas objects that this paradox of rationalization does *not* express an internal *logic* (or dialectic) of modern rationalization processes; it is, strictly speaking, not a paradox of *rationalization*, if we use this term in the broad sense of a post-traditional conception of rationality which, as Habermas shows, we have to substitute for Weber's restricted conception of rationality. From the perspective of an action theory in Weber's sense, then, there would neither be a paradox of rationalization nor a "dialectic of enlightenment"; rather it would be more adequate to speak of a "selective" process of rationalization, where the selective character of this process may be *explained* by the peculiar restrictions put upon communicative rationalization by the boundary conditions and the dynamics of a capitalist process of production (ibid., II, 485). Because Weber for conceptual reasons could not distinguish between systemic and communicative rationalization processes, he could not even identify those elements of communicative rationalization which have been institutionalized or preserved in the universalist principles of modern constitutions, in democratic forms of political organization, in forms of scientific, political, or aesthetic discourse, or in the self-interpretations and goals of social movements which fight for the rights of individuals, the integrity of the life-world, or the democratic organization of collective will formation. For Weber those elements of communicative rationalization, as far as he could not integrate them into his conception of formal and bureaucratic rationalization, in the end appeared as residues of irrational life forces in a rationalized world or as irrational counterreactions against the constraints of modern rationalism. Once we acknowledge these elements of – or impulses toward – communicative rationalization in the modern world *as what they are*, we can also recognize the essential *ambiguity* of the world-historical process of modernization, a kind of ambiguity without which it would indeed be impossible to combine – as Horkheimer and Adorno tried to do – a Weberian perspective on economic and bureaucratic rationalization with the Marxian perspective of an emancipated society.

Habermas's basic thesis against Weber as well as Horkheimer and Adorno is that given the emergence of a post-traditional form of rationality in modern European history, the *actual* course which the process of rationalization has taken in the modern world was only *one* among a number of different possible courses (ibid., I, 338–9), corresponding to different possible constellations concerning the relationship between system and life-world. Given the fact, however, that all possible constellations of system and life-world in the modern world have as their basis a post-traditional form of rationality, we can say – without going beyond the normative structures embodied in the basic institutions of modern societies – that only those constellations conform to a modern idea of rationality, in which the processes of systemic rationalization are brought under the control of a rationalized life-world. It is precisely in this sense that Habermas reinterprets Marx's idea of an emancipated society: in an emancipated society the life-world would no longer be subjected to the imperatives of system maintenance; a rationalized life-world would rather subject the systemic mechanisms to the needs of the associated individuals. Only then, to put it in Marx's terms, would the dependence of the "superstructure" on the "base"– i.e., the dependence of the life-world on the system – come to an end.

V

In Habermas's reconstruction of Critical Theory, Marx's idea of a free association of the producers is reinterpreted as the idea of a fully rationalized life-world. The basic direction concerning changes in the forms of social integration which is indicated by the notion of communicative rationalization is, as I have indicated before, such that the process of communicative action itself becomes more and more the decisive "mechanism" for the securing of consensus and the coordination of action (ibid., II, 268–9). The utopian perspective inherent in the conception of communicative rationalization therefore is the idea of a state of society in which "the reproduction of the life-world is no longer only *channeled through* the medium of communicative action" (ibid., II, 218–19), but in which this reproduction is *brought about* by the communicative and interpretive acts of the individuals. "The universal discourse points to an idealized life-world, reproducing itself through a mechanism of communicative action which has become largely independent of normative contexts and is based on rationally motivated Yes/No-decisions." (ibid., II, 219). Habermas also speaks of a "communicative fluidization" of traditions, normative structures and ego-identities (ibid., II, 219–20).

While the idea of an "idealized life-world" spells out the utopian perspective inherent in the idea of communicative rationality, it is not meant to provide an answer to the question of how an institutionalization of freedom in a post-capitalist society would look. Habermas's notion of communicative rationalization has rather built into it a categorial distinction between the regulative idea of a fully rationalized life-world, on the one hand, and the organizational principles which would express the institutional structures of communicatively rationalized societies at a given point in history, on the other.

Historically speaking, the problem posed by the disproportion between "system" and "life-world" in present-day industrial societies would be the problem of an adequate "objectification" of communicative rationality in new social and political *institutions*; by institutions, i.e., which, on the one hand, would represent the normative anchoring of the system in the life-world, and, on the other, would protect the communicative structures of the life-world themselves and secure a rational and democratic control of the system by the life-world. Habermas does not try to answer the question how such institutional structures would look in a post-capitalist society. This is quite consistent with his general position; it is not the task of the theoretician to determine what the content of a future social consensus will be.

Speaking about conceptual strategies, I think it is one of the great achievements of Habermas's reconstruction of Critical Theory that it mediates between the theoretical perspectives of Hegel, Marx, and Weber in a more successful way than did older versions of Critical Theory. In particular, Habermas's theory first bridges the gap between a "Hegelian" perspective on the differentiation processes of modern societies, on the one hand, and the utopian perspective of Marx's critique of political economy, on the other. It allows us to understand the Marxian problem of emancipation as the political and historical problem of a new *institutionalization* of freedom in the modern world, while at the same time making intelligible the utopian perspective inherent in this *historical* project. And Habermas's theory secondly bridges the gap between a Weberian perspective on modern rationalization processes, on the one hand, and Marx's view of historical progress, on the other. For it establishes an intelligible link between the *negative* dynamic of progress in present-day capitalism and an emancipatory historical *project* in the Marxian sense.

These are large claims, which will be disputed by Hegelians, hermeneutic philosophers, functionalists, and conservative political philosophers alike, and which I cannot really defend in this essay. However, I want at least to put forward a few arguments concerning the relationship between the historical project of a new institutionalization of freedom in the modern world and the *utopian* perspective of an "idealized life world." A criticism, as it is often put forward against "utopian rationalism" by philosophers with an Aristotelian or hermeneutic background, is that democratic legitimacy, although it must be conceived of as being based on a consensus of basic norms, institutions, and values, cannot be understood as being based on a *rational* consensus. The upshot of this criticism is that communicative action and rational discourse ultimately cannot generate legitimate institutions (legitimate power), but that only legitimate institutions (legitimate power) could set free communicative action as a mechanism of social coordination. As far as the legitimacy of institutions is concerned, however, there can be no ideal limit; there is rather an irreducible element of "voluntas" as against "ratio," or, to put it in Hannah Arendt's terms, legitimate power can only be based on "opinion." This means, however, that (1) there is no internal link between the ideas of rationality and radical democracy, and (2) that normative idealizations like that of an "idealized life-world" are, strictly speaking, meaningless. In short, there is no *rational* solution to the problem of an institutionalization of freedom.

The argument, as I have presented it here, might be called "left-Aristotelian" or "left-hermeneutic." In my response I do not wish to elaborate and defend Habermas's consensus theory of truth, nor do I wish to go into more details of his theory of communicative action. I rather want to take an indirect line of defense, showing that what the critic *accepts* is enough to validate Habermas's general position.

Let us first take the consensus on basic norms, institutions, and values. Certainly nothing prevents us from assuming that part of this consensus is a principle saying that in cases of disagreement on practical matters agreement ought to be brought about by argument as much as possible Under these conditions communicative action *might* become the primary mechanism of action coordination. This does not necessarily mean that there are, e.g., no majority decisions; it simply means that in cases of normative disagreement *some* kind of agreement is brought about which is considered as "fair" or "just" by all individuals involved (e.g., that a majority vote should be taken and accepted by all). This means, evidently, that nobody is *forced* to do or to tolerate what he is not convinced he/she *should* (morally should) do or tolerate.

By free agreements we mean, of course, agreements which are not the result of manipulation or internalized pressure. Although this is not a trivial qualification, it is enough to state it here, since we may assume that the individuals involved know how to apply the distinctions in question. Since the basic agreement is never put into question, although nobody is prevented from putting it into question (actually nobody sees a reason to do so), this agreement can be called rational at least in the sense that no arguments are brought forward *against* it (and none are suppressed). The basic agreement being stable means that the individuals experience their form of life as a good form of life. We need not know how this agreement has come into being; it could, e.g., have been the result of a long struggle for recognition between different factions or groups in society.

Here we have Habermas's "idealized life-world." Since coordination by rational agreement is its all-pervasive principle, it seems almost paradoxical to ask why it should be called a *rationalized* life-world. The question, however, was whether such an organization of society coud be called rational as a whole (not having an *irrational* basis). Basically this is question, whether the (successfully applied) principle of consensual action coordination is but *one* among many possible contents of a democratic consensus. Now I think that this question has to be answered in the negative precisely insofar as we believe that rational argument about practical matters or norms is – in principle – *possible*. For insofar as we believe *that*, granting equal rights and liberties to everybody, including equal rights of political participation, is tantamount to accepting a principle of consensual action coordination. Without going into the question of whether the democratic principle is itself rooted in the structures of speech as such, we must say that if the principle of rationality is *combined* with the democratic principle, a principle of consensual action coordination becomes unavoidable insofar as we believe in the *possibility* of rational argument. Consequently the question under debate boils down to the question, whether there are any limits of rational argument *in principle*, i.e., limits of rational discourse where the idea of a rational agreement with respect to controversial issues *does not make sense* any more. At this point, however, the Aristotelian or hermeneutic defender of democracy is in a weak position: for the idea of a democratic consensus on basic norms, institutions, and values does hardly make sense, if it is not conceived as being *also* a consensus on the *application* of basic rules and norms and on basic *criteria* of justice or fairness. But then on the *basis* of this consensus rational argument about normative matters *must* be possible. If that much is granted, however, to deny the rationality of the *basic* consensus amounts to drawing an arbitrary boundary line between questions concerning the basic framework of norms, institutions, and interpretations, on the one hand, and questions which are internal to this framework, on the other. I say "arbitrary," not because I deny the qualitative difference between questions internal to a conceptual framework and questions concerning the conceptual framework as a whole, but because in the continuum of problems which stretches from problems of one kind to those of the other we cannot fix a boundary line beyond which the notion of "rational argument" ceases to apply. That much, I think, has been shown by recent debates in the philosophy of science. If this is granted, however, the basic consensus, which I have presupposed in my argument, deserves to be called "rational" precisely inasmuch as the principle of coordination by rational agreement, which is part of this consensus, is not restricted in its application to any particular level of societal life, i.e., if no norms, institutions or interpretations are in principle exempt from the possibility of critical examination.

The upshot of my considerations is that the principle of consensual coordination must be considered as the normative core of the very democratic consensus, which the critic took for granted; *and* that we cannot draw any definite line of demarcation between "internal" rational agreements and "external" agreements based on mere "voluntas." But then an "idealized life-world" in Habermas's sense begins to appear as the normative "center of gravitation" of *any* democratic and egalitarian form of social and political organization. By this I mean that the more a consensual mode of action coordination has already become real in the institutions and practices of a society, the more a society will gravitate toward dissolving the remnants of brute force and mere compulsion. Accordingly, I would think that the utopian perspective inherent in the democratic tradition should not so much be considered in analogy to geometrical idealizations, which can never be perfectly embodied in the recalcitrant material of physical bodies (one might rather think of an infinite process of possible approximations), but rather as the center of gravitation of democratic forms of organization, the attractive force of which becomes proportionately stronger as a relationship of mutual recognition is already embodied in consensual forms of action coordination.

Conversely, I think it is obvious that for democratic legitimacy to be kept alive a consensus about basic procedural norms and rules irrespective of any chances of rational agreement is not enough; for beyond a certain point disagreement about substantive matters will necessarily turn into disagreement about procedural rules or a disagreement about the interpretation of basic norms. (The new social movements provide ample material for illustration.) This again shows that there is a "more" or "less" with respect to democratic legitimacy; and the (internal) standard of this "more" or "less" is expressed precisely by the normative idealization which Habermas derives from his notion of communicative rationality. This means, however, that communicative action in the ideal case would become the exclusive mechanism – not of action coordination, since we suppose systemic forms of integration to persist, but – of securing consensus and of dealing with dissensus. Needless to say, that such a form of life may never become true; what is important at this point is not what will be historically *possible*, but how the "depth-grammar" of our *historical* projects is to be understood.

The idea of communicative rationalization with its inherent utopian perspective does not put into question the differentiation processes of modern societies as such, not even the differentiation of "systemic" from "social" integration. And yet it enables us to give a new, more precise meaning to the old ideas, inseparable from the Marxist tradition, of a "sublation" (*Aufhebung*) of the bourgeois form of law, of politics, or of art in an emancipated, postcapitalist society. Underlying these ideas, as they were expressed not only in the Marxist tradition up to Marcuse and Adorno, but also in avant-garde movements of art and by rebellious students, has always been the awareness that those specific forms of systemic and functional differentiations as they have grown out of the capitalist rationalization process, have become obsolete and oppressive: politics being separated from the life-world, the sphere of formal law being disconnected from the sphere of moral discourse, autonomous art being separated from the life process of individuals, and finally the life-world as such being increasingly subjected to the dynamics of economic and administrative processes, which more and more threaten to push individuals to the fringes of a reified social system. I have indicated above that we have to distinguish between those irreversible differentiation processes, which signify the end of traditional society and the emergence of specifically modern, universalist conceptions of rationality, freedom, and democracy, on the one hand, and the specific form in which these differentiation processes have been articulated and institutionalized in capitalist societies. It is obviously to the *latter* only that the ideas of a sublation of formal law, politics, or art can meaningfully apply. What they can mean is what could be called a new "permeability" of the relatively autonomous subsystems or cultural spheres for each other: The formalized processes of administration, legislation, and jurisdiction would then enter into a new constellation with nonformalized – or not necessarily formalized – processes of communication and will-formation, so that the formalized decision processes would become permeable to the need-interpretations, moral impulses, or aesthetic experiences articulated beneath the level of formal organizations. The arts, without losing their autonomy, would become a medium of communication, objectifying as well as transforming the experience and self-experience of the individuals; they would reenter into the life process by affecting the articulation of needs and the self-interpretations of individuals, who otherwise would become mute and blind vis-à-vis their own internal nature. The critique of autonomous art, then, would not question the *autonomy* of art – although it was often misunderstood in this way; its genuine impulses are rather directed against art as a bourgeois institution, against art as commodity and as a part of mass culture, and against art as a self-contained sphere of ideological consolations.

As far as the Marxist critique of formal law is concerned, the point under debate can be made a little clearer if we contrast the idea of a *reconciliation* of the legal and the moral sphere, as it is contained in the notion of communicative rationalization, to the practice of *negating* the differentiation of legality from morality, as it can be found in modern totalitarian systems. I think that the latter, i.e. the repressive abolition of a differentiation process constitutive of modern societies, should be seen as a regressive counterfeit of that reconciliation of morality with legality, which would be brought about where legal norms and political institutions would lose their repressive character and would no longer be in conflict with moral demands. The latter *presupposes* the differentiation of morality from legality, but tries to adjust formal law to moral principles; the former is meant to *undo* this differentiation by subjecting moral consciousness to the demands of positive law. Seen from the perspective of communicative rationalization, therefore, the critique of the bourgeois form of law, as it was prominent in the Marxist tradition up to Adorno's *Negative Dialectics*, can be seen in its proper light and as being continuous with the tradition of Enlightenment. This applies in particular to the critique of the formal character of the principles of bourgeois constitutions: Not the *abolition* of formally guaranteed liberties and rights – the great achievement of the bourgeois revolutions – is what is aimed at in this critique, but their becoming the true fundament of a liberated social life for all individuals in modern societies. This is certainly what Marx *meant* when he said (in *On the Jewish Question*) that "human emancipation will only be completed when the real, individual man has absorbed into himself the abstract citizen; when as individual man, in his everyday life, in his work and in his relationships, he has become a species-being; and when he has recognized and organized his 'forces propres' as social powers so that he no longer separates his social power from himself as political power."

Coming finally back to Adorno, I might now rephrase my objections against his aesthetic interpretation of a utopian perspective as follows: The "disintegration" of objective reason into its partial moments (Habermas) – scientific–technical rationality, practical–moral rationality, and aesthetic rationality – which went along with the process of modernization, cannot possibly be "overcome" by a transformation of society, for which *one* moment of reason – aesthetic rationality – would provide the model. Of course, Adorno would never have said it in this way. However, the specific rationality of aesthetic production certainly became for him the dominant model in terms of which he tried to conceive of a "sublation" of instrumental rationality into a nonrepressive form of reason. The idea is tempting, since art – in particular, music – *does* obviously contain an element of "instrumental" rationality, of technique and of construction, and therefore provides a model for instrumental reason being sublated into a field of forces which is ruled by a logic higher than that of "identifying" thought and instrumental action.

Through integrating instrumental (and discursive) rationality as a sublated moment, the work of art for Adorno was able to achieve its specific, nonrepressive – i.e., aesthetic – unity out of a manifold of its individual elements. *Therefore* the authentic work of art could appear to him as a semblance of reconciliation. However, the interplay between mimetic impulses and rational elements, constitutive of the aesthetic integration of elements into a whole, could not possibly provide an image of what the "domestication" of instrumental reason could mean with respect to the problem of bringing about a nonrepressive form of *social* integration. Adorno, then, had good reasons also to *distrust* aesthetic experience if it was left on its own: he insisted, paradoxically, that only philosophy can bring out what the truth of aesthetic experience really is. I think it would be better to concede that art in itself cannot be the bearer of a utopian perspective. As far as a semblance of reconciliation *is* constitutive of the work of art, it might rather be suspected that this reconciliation is one *beyond* reason, a stepping out of the confines of space, time and causality, ecstatic rather than anticipatory. Perhaps for Adorno these ecstatic moments of aesthetic experience were the only genuinely transcending impulses he could detect in a closed universe of instrumental reason; so he tried to decipher them as meaning reconciliation in space and time, utopia in the materialist, Marxian sense. The price for this, however, was that the *political* dimension of the historical project of emancipation was lost again.

And yet, there is another sense in which aesthetic experience *can* be related to the utopian perspective of Critical Theory. Adorno himself has occasionally interpreted the utopian potential of art as residing in its speechlike character: art can say what *we* cannot say. At this point, however, aesthetic experience *can* be seen as being related to the utopian perspective of unblocked communicative relationships – *between* the individuals as well as *of* the individuals *with themselves*. If we take the work of art as providing a *medium* rather than a *model* of such communicative relationships, we can, I think, better understand why Adorno insisted on the *transcending* elements in genuine aesthetic experience, transcending, that is, the confines of mere aesthetic pleasure. But the *beyond* of art, to which it points and to which it is related, is not something superseding art *as* art, but the social life process itself as it can be *affected* by aesthetic experience. Understood in this way, aesthetic experience, by illuminating our life praxis and our self-understanding, by pushing back the boundaries of muteness and inarticulate silence, and by making accessible the hidden depths of our lives to ourselves, *is*, as Adorno thought, the presence of a utopian perspective.

Evidently there *is* a sense in which the old radical ideas of a "supersession" of bourgeois politics, of the bourgeois form of law, or of bourgeois art, can be adopted without questioning irreversible differentiation processes as they are constitutive of the "project of modernity." To adopt these radical ideas can, however, only mean to reinterpret them, i.e., to place them into a new theoretical context and to fill them with new and more complex connotations. To reinterpret them as I have suggested in this essay might be useful if we try to understand what is progressive (and what is regressive) in those new social movements which have sprung up everywhere in the Western world during the past twenty years; in particular if we try to understand them not only as defensive movements, but in their possible meaning with regard to the historical project of a postcapitalist institutionalization of freedom. By this I mean above all the institutionalization of public spaces for political participation and communal action, which would not only provide a basis for a democratic control of economic and administrative processes, but which would also provide the social basis for a viable identity of the individuals who are increasingly threatened by anomie and alienation. Last but not least, such an institutionalization of freedom would provide the basis for transforming alienated labor into meaningful work. The old communist slogan "to each according to his needs" could, after all, still become true if human need, instead of being determined by the process of material production, would begin to determine its direction as well as its form of organization; i.e., if the disastrous dynamics of the capitalist production process, which at present leads to an increasing destruction of the human habitat, an increasing reification of consiousness and of social relationships, a mindless overconsumption for the privileged and a degrading poverty for the rest, could be brought to a halt. I do not know whether we should still use the old and much-discredited term "socialism" for this historical project. If we do, I think one might say that the signs are increasing again that the only alternative for the capitalist world, after all, still is: Socialism or Barbarism. Provided we still have time enough to choose.

2

Psychic Thermidor and the Rebirth of Rebellious Subjectivity[1]

JÜRGEN HABERMAS

We all remember what Herbert Marcuse kept denouncing as the evils of our age: the blind struggle for existence, relentless competition, wasteful productivity, deceitful repression, false virility, and cynical brutality. Whenever he felt that he should speak as teacher and philosopher he encouraged the negation of the performance principle, of possessive individualism, of alienation in labor – as well as in love relations. But the negation of suffering was for him only a start. No doubt, Herbert Marcuse claimed negation to be the very essence of thinking – as did Adorno and Horkheimer; but the driving force of criticism, of contradiction and contest carried him well beyond the limits of an accusation of unnecessary mischief. Marcuse moved further ahead. He did not hesitate to advocate, in an affirmative mood, the fulfillment of human needs, of the need for undeserved happiness, of the need for beauty, of the need for peace, calm, and privacy. Although, certainly, Marcuse was not an affirmative thinker, he was nevertheless the most affirmative among those who praised negativity. With him negative thinking retained the dialectical trust in determinate negation, in the disclosure of positive alternatives. Marcuse did not, in contrast to Adorno, only encircle the ineffable; he made appeals to future alternatives. I am interested in this affirmative feature of Herbert Marcuse's negative thinking. In this lecture, let me illustrate what I mean by "affirmative feature" with reference to a rather personal reminiscence. I have just reread the two lectures which Marcuse gave when I first met him. For us it was a surprisingly new tone when we heard the following sentences: "The order of values of a nonrepressive principle of progress can be determined on almost all levels in opposition to that of its repressive counterpart. Men's basic experience would be no longer that of life as a struggle for existence but rather that of the enjoyment of life. Alienated labor would be transformed into the free play of human faculties and forces. In consequence all contentless transcendence would come to a close, and freedom would no longer be an eternally failing project . . . Time would not seem linear. . . , but cyclical, as the return contained in Nietzsche's idea of 'the perpetuity of pleasure'."

This is not quoted for the Marcuse of 1967, who came to Berlin for intense discussions on violence and the expected end of utopia and who, at that time, was hailed by the protesting students as their inspirational intellectual leader. Neither is that quote from the Marcuse of 1964, who came to the Max Weber centennial in Heidelberg, made his professional appearance as an important emigre social theorist and immediately aroused excited discussions. I am speaking of the Marcuse of 1956, who came to Frankfurt for another centennial: the commemoration on the occasion of Freud's 100th birthday was the date of Marcuse's first academic return to Germany. I should mention that the international conference of *Freud in der Gegenwart*, where Marcuse lectured side by side with famous analysts such as Alexander, Balint, Erikson, and Spitz, was the first opportunity for young German academics to learn about the simple fact that Sigmund Freud was the founding father of a living scientific and intellectual tradition. In this context Marcuse opened his first lecture with sentences which, at a time when Freud and Marx were "dead dogs" and practically unknown at German universities, sounded strange and radical: "The psyche appears more and more immediately to be a piece of the social totality, so that individuation is almost synonymous with apathy and even with guilt, but also with the principle of negation, of possible revolution. Moreover, the totality of which the psyche is a part becomes to an increasing extent less 'society' than 'politics.' That is, society has fallen prey to and becomes identified with domination."

For us, the research assistants at the Institute of Horkheimer and Adorno, this was the moment when we first faced an embodiment and vivid expression of the political spirit of the old Frankfurt School. As a school it had been alive only during a few years of American exile. If there ever has been a Frankfurt School, it did not exist in Frankfurt, neither before nor after the Nazi period, but during the thirties, in New York. I was reminded of this fact when Herbert, before his death in Starnberg, while he was, after a stroke, already somewhat inhibited in his verbal fluency, did not speak his mother tongue: the language of his last days was English. But let me return to our first encounter. What, in 1956, made a stunning impression was the forthright style of Marcuse's thought and presentation. You know better than I that Herbert Marcuse's spoken English never quite lost the mark of a Berlin accent, that his written English was never completely stripped of the clumsiness of the German grammar underneath. But with his German it was the other way round. By the standards of the jargon of German philosophers Marcuse spoke a straight, affirmative language, easy to understand and without the rhetorical loopholes where the more shocking consequences of a dialectical argument might have found a hiding place. Although rather a shy person, Marcuse was never afraid of being outspoken and for taking the responsibility for what he said, even for taking the risk of oversimplification, if there seemed to be no other way to address an important issue. In the following years, when I became closer to Herbert Marcuse and learned more about the first generation of critical theorists, that affirmative feature which struck me from the very beginning became even more obvious. Compared with Horkheimer, Lowenthal, and Adorno, with whom he had formed the inner circle, Marcuse represented a singular combination.

Since he first joined the Institute, Marcuse had made the most "orthodox" contributions to Critical Theory. This is true of his essays in the *Zeitschrift* were Marcuse was chosen to write the article "Philosophy and Critical Theory," counterpart to Horkheimer's famous position paper on "Traditional and Critical Theory." But it is also true of his later writings including the very last: in *Reason and Revolution*, in *One Dimensional Man* and in *The Aesthetic Dimension*, Marcuse elaborated themes and arguments, pursued lines of reasoning which were more or less shared by the whole group. This orthodoxy is, however, only one side of Marcuse's work. His work reflects, on the other side, quite distinct features which set it apart from the background tradition. Marcuse received his philosophical training in Freiburg with Heidegger, and he never lost contact with existential phenomenology. Marcuse was, among his colleagues, the most professional in attitude; his major works, *Reason and Revolution, Soviet Marxism*, and *Eros and Civilization*, are all well placed in the context of related disciplines and exemplify an almost conventional type of systematic academic presentation.

Marcuse's personal history followed, as compared to the biographies of those next to him, including Neumann and Kirchheimer, an almost opposite trend; he, who started from a rather conservative theoretical position, became in the course of his life more and more radicalized – he was, moreover, the only one who assumed a direct political role; supported by his wife Inge, he deliberately took this role and played it at times with a considerable sense for the imponderables of political activism.

Take one example: when Marcuse was in Berlin in 1967, he was asked about his relation to the heroes of the Third World and, in his inimitable manner, gave the answer: "I would not have mentioned Fanon and Guevara as much as a small item that I read in a report about North Vietnam and that had a tremendous effect on me, since I am an absolutely incurable and sentimental romantic. It was a very detailed report, which showed . . . that in the parks in Hanoi the benches are made only big enough for two and *only two* people to sit on, so that another person would not even have the technical possibility of disturbing."

Here, again, we encounter something very affirmative. Imagine, for the moment, that Adorno in a similar situation would have wanted to express a similar intention! He probably would have made a cautious appeal to a poem of Eichendorff while anticipating what all of us today, after the Vietnamese invasion into Cambodia, do think: that the facts will reveal as an incurable romantic one who tries to affirmatively spell out utopia in terms of particular examples, as Herbert did. What I have called the affirmative feature is documented by a type of self-confessed romanticism which is lacking in Adorno and Horkheimer, and even in Benjamin.

The question which I would like to pursue is whether this peculiar feature should just count as a trait of Herbert Marcuse's personality or whether it is due to a theoretical position which separates him from his close friends. Since there is a good deal of manifest agreement among the members of the inner circle, we tend to think that the affirmative feature of Marcuse's negative thinking indicates a difference rather in style and character than in theory. How otherwise could we explain the fact that the author of the deeply pessimistic *One Dimensional Man* – a book which ends with the quote from Benjamin that it is only for the sake of those without hope that hope is given to us – that this man, less than one year later, inspired the student movement with his hope? I think there is another explanation. In Marcuse's version of critical theory we find a twist on an argument which well can explain why Marcuse was different. In order to identify this twist I will briefly outline the main stages of the thought of Herbert Marcuse.

II

I will start with (A) the transition from Heidegger to Horkheimer, and then (B) indicate the classical position of Critical Theory in the mid-thirties, with a subsequent shift marked by Horkheimer and Adorno's *Dialectic of Enlightenment*. From this perspective we will see (C) the route which Marcuse took as his way out of the dilemma posed by the alleged totalization of instrumental reason. He discovered this way with *Eros and Civilization*, the book which appeared in 1955 and the substance of which was contained in the two Freud lectures given at Frankfurt one year later.

(A) *Hegels Ontologie und die Grundlegung einer Theorie der Geschichtlichkeit*, published in 1932, was planned as *Habilitations-Schrift*. The aspired *Habilitation* did not work out – Heidegger was soon to become one of the Nazi Rectors of the first hour. That Hegel book was written by one of the brightest students of Heidegger; it is the document of an attempt to interpret dialectical thinking from a peculiar Heideggerian point of view. Hegel is here presented as another ontologist who conceived being as the essence of becoming – *Sein als Bewegtheit*. Heidegger had a lasting impact on Herbert Marcuse – as much in terms of personal loyalty, bridging the political abyss, as in terms of certain philosophical motivations. For Marcuse, Heidegger remained the one of *Being and Time*, moreover that Heidegger whose analysis of *Dasein* was received as a radicalized transcendental approach. Of course, after the period of *Being and Time*, both Heidegger and Marcuse moved in opposite directions. While Heidegger made *Dasein*, the abstract structures of the human world, dependent on some metahistorical fate, of an even more abstract *Sein* or fateful being, Marcuse, on the other hand, tried to link the ontological structures of the life world to the ontic, that is, to the contingent and concrete processes of society and history; he looked out for the differentiation of the ontological difference. It was no accident that Marcuse, in this transitional period, did not move away from Heidegger by way of a critique of Heidegger. For the preparation of this lecture, Leo Lowenthal lent me his copy of *Hegels Ontologie*, and in this old copy I found a yellowed cut out from the feuilleton of the *Vossische Zeitung* with a long and intense review of the three volumes of Karl Jaspers' *Philosophie*, written by somebody with the initials H.M., dated Dec. 14, 1933. It is in this context of a criticism of Jaspers that we find a passage which indicates, still guarded by clauses, Marcuse's detachment from Heidegger. Here, Marcuse insists that the formal properties of historicity conceal rather than disclose the substance of history. He raises the question, "Whether it is not the case that particular and contingent situations can destroy the authenticity of human existence, can abolish freedom or transform it into sheer illusion." Any talk about historicity, he continues, "must remain abstract and uncommitted until the analysis focuses on the concrete, 'material' situation." (*Vossische Zeitung* Nr. 339, Dec. 14, 1933.)

The term "material" is printed in quotes, thereby inconspicuously referring to an earlier article of the same author on the recently discovered Paris Manuscripts, not by Karl Jaspers but by Karl Marx. This article shows how young Marcuse appropriated young Marx from the viewpoint of existential phenomenology, taking the very notions of *Praxis* and *Lebenswelt* as guidelines for the liberation from alienated labor. Marcuse was the first Heideggerian-Marxist, anticipating the later phenomenological Marxism of Jean-Paul Sartre, Karl Kosík, Enzo Paci, and the Yugoslav *Praxis* philosophers.

(*B*) In the meantime, Marcuse had joined the Frankfurt Institute on its way to the United States. In his famous essay on "Philosophy and Critical Theory," published in 1937, Marcuse presents himself at the center of the Frankfurt School's theory. The vacant place of *Dasein* and *Geschichtlichkeit*, of the abstract structures of the human world, is now filled with a historically situated reason: "Reason is the fundamental category of philosophical thought, the only one by means of which it has bound itself to human destiny." The abstract and ahistorical concept of reason which is at the heart of idealistic philosophy lends itself to all forms of ideology, but the bourgeois ideals, of cognitive and moral universalism on the one hand, of expressive subjectivism on the other, carry also a utopian content which transcends the limits of false consciousness. For Critical Theory those ideals "are exclusively potentialities of the concrete social situation. They become relevant only as economic and political questions and as such bear on human relations in the productive process, the distribution of the product of social labor, and men's active participation in the economic and political administration of the whole." The demand for reason simply means, resonating indeed to an ancient truth, a demand for "the creation of a social organization in which individuals can collectively regulate their lives in accordance with the needs."

At the time when he wrote this, Marcuse was already aware of, and explicitly referring to the fact that, with fascism and, moreover, with Stalinism, history had taken a course quite contrary to the predictions of Marxist theory. He therefore stressed the constructive as against the descriptive and explanatory role of theory, admitting that Critical Theory "must concern itself to a hitherto unknown extent with the past." But Marcuse did not yet question the revolutionary dynamic of the productive forces developing in the womb of capitalism. The stifling of the proletariat, its lack of revolutionary consciousness, is still explained in the old vein: "Fettering the productive forces and keeping down the standard of life is characteristic of even the economically most developed countries."

In the following years Marcuse elaborated the classical position of Critical Theory in careful studies on Hegel and the rise of social theory. At the same time, Horkheimer and Adorno, who had moved to Santa Monica, had already taken a somewhat different line. With *Dialectic of Enlightenment* they definitely lost their trust in the revolutionary dynamic of the productive forces, and in the practical impact of negative thinking. Both the productive forces and critical thought were seen in the perspective of merging with their opposite, with the forces of domination. As they develop they become regressive, more and more subordinated to the imperatives of an instrumental reason which is no longer instrumental for the satisfaction of human needs, but gaining the autonomy of an end in itself. The totality of instrumental reason finds its expression in totalitarian society. I will not go into the subtleties of this gloomy exposition which Marcuse soon adopted. In the foreword to an English translation of his old essays, published three decades ago in the *Zeitschrift*, Marcuse declared the break in his thinking: "That . . . this was written before Auschwitz deeply separates it from the present. What was correct in it has since become, perhaps not false, but a thing of the past . . . : remembrance of something that at some point had lost its reality and had to be taken up again . . . The end of a historical period and the horror of the one to come were announced in the simultaneity of the civil war in Spain and the trials in Moscow."

Marcuse described this new period as a totalization of instrumental reason, that is, in the light of his own analysis in *One Dimensional Man*: "Productivity and prosperity in league with a technology in the service of monopolistic politics seem to immunize advancing industrial society in its established structure." He then asks the central question: "Is this concept of immunity still dialectical?"

Adorno answered this question with a qualified "No"; he explained this reaction in terms of his "Negative Dialectics." Marcuse, on the contrary, still stuck to an affirmative answer. According to Marcuse, the earlier theory, with its concept of a free and rational society, made only one mistake – it did not promise too much but rather too little.

(C) The reasons why Herbert Marcuse could both accept Horkheimer's and Adorno's analysis of the eclipse of reason and yet remain faithful to the political intention of early Critical Theory are laid out in *Eros and Civilization*, among Marcuse's books the most Marcusian one.

Let me first state the question at issue. Marcuse agreed with Horkheimer and Adorno in their assumption that with the expansion of capitalism the project of instrumental reason would shape the entire universe of discourse and action, intellectual and material culture: "In the medium of technology, culture, politics, and the economy merge into an omnipresent system which swallows up or repulses all alternatives." On the other hand, Marcuse still maintained that the same project does undermine the stability of a domination which fuses technology with practical rationality, since "The progressive reduction of physical labor power in the production process . . . suggests possible liberation from alienated labor." If these objective possibilities are at all suggestive, we must, however, rely on a subjectivity which is still sensitive to a utopian horizon. This is the question then: how could Marcuse believe in the rebirth of rebellious subjectivity if he accepted the first of the two arguments, in fact the core argument of *Dialectic of Enlightenment*, that with each conquest over external nature the internal nature of those who gain ever new triumphs is more deeply enslaved?

It is at this point that Marcuse shows reservations based on his distinctive reading of Freud's theory of instincts. To put the argument in a nutshell: even if the individual, the sole bearer of reason, is more and more swallowed up by a totalitarian society, and even if this shrinkage of the ego is without any limits, we still may hope for the rebirth of rebellious subjectivity from a nature which is older than, and arises from below the level of, individuation and rationality. Marcuse has a chiliastic trust in a revitalizing dynamic of instincts which works through history, finally breaks with history and leaves it behind as what then will appear as prehistory. Let us recall how he interprets Freud's theory of patricide:

> This dynamic of domination, which begins with the institution of despotism, leads to revolution and ends after the first attempt at liberation with the reestablishment of the father in internalized and generalized, i.e. rational form, repeats itself . . . during the entire history of culture and civilization, although in diluted form. It does so as the rebellion of all sons against all fathers in puberty . . . and . . . in the ever recurring dynamic of revolutions in the past. . . . Insurrection succeeds and certain forces attempt to drive the revolu-

tion to its extreme point, from which the transition to new, not only quantitatively but qualitatively different conditions could perhaps proceed. At this point the revolution is usually vanquished and domination is internalized, reestablished, and continued at a higher level. . . . we can raise the question whether alongside the socio-historical Thermidor . . . there is not also a *psychic* Thermidor. Are revolutions perhaps not only vanquished, reversed, and unmade from the outside, is there perhaps in individuals themselves already a dynamic at work that *internally* negates possible liberation and gratification and that supports external forces of denial?

At a first glance, this consideration is nothing but a translation, of what the dialectic of instrumental reason means, into Freudian language. On a careful reading, the difference however comes to the fore – the difference is in the move to keep separate the internal or instinctual from the external or social forces of domination. If the psychic as compared with the socio-historic thermidor gains a dynamic of its own, it is no longer social theory alone, but the theory of instincts which also provides the key. The question, whether the psychic termidor must be repeated again and again, gains an almost existentialist dignity, since the answer to this question no longer depends on whether or not late capitalism, as an economic and a political system, can contain its inner conflicts.

From the metahistory of instincts Marcuse defends two related propositions. (1) There is no final opposition between Eros and Thanatos; in spite of their antagonism both are conservative in nature, both strive for pacification, and both are unproductive and similarly directed against a relentless struggle for existence. (2) As soon as the progress of civilization, which is based on the repressive modification of the instincts, increases, the existence of a surplus product not leading to individual gratification provokes a reaction from both Eros and Thanatos. Once instinctual repression loses its function for necessary self-preservation, the two conservative powers behind the scenes of civilization form a coalition and demand the recalling of energies from alienated labor.

III

This theory has the weakness that it cannot consistently account for its own possibility. If rebellious subjectivity had to owe its rebirth to something that is beyond – a too deeply corrupted – reason, it is hard to explain why some of us should at all be in a position to recognize this fact and to give reasons in defense of it. In this respect, Adorno was the more consistent thinker. However implausible the argument may seem, it had the function to preserve in Herbert Marcuse one of his most admirable features – not to give in to defeatism. But there is more to the search for an "instinctive" base of socialism. This effort is, after all, the result of a true philosophical intention. Marcuse did not want to fall back into existentialism, he did not want just to appeal to the vital needs of freedom or merely to evoke the pathos of emancipation. He felt the obligation to give theoretical explanations and thereby to ground action in reason.

Moreover, Marcuse was one of the few philosophers who were severely and chronically rebuked for the seriousness of their philosophical attitude. In summer 1967, at the Free University, Marcuse was exposed to a situation where he knew that any single word could have irrevocable consequences. He was invited to talk about the use of violence, and he had just declared the unity of moral, sexual, and political rebellion, when he found himself confronted with questions about the doubtful nature of moral justifications. Some of the questions indicated a then–widespread inclination, on the side of the students, to free political activism from the painful hesitations of moral–practical reasoning. One student complained about difficulties he had experienced in discussions with a worker: "What does this worker care about the terror in Vietnam? Humanitarian arguments wouldn't do, since humanity itself gave rise to terror." The student apparently referred, although in an elliptic and misleading form, to the core of the analysis of the eclipse of reason. But Marcuse was not irritated at all. "As to your suspicion about humanitarian arguments . . . We must finally relearn what we forgot during the fascist period, or what you, who were not even born . . . have not fully become conscious of: that humanitarian and moral arguments are not merely deceitful ideology. Rather, they can and must become central social forces." Another student countered this straight answer with a moral skepticism which in my country often reveals the strong influence of Carl Schmitt even on the left: "On the right of resistance: in your essay on tolerance you put this right in quotation marks, but now you have interpreted it as an ancient principle. What is this right based on? Is it a romantic relic of natural law, or is it a self-posited right and, if so, how can the opposition invoke a right which it must first generate?" In this moment, Marcuse decided to be inconsistent rather than irresponsible. He swept aside his own doubts on a corrupted practical reason which supposedly had been absorbed into a totality of instrumental reason. His answer was clear, without the slightest ambiguity: ". . . appealing to the right of resistance is an appeal to a higher law, which has universal validity, that is, which goes beyond the self-defined right and privilege of a particular group. And there really is a close connection between the right of resistance and natural law. Now you will say that such a universal higher law simply does not exist. I believe that it does exist. Today we no longer call it Natural Law . . . If we appeal to humanity's right to peace, to the right to abolish exploitation and oppression, we are not talking about self-defined, special, group interests, but rather and, in fact, interests demonstrable as universal rights."

Before his eightieth birthday, and in preparation for an interview on that occasion, Marcuse and I had a long discussion on how we could and should explain the normative base of Critical Theory. Last summer, when I saw him for the first time since that discussion, Herbert was under intensive care in a hospital in Frankfurt, all types of controlling apparatuses on his left and on his right. None of us knew that this was the beginning of the end. On this occasion, indeed our last philosophical encounter, Herbert made the connection with our controversy two years ago, telling me: look, I know wherein our most basic value judgements are rooted in compassion, in our sense for the suffering of others.

3

Neoconservative Culture Criticism in the United States and West Germany: An Intellectual Movement in Two Political Cultures

JÜRGEN HABERMAS

It is an accomplishment of the neoconservatives in the United States that a conservative government is able to rely on theoretical perspectives and not merely on pragmatic considerations and the general climate. That explains the interest of the European conservative parties in this intellectual movement: an example is the conference sponsored by the Konrad Adenauer Foundation in September of 1981, which brought together German and American neoconservatives.[1]

In the United States as in the Federal Republic, neoconservatism is a matter of loose groupings of intellectuals with common orientations. The neoconservatives in both countries share a collection of critical positions and conceptions which resulted from similar disappointments. Since the middle of the sixties these social scientists and philosophers confronted economic, political, and intellectual developments which did not conform to their rather affirmative image of Western industrial societies. In this sense, neoconservatism emerges from a response to a disappointment. Nevertheless, the profiles of neoconservative thought in the United States and the Federal Republic differ as much as do the theories and diagnoses with which these intellectuals, in both countries, commenced during the fifties.

I

The theoretically productive center of American neoconservatism is composed of well-known, scholarly recognized sociologists such as Daniel Bell, Peter Berger, Nathan Glazer, Seymour Martin Lipset, Robert Nisbet, and Edward Shils. They make no secret of their leftist and liberal pasts. During the fifties many belonged to the strictly anticommunist circle around the American Committee for Cultural Freedom, took part in related congresses and published in the journal *Encounter*, the English counterpart to *Preuves* and *Monat*. Given this political background, the intellectual continuity of the American neoconservatives becomes evident. They continue to maintain two important positions advocated during the fifties: on the one hand, anticommunism, understood in terms of the concept of totalitarianism, and on the other, antipopulism, based on the theory of democratic power elites. Neither theory was uncontroversial in the social sciences of the fifties, but both were widely accepted. The theory of totalitarianism highlighted the negative traits of the enemy's political system by emphasizing the similarities between fascist and communist one-party systems; with the other theory, intellectuals explained the advantages of their own political system by claiming that the representative character of the constitutional state with a balance of powers guaranteed both the pluralism of social interests as well as the optimal selection of the leadership cadre. This was the common denominator of liberal social theories in which the understanding of modernization processes implied that the industrially most advanced society, i.e., the United States, was exemplary.

This normative distinction of the status quo could not, of course, withstand the realities of the sixties and seventies. Hence the self-understanding of Irving Kristol who sees himself as "a liberal disillusioned by reality." Peter Glotz paraphrased this definition: "Neoconservatism is the net into which the liberal can fall when he begins to fear his own liberalism." What frightened the liberals?

The social and economic changes that brought about the end of the New Deal era and destroyed the old New Deal coalition (in part through upward mobility) cannot be treated here. The changes in foreign policy were more tangible; the neoconservatives reacted to the defeat in Vietnam and Kissinger's détente policies with the feeling that America's resistance to world communism was being crippled by a sort of moral disarmament. As little as the international developments fit into the anticommunist project, the domestic mobilization which gripped society in the wake of the civil rights movement, the student protests, the New Left, the women's movement, and the escapist countercultures did not correspond to the wholesome world of a nonideological power elite.

In addition, the thematization of poverty in the middle of the sixties fractured the rather harmonious picture of the affluent society. The undesired byproducts of the social programs implemented bureaucratically under Johnson soon began to appear. Where these programs nevertheless functioned well, they displeased the neoconservatives even more, since they endangered the formal principle of equal opportunity via the improvement of the collective chances of ethnic minorities and women.

The formerly liberal neoconservatives are concerned with the alleged loss of authority of the central institutions, especially the political system. This phenomenon is presented suggestively with key terms like ungovernability, decline of credibility, the loss of legitimacy, etc. The explanation begins with an "inflation" of expectations and claims, heightened by the competing political parties, the mass media, and pluralist interests. This pressure of popular expectations "explodes" in a drastic expansion of state activities. The steering instruments of the administration are consequently overburdened. This overburdening, in turn, leads to a loss of legitimacy especially when the possibilities of state activity are limited by preparliamentary power blocks and when the citizens blame the government for tangible economic losses. This is increasingly dangerous, the more the loyalty of the population depends on material compensations.

Interestingly the beginning and end of this spiral are marked by cultural resources: the so-called *inflation of expectations* and *the lack of a willingness to acclaim and obey*, which is based on tradition and is immune to variations in (state) services. This point was formulated by Peter Steinfels in his 1979 book *The Neo-Conservatives*: "The current crisis is above all a cultural crisis . . . The problem is that our convictions are full of holes, our morals and our manners corrupt."[2]

Certain therapeutic proposals result from this analysis. The state bureaucracies need relief: hence those problems, which burden the governmental budget, are to be returned from the state to the market. Because simultaneously investment activity is supposed to be heightened, the reduction of the volume of tasks must lead to a restriction of public social services and consumptive spending in general. At this point, support for a monetarist and supply-side economic policy, designed to stimulate investment activity through tax reductions, merges easily into the neoconservative vision. The more the state retreats from the economic process, the better it can escape the legitimation demands, which arise from its general responsibility for the burdens resulting from a crisis ridden accumulation process.

Other proposals aim directly at the suspected causes. The neoconservatives recommend a stronger decoupling of the executive from the broad political will formation and even a moderation of those democratic principles which "excessively" heighten the level of legitimation.[3] Behind the "utopian" exaggeration of the democratic level of justification, behind the "luxuriating" expectations-pressure, which is passed on to the state through decision-making channels open at the base, certain cultural orientations are operating. The overstimulation of these cultural resources must ultimately be blamed on an enemy – the "new class" of intellectuals. They release, be it through negligence or design, the explosive contents of cultural modernity; they are the advocates of an "adversary culture," i.e., adversary, as it seems, from the perspective of the functional exigencies of state economy. Thus the intellectuals become the most visible target of neoconservative criticism: "The new class and its hostile culture must be tamed or forced out of all sensitive areas."[4]

I do not want to present an extensive critique of the research on ungovernability. The theoretical weakness of these analyses is based on their confusion of cause and effect, as Joachim Heidorn has correctly shown.[5] A crisis which arises in the economy and the state is presented as a "spiritual–moral" crisis – also presented, by the way, in this manner by the leader of the opposition, Helmut Kohl, in the Bundestag debates of 9 September 1982. More interesting than this argument however is the fundamental cultural theory, especially the interpretation of the cultural crisis which Daniel Bell first presented in 1976 in his book *The Cultural Contradictions of Capitalism.*[6]

II

Bell starts from Max Weber's claim that by destroying the Protestant ethic, capitalist development undermines the motivational prerequisities for its own continuity. Bell explains the self-destructive pattern of this development in terms of a spilt between culture and society. He analyzes the tension between a *modern* society, unfolding in terms of economic and administrative rationality, and a *modernist* culture, which contributes to the destruction of the moral bases of rationalized society. In both cases modernity depends on the process of secularization; but what is good for *secularized* society, i.e., capitalist modernization, is catastrophic for culture, since a culture rendered *profane* evokes subversive attitudes; in any case, it contrasts with the willingness, anchored in religion, to achieve and obey, on which an efficient economy and a rational state administration functionally depend.

The affirmative stance toward *social* modernity and the denigration of *cultural* modernity are typical for the evaluative schema implicit in *all* neoconservative diagnoses of the contemporary situation. But Bell has a complex mind and is a good social theorist – in his analysis of the causes of the cultural crisis he does not proceed at all in a neoconservative manner.

The concept of the new class, which according to neoconservative tenets allegedly establishes the predominance of the principle of unlimited self-fulfillment, is rejected by Bell as confused. The so-called new class is composed of individuals who carry the "logic of modernism" to its conclusion in their radical lifestyle but who exercise no significant power. The development of capitalism is determined by very different factors: military needs, technical innovations, social upheavals, and so forth. In addition to these structural transformations, a new hedonism has spread, which is modeled after examples from aesthetic modernity. According to Bell in a 1979 essay, only "the machine of modern capitalism assimilated and commercialized these (countercultural) lifestyles. Without this hedonism stimulated by mass consumption, the consumer goods industry would collapse. The cultural contradiction of capitalism ultimately amounts to the following: once capitalism lost its original legitimations, it adopted the legitimations of a formerly antibourgeois culture in order to maintain the stability of its own economic institutions."[7]

In this essay, Bell is not all guilty of the usual confusion of cause and effect. He does not explain the split between culture and society with the claim that the crisis of authority can be simply ascribed to a culture whose advocates exacerbate the hostility toward the conventions and virtues of the rationalized everyday life of economy and administration. Nevertheless his analysis of modernism is somewhat distorted.

On the one hand, Bell fully comprehends the development of modern art and literature since the middle of the nineteenth century as the unfolding of a consistent pattern, which is specific, in Max Weber's terms, for the "sphere of aesthetic value." The avant-garde artist gives authentic expression to experiences, which he makes via a decentered subjectivity freed from the pressures and exigencies of everyday knowledge and practice. The specificity of the aesthetic appears on the condition of avoiding the everyday structures of time and space, of the break with the conventions of perception and goal-oriented activity, and it is revealed in the dialectic of revelation and shock, which breaks down taboos and purposefully wounds moral sentiment.

On the other hand, Bell is less interested in the new sensibilities and experiential genres of aesthetic modernity; he stares at the subversive power of a consciousness which rejects the normalization achievements of the tradition. Bell does not see that the aestheticist neutralization of the good, the useful, and the true – the aesthetic rebellion against all norms – is only the result of a radical differentiation and specification of this value sphere; the avant-garde cleanses, so to speak, aesthetic experience from contamination from different values spheres. The sociologist's attention is directed solely toward the disturbingly anarchistic lifestyles which are spreading everywhere and in which the new mode of experience becomes the center of a subjectivist lifeform concentrated on self-experience and self-realization. Therefore the central claim coincides fully with the neoconservative line of argument: that the bohemian lifestyles with their hedonistic and unlimitedly subjective value orientations are spreading and eroding the discipline of bourgeois everyday life.

On closer examination, the complaint about the anomic effects of avant-gardist art can refer only to the surrealist *program* of an unmediated transformation of art into life. These attempts at a false supersession of art failed long ago. If one examines empirical research into changing values in Western societies, one observes something very different in terms of new attitudes and the shift of the whole spectrum of values – especially in the younger generation.

The "materialist" needs for security and subsistence are receding behind "postmaterialist" needs.[8] This label covers a variety of issues: an interest in an expanded space for self-realization and self-realization and self-experience, an increased sensitivity for the need to protect natural and historical environments, as well as a heightened sense for vulnerable interpersonal relations. Certainly Daniel Bell could link these *expressive* attitudes to the dimension of aesthetic experience. However in the postmaterialist scale of values, one also finds orientations characteristic of *moral* sensibility – for example, the interest in the protection and extensive use of civil rights and democratic self-determination are *two equal*, mutually complementary components, which are *equally rooted* in cultural modernity. Bell does not see the implications of the fact that modern culture is no less characterized by the universalization of law and morality than by the autonomization of art.

Bell himself uses these moral ideas at the end of his book where he claims that the economic contradictions of capitalism, evident in the governmental budgets, can be solved only with the help of a renewed social contract. He is not satisfied with the neoconservative demand to limit democracy in order to meet the imperatives of an economic growth based on an unchanged incentive mechanism. As a consistent liberal, rather, he considers a consensual *concept of equality* necessary, "which gives all persons a sense of fairness and inclusion in the society and which promotes a situation where, within the relevant spheres, people become more equal so that they can be treated equally."[9] On this basis, the historically established terms, under which the social product is achieved, distributed and used, would have to be negotiated anew.

III

The social questions of the eighties, for which no one can offer a simple solution, might be discussed on that sort of basis. However in the Federal Republic, those neoconservatives who, like Richard Löwenthal and Kurt Sontheimer, could be regarded as the intellectual counterparts to their American colleagues, do not set the tone. Rhetoric and a politics of ideas determine the controversy in Germany more strongly than does social scientific analysis. In addition to a few historians, the spokesmen are largely philosophers. In the wake of neoconservative positions, sociologists are declaring themselves "antisociologists" – a very German phenomenon.

Yet the differences in the styles of thought and discussion depend less on the initial disciplines than on the lines of tradition in the two political cultures. The philosophical proponents of German neoconservatism – and I will restrict my discussion to this clearly defined central group – did not identify with social modernity via the concepts of an unambiguous liberal theory which subsequently gave way to disappointment. The theories with which they *commenced* had rather a young conservative tone and thereby a specifically German background. They relied on a generation of teachers who had inherited the young conservatism of the Weimar period. After 1945 these figures reconciled themselves to civilization progress but maintained the cultural criticism. This compromise, the halfhearted acceptance of modernity, separates the Germans from the Americans, the formerly young conservatives from the formerly liberal neoconservatives.

For authors like Joachim Ritter, Ernst Forsthoff, and Arnold Gehlen, the compromise meant that they only conditionally accepted social modernity, refusing to affirm cultural modernity. In his equally fascinating and influential interpretation of Hegel's political writings, Joachim Ritter described the modern "bourgeois society" which emerged from the French Revolution as the locus of both emancipation and estrangement. The devaluation of the traditional world, the estrangement from the historically transmitted life order, is seen on the one hand positively as the form in which the *citizens* (*Bürger*) of the modern world achieve and maintain their subjective freedom. On the other hand, modern economic society reduces *human beings* (*Menschen*) to the status of agents of production and consumption. Because of its tendency to reduce *persons* to their structure of needs, encompassing socialization which negates its own historical conditions would also destroy the achievements of subjective freedom. In the context of estrangement, freedom can be guaranteed against the danger of total socialization, if the devalued powers of tradition "as powers of personal life, subjectivity and provenance" still maintain the strength to compensate for the unavoidable abstractions of bourgeois society. Therefore in order to stabilize social modernity, a renewal of its own historical substance is necessary, in other words, a desperate, because paradoxical, effort of an historical enlightented traditionalism.

Conservative constitutional theory attempts to find a different solution with the help of Carl Schmitt's concept of sovereignty. In the early fifties a discussion arose over the constitutional significance of the social-state clause in the West German constitution. Ernst Forsthoff put forward the position then that the norms which established the constitutional-state character of the Federal Republic had to maintain absolute priority over the social-state clause, understood merely as a political recommendation. The historico-philosophical content of this legal–dogmatic controversy[10] becomes evident only if one recalls the premise which is reminiscent of Ritter's interpretation of Hegel: that the society which represents the substrate of welfare-state mass democracy cannot achieve stability immanently and requires compensations. For Forsthoff, however, this social dynamic cannot be retarded by the counterforce of a rhetorically invoked tradition but only by the sovereign state. The constitutional state still has, as its substantial center, sovereign power, and this state can develop the power necessary to stabilize social modernity only if, in extreme cases, it is immune to arguments presented in the name of social interests. The guardians of the commonwealth must have the political power *not* to argue but instead to decide. In this view, social modernity ceases to be a danger only for a state power whose sovereignty is not threatened by moral disarmament. In later works, Forsthoff confronted technocratic conceptions.[11]

Arnold Gehlen follows this third line of argumentation. His important anthropology from the early fifties emphasizes the extreme plasticity and vulnerability of a human nature which is not fixed by instincts and therefore depends on the regulating force of archaic-natural institutions.[12] From this perspective, the dismantling of sacred institutions, the loss of authority by the church, the military, and the state as well as the erosion of the latter's sovereign substance appear as signs of a pathological development. This explains the harsh cultural criticism which Gehlen initially articulated after the war.[13] Every step toward emancipation robs the individual of automatic regulations, abandons him without protection to his desultory motivations, strains him with excessive demands for decisions, and renders him increasingly unfree, the more the ideals of self-determination and self-realization are extended.

The tenor of the argument changes in the course of the fifties when Gehlen adopted a technocratic thesis which allowed him to view modern society in a new light. According to this idea, economy and state administration, technology and science coalesce in the iron cage of modernity and become a self-regulating system of laws which are apparently subject to no influences and which can substitute the dismantled institutions. The anthropologically soothing tendency to unburden the individual (*Entlastungstendenz*) can continue on the level of this system and its *Sachgesetzlichkeiten* because time has run out for cultural modernity: the premises of the Enlightenment, so Gehlen argues, are dead, and only its consequences continue. A traditionalist revival of former powers no longer provides the prescription for the deactivation of modern ideas; the key term is rather "crystallization." Gehlen calls modern culture "crystallized" because "the fundamental contents and all the immanent possibilities have been exhausted."[14]

IV

Given this background, it becomes clear that the changed scene of the sixties – the revival of a militant social criticism and a broadly

mobilized Enlightenment tradition, an antiauthoritarian movement, a new outbreak of the avant-garde in the arts and an
aesthetically inspired counterculture – revived everything which
the conservative theoreticians had considered dead. Theoreticians
like Ritter, Forsthoff, and Gehlen had only recently reconciled
themselves with social modernity on the assumption of an immobilized culture modernity. While American liberals were forced to
search for new arguments for an unforeseen situation, the philosophers among the German neoconservatives were faced with a
relatively easy task. The argumentative arsenals of their teachers
supplied the necessary ammunition: whatever contradicted their
theory was to be combatted in *practice* as the machinations of a
domestic enemy. They needed only to name the agents who were
responsible for the disagreeable phenomena, which seemed to shake
the foundations of the compromise, and who had unleashed a
cultural revolution. This turn to practical polemics explains why
the German neoconservatives could tread the beaten path and were
not compelled to offer much that is new. A new element however,
is the type of professor who courageously takes his stand in the
semantic front of the civil war.

The neoconservative doctrine which during the seventies filtered
through the press into the everyday politics of the Federal Republic
is based on a simple pattern. The modern world appears as the
world of technical progress and capitalist growth; all social
dynamic, which is ultimately based on private investments, is
modern and desirable; the motivational resources on which this
dynamic thrives are in need of protection. Danger lies in cultural
transformations, motivational and attitudinal changes, and shifts
in patterns of values and identities, which are attributed to the
entry of cultural innovations into more or less traditional forms of
life. Therefore the legacy of tradition has to be preserved as far as
possible.

The therapeutic suggestions which in recent years in the Federal
Republic have penetrated into everyday politics can be derived
from three elements. (1) All phenomena which do not correspond to
a compensatorily immobilized modernity are personalized and moral-
ized, i.e., blamed on Left intellectuals, who allegedly are carrying on
a cultural revolution in order to insure their own authority, the
"priestly rule of a new class." (2) The explosive contents of cultural
modernity, which nourish this cultural revolution, must be deactivated, hopefully by declaring them passé. We have actually reached
the safe shores of posthistory, the postenlightenment or postmodernism. Only the slowpokes still caught up in the dogmatic slumber of

a "humanitarianism" have not yet recognized the new situation. (3) The socially undesirable byproducts of an economic growth lacking political direction are transposed to the level of a "spiritual–moral crisis"[15] and need the compensation of a straightforward common sense, historical consciousness, and religion. I want to comment on these three recommendations separately.

(1) The *critique of intellectuals*, to which Arnold Gehlen devoted the work of his last decade and which Helmut Schelsky expanded into a theory of the new class, draws on three sources.[16] First, it mobilizes the clichés which have accumulated during the "history of an insult" since the days of the campaign against the Jewish Captain Alfred Dreyfus (1894). Dietz Bering traced this history, and his study provides a lexicon of aggressive and coded terms, such as abstract, abstruse, agitator, decadent, formalist, free-floating, critical, mechanistic, opportunistic, radical, racially foreign, revolutionary, cutting, arrogant, soulless, self-glorious, substanceless, degenerate, unworldy, rootless, immoral, cynical.[17] Once one has glanced through this register of nearly one thousand terms, the new critique of intellectuals turns out to be less than novel.

In addition, the allegation of an intellectual theocracy is based on certain trends; for example, in postindustrial societies the proportion of academic occupations grows, and the significance of the scientific and educational systems generally increases. Among the intellectual professions, Schelsky of course points especially to teachers and publicists, ministers and social workers, humanists and philosophers, and stylizes them as an exploitative class of mediators of meaning (*Sinnvermittler*) – while others do the real work. Richard Löwenthal provides a convincing critique of the false conclusions implict in this extraordinary concept of the new class: "The first false equation is between a social sector and a class. The second false equation is between influence and power. The third false equation is between eschatological hopes, implying necessarily a short-term outbreak of chiliastic faith, and a long-term religion capable of culturally forming everyday social life."[18]

The last element is the relationship of intellectuals to the crisis of the educational system. The educational reforms, necessitated by sociostructural changes but long postponed in the Federal Republic, did indeed take place in a period during which educational policy was influenced by liberal and moderately Leftist goals. And it was in fact the reformist practice itself which led to the recognition of the dangers of legal regulation and bureaucratization as well as the dangers of a scientificization of pedagogy. But the neoconservatives misrepresent these unintended consequences as cultural revolutionary intentions, and they were able to use these consequences, which met with general disapproval, as an excuse to mobilize middle-class ressentiment, because anti-intellectual agitation provided the missing link needed to suggest the fatal nexus of social criticism, educational reform, and left-wing terrorism.[19] Subsequent biographical analyses of terroristic careers have dissolved this fantasy into thin air.[20]

(2) The thesis of an *exhaustion of cultural modernity* refers to all three components: technically successful sciences, avant-garde art, and universalist morality as conceptualized by Rousseau and Kant.

As far as science is concerned, the message is simple. If scientific progress has become "uninteresting for a politics of ideas," if the solution of scientific problems no longer touches our life problems,[21] then the encapsulated expert cultures have little more to offer everyday life – except technical innovations, and sociotechnical recommendations. An ability to orient practice is ascribed only to historical sciences, where narrative means reactualize traditions and guarantee continuities. Hence the revaluation of narrative procedures in the humanities as well as the distrust of history as a social science and a devaluation of sociology – this would never have occurred to the American neoconservatives, since their spokesmen are nearly exclusively sociologists.

In addition, the thesis of a post-Enlightenment is anything but convincing. Certainly, the empirical sciences provide no substitute for metaphysical and religious world views. Yet the wide distribution of popular scientific literature proves that cosmological findings regarding the origin and development of the universe, biochemical discoveries about the mechanisms of heredity, and especially anthropological and ethnological insights into the natural history of human behavior and the evolution of our species, psychological findings on the development of intelligence in children, the development of moral consciousness, affects, and motivations, the psychology of mental illness, and social scientific insights into the origin and unfolding of modern societies – all this still touches the self-understanding of contemporary subjects. These findings also change the standards of discussion for life problems, for which the empirical sciences themselves have no ready answers.

It is of course important to exercise caution by treating hypothetical, i.e., provisional knowledge, carefully; a healthy dose of skepticism is also called for regarding the extent and efficiency of sciences which depend on a hermeneutic access to their object domain; and the concern is certainly legitimate that the life-world autonomy of everyday practice needs to be protected from the unmediated, professionally largely unregulated interventions of experts – in the family and at school no less than in the gray zone of often questionable psychological services and therapies.

With reference to the *fine arts*, Gehlen claimed as late as 1960 that the avant-garde had lost its contagiousness – we, so he thought, have learned to live *beside* today's art. Looking back over the past two decades, Hans Sedlmayer comes to different conclusions. He is convinced that "aesthetic anarchism [is] much more dangerous than political [anarchism]."[22] Sedlmayer sees "a black line" linking the early romanticism of Jena with contemporary avant-garde art via Baudelaire and surrealism. He conjures up the dangers of an artistic practice which begins by abstracting from all extra-aesthetic orders and which banishes from art justice and truth as well as beauty in order to break the borders of the aesthetic work and become subversively active in the everyday bourgeois world. The uniformity of modern architecture appears simply as the other side of anarchism in painting, music, and literature: "The rejection of art, logic, ethics, shame; the church, the state, the family; the classical European tradition and all religion – has penetrated newspapers and journals, film and television, theater and happenings and the practice of life." Of course it is not the complaint which is neoconservative, but the reaction to it – the programmatic dismissal of cultural modernity and the proclamation of the "postmodern." This expression implies the claim that avant-garde art, having exhausted its creativity, has reached its end and is trapped revolving in unproductive circles.

"Postmodern" is also the key term in a debate in recent years in the field of architecture. One might concede that contemporary post-avant-garde art, whichas given up the surrealist dreams, does not emit any clear signals. But where are the works which might fill the negative slogan of "postmodernism" with a positive content?

From a neoconservative standpoint, it is not only necessary to deny the sensitivization potential in contemporary art and to downplay the enlightenment potential of the sciences; it is above all the explosive force of the *universalistic principles of morality* which must be deactivated. A morality is universalistic if it permits only norms of which all those concerned could approve on the basis of full consideration and without duress. No one will object to that – the basic rights and the principles of our constitutions are norms which we may assume everyone could affirm. I do not want to treat the problems which result when such abstract principles are applied to concrete life situations. Only *one* aspect of the relationship of morality and ethical life is of interest, for it especially arouses the suspicion of the conservatives. A universalistic morality naturally recognizes no limits; it even subjects political action to moral scrutiny. In contrast, the neoconservatives desire to minimize the burden of moral justification incumbent on the political system.

Following Hobbes and Carl Schmitt, some proceed from the claim that the state must legitimize itself above all by accomplishing its central task of guaranteeing the peace, i.e., the defense against foreign and domestic enemies. Hence the priority of the problem of internal security and especially the stylization of a purported competition between demands of the legal state and of democracy. Others proceed from the technocracy thesis that the state must act primarily as an arbitrator guaranteeing an appropriate separation of jurisdictions so that the relevant laws of the functionally specific sectors can operate "independent of the general political will formation."[23] Hence the preference for depoliticized steering institutions (like the *Bundesbank*) and especially the stylization of a purported competition between the principle of a balance of powers, on the one hand, and democracy, on the other. In both cases, the arguments point to a separation of the administration from the democratic discussion of sociopolitical goals and social justice.

The relevance of these considerations is obvious in a situation in which the central issue is the degree of social injustice we are prepared to accept, given the fiscal crisis of the state, in order to reinstigate an economic growth, the propelling mechanism of which remains unchanged. This capitalist propelling mechanism requires, for example, that the distribution of jobs be regulated solely by the job market, even if the reserve army of the unemployed continues to grow.

(3) The programmatic dismissal of cultural modernity should make room for a *healthy sense of tradition*. As soon as cultural modernity closes all the gates open to everyday practice and the expert cultures are also sufficiently sequestered, the *preserving powers* of common sense, historical consciousness, and religion come into their own. However the birth pains of the post-Enlightenment call for the midwifery of neoconservatism. It concentrates on a "courage to educate," i.e., an educational policy which tailors elementary education to basic skills and secondary virtues (industriousness, discipline, and cleanliness). Simultaneously it emphasizes a "courage for the past" in schools, the family, and the state. The neoconservatives see their role, on the one hand, in the mobilization of pasts which can be accepted approvingly and, on the other, in the neutralization of these pasts, which would provoke only

criticism and rejection. Walter Benjamin called the "empathy with the victor" one of the signs of historicism. When, in the spirit of Benjamin, Gustav Heinemann called for the adoption of the perspective of the defeated, the unsuccessful rebels and revolutionaries, he had to put up with the rejoinder (from Hermann Lübbe) that this orientation toward the ideals of his own past was merely a "fixation of immaturity."[24] In this context, one also finds the attempts to interpret the National Socialist period so artificially that any reference to fascism can be denounced as a symptom of a "universal domination of sophistry."[25]

Of course the simple truths of common sense and historical continuities cannot alone carry the burden of the envisioned spiritual-moral regeneration. The appeal to the cohesive powers of religion is most important. In fact the Enlightenment was incapable of fulfilling or ending the need for comfort. It also never answered the central question: whether, after the collapse of the religious world views, additional elements beyond the profane principles of a universalist ethic of responsibility could be salvaged – and as this implies, appropriated with good reason, based on insight.

With this question, we are of course still in the realm of modernity, including modern theology. It leads away from a traditionalist revival of religious consciousness, and it compels us to understand the whole spectrum of movements and impulses which, for example, are filling contemporary church conclaves in West Germany. Even religious fundamentalism thrives on very heterogeneous sources; meanwhile the nonfundamentalist currents release exactly those forces of problematicization which the neoconservatives want to impede, as can be seen in the religiously motivated sections of the peace movement. It is precisely here that Schelsky's sense-mediators are congregating along with Lübbe's ideological guides, horizon-openers, experts on goal-selection and pathfinders.

While Daniel Bell unbiasedly analyzed the different orientations of new congregational and communitarian religiosity inside and outside the churches,[26] the German neoconservatives are often concerned only with one issue: the powers of social cohesion implicit in an inherited belief which they understand solely as a substantial tradition unburdened by any demands of proof. Lübbe considers this functionalist interpretation of religion as a "practice of over-coming contingencies" advantageous precisely because it ignores the aspect of the legitimacy of religious belief.

However, traditions cannot be revived simply by demonstrating their beneficial effects. The retreat into functionalism does not solve the quandary in which every mere traditionalism has been entangled since the historical Enlightenment. Horkheimer pointed this out in 1946: "Precisely the fact that tradition must be invoked today shows that it has lost its power."[27]

I do not want to be misunderstood: the nonrenewable resources of our natural environment and the symbolic structures of our life-world – both the historically developed and the specifically modern life-forms – need protection. But they can be protected only if we know *what* is threatening the life-world. The neoconservatives confuse cause and effect. In the place of the economic and administrative imperatives, the so-called objective exigencies, which monetarize and bureaucratize growing dimensions of life and increasingly transform relationships into commodities and objects of administration – in the place of these real sources of social crisis, they focus on the specter of an expansive and subversive culture. This false analysis explains why the neoconservatives, when they have the choice, do not regard the life-world, including the family, as so sacred as they otherwise claim – for example, in the case of the Christian Democratic media policy.

V

The political culture of the Federal Republic would be worse today if it had not adopted impulses from American political culture during the first postwar decades. The Federal Republic opened itself for the first time to the West without reservations: we adopted the political theory of the Enlightenment, we grasped the pluralism which, first carried by religious sects, molded the political mentality, and we became acquainted with the radical democratic spirit of the American pragmatism of Peirce, Mead, and Dewey. The German neoconservatives are turning away from these traditions and drawing on other sources. They are reaching back to a German constitutionalism, which reduces democracy to little more than the rule of law, to a Lutheran state ecclesiasticism rooted in a pessimistic anthropology, and to the motifs of a young conservatism, whose heirs could achieve only a half-hearted compromise with modernity. Bismarck broke the back of political liberalism in Germany. It is no historical accident that the domestic political shift to neoconservatism was brought about by the national-liberal wing of the FDP. For German political culture, this change threatens to close a fatally vicious circle. The rejection of cultural modernity and the admiration for capitalist modernization will corroborate a general anti-modernism ready to throw out the baby with the bathwater. If modernity had nothing to offer beside the praises of neoconservative apologetics, one could understand why parts of today's intellectual youth are returning (via Derrida and Heidegger) to Nietzsche, searching for salvation in the portentious moods of the cultic rejuvenation of a young conservatism not yet distorted by compromise.

Translated by Russell A. Berman

4

Reason Without Revolution? Habermas's *Theorie des kommunikativen Handelns*[1]

ANTHONY GIDDENS

Appropriately enough, for an author concerned with the expansion of the public sphere and the fostering of debate, Habermas's writings have from the beginning of his career attracted widespread attention. Habermas has been a public figure in German life since his early association with — and disassociation from — the student movement of the late 1960s. His work has drawn sharp, even bitter, criticism from both Right and Left for Habermas's writings are not easy to place, intellectually or politically. Self-professedly working within Marxist traditions, Habermas's work is far too revisionist to appeal to most others who would call themselves "Marxists." Yet his connections with the Frankfurt School have made him an object of deep suspicion to those affiliated with conservative perspectives. Habermas's thinking has been shaped in considerable degree by the controversies in which he has been involved. The accusation which Habermas directed against certain sections of the student movement — "Left fascism" — has reverberated through his subsequent intellectual career. His preoccupation with isolating the conditions of rational decision-making and of specifying the conditions under which a consensus, governed purely by the "force of the better argument," can be brought about, evidently in some part represents a protracted attempt to come to terms with the implications of this notorious remark. Successive confrontations with Popper, Gadamer, Luhmann, and others have also left a deep imprint on his thought.

But it would clearly be wrong to regard Habermas primarily as a polemicist. He is a systematic thinker who has consistently sought to come to terms with a number of basic issues in philosophy and social theory. Habermas's writings range over an extraordinary variety of topics, and it would be easy to see in this a diffuse eclecticism. Certainly he does incorporate into his own theories ideas taken from a variety of apparently incompatible approaches. Anyone who has the least bit of sympathy with Habermas's overall project, however, must recognize that he employs such ideas in a highly innovative and disciplined fashion.

Habermas's work can be divided, broadly speaking, into two main phases. The first culminated in the publication of *Erkenntnis und Interesse* (*Knowledge and Human Interests*) in 1968. Although the views Habermas expressed therein have been influential in the social sciences and philosophy, the book also received a barrage of critical attacks. This critical onslaught undoubtedly did indicate some serious shortcomings in the work, and in Habermas's standpoint more generally. Habermas sought to advance a novel conception of critical theory, on the basis of the constitution of knowledge through interests. But the "interest in emancipation" seemed to exist only as a moment in the conjunction of the other two knowledge-constitutive interests. Habermas's later work can be seen as an attempt to give flesh to the emancipatory potential of social analysis. This endeavor has led Habermas away – just how far, he has yet to specify – from the framework adopted in *Erkenntnis und Interesse.* It seems apparent that Habermas would now regard the attempt to found critical theory upon epistemology as misleading if not actually mistaken. Epistemology, he insisted in *Erkenntnis und Interesse*, is possible only as social theory: social theory which examines the conditions under which, in Habermas's words, "reason that becomes transparent to itself" is disclosed. However, if the traditional search for a transcendental basis of knowledge – a "first philosophy" – is to be abandoned, why approach critical theory through the theory of knowledge at all? Habermas seems today to hold that his excursion into epistemology was something of a detour in his endeavor to ground critical theory: the more direct route is through the embedding of reason in *language* in general, and in *communication* in particular.

Habermas's newest publication, *Theorie des kommunikativen Handelns*, is a synthetic statement and an elaboration of the ideas developed in this second phase of his writings. Consisting of two large volumes, each of somewhere near six hundred pages, it is a sprawling, uneven work. It is, I would say, quite unnecessarily long. Purposes of communication would surely have been better served, and the main theses of the book would have stood out in greater relief, if Habermas had taken a razor to some of his material. The work is like a bumper edition of Habermas's *Zur Logik der Sozialwissenschaften*, which appeared fifteen years ago, and in which he offered an analysis of a variety of leading contributions to social theory. His new book contains reassessments of most of the traditions of thought he discussed before. The differences are that these traditions are now considered in much more detail; Max Weber occupies a considerably more prominent position; and the exegetical material is more directly focused upon the conceptual schema of Habermas's own thought. I don't think confirmed Habermas-watchers will learn a great deal from this massive work, for nearly all of the main theorems it advances have been introduced in more minor contexts over recent years. But it does bring these together in a central source, and provides a useful opportunity to appraise the current trend of Habermas's thinking.

The theory of communicative action, Habermas asserts in the opening section of the book, is neither a metatheory nor a continuation of the theory of knowledge by other means. The analysis of communicative action allows us to connect three levels of rationality relevant to social analysis (Habermas is fond of talking in threes; the tables and classifications with which the book abounds are often based on threefold distinctions). One concerns "rationality" as debated in hermeneutics and Anglo-American analytical philosophy, related particularly to issues of relativism. If divergent cultures or forms of life have their own inner criteria of rationality, in what sense is it possible to make comparisons of them – and subject them to critique – in terms of universal standards? Another concerns the rationality of action: how are we to grasp the distinctively meaningful character of human conduct? This touches upon questions of the significance of *Verstehen*, and of the role of the social sciences in claiming superior explanations to those which actors themselves already are able to provide as "reasons" for their behavior. Finally – and large segments of the book are given over to this – Habermas is concerned with the social expansion of rationality as the rationalization of society characteristic of the modern West. Here is where he makes particular appeal to the writings of Max Weber, seeking to reformulate the conception of reification that links Weber to the early Lukács and to the Frankfurt School.

In defending an overall conception of rationality in each of these domains, Habermas evidently has a strong sense of swimming against the stream. He proposes universal criteria of reason at a time when relativistic styles of thought have become fashionable in various areas of intellectual discourse – as, for example, in "poststructuralism." He wants to offer a vindication of enlightenment and modernity when for many these have become effectively discredited. The rise of neoconservatism is particularly important here. *Theorie des kommunikativen Handelns* is written at a characteristically Habermasian level of high abstraction; but there is also a directly political *motif* that runs through the book. Both neoconservatives, who place primacy upon the achievement of economic growth through the revival of market forces, and the ecological critics of growth, turn against the heritage of Western rationalism. Habermas wants to criticize both standpoints, while seeking to understand why they have come to the fore in the current era. In a recent interview (*Äesthetik und Kommunikation*, no. 45/6, 1981), he says that his "real motive" in writing the book was to make clear how "the critique of reification," of rationalization, can be reformulated to offer a theoretical explanation for the decay of the "welfare-state compromise" on the one hand, and on the other the critical potential embodied in new movements – without discarding the project of modernity or relapsing into post- or anti-modernism.

Philosophy, Habermas argues, has always had as its main task reflection upon reason. But contemporary philosophy has become a diverse array of specialisms, no longer seeking to provide a unified world-view. This situation is partly a result of the collapse of attempts to found a "first philosophy": all attempts to provide indubitable foundations for philosophical reason have broken down. Habermas accepts some of the implications of this. Philosophy can no longer hope to develop the sort of grand metaphysical schemes such as were sought after by Kant and Hegel. A new relation therefore has to be established, and is already becoming established, between philosophy and both the natural and social sciences. The procedure of "rational reconstruction" Habermas takes as a key element in this: the process of reconstructing what can be regarded, after the event, as the rational content of a field of research or subject area. He takes Piaget's developmental psychology as a type-case. Piaget reconstructs psychological development not just as a sequences of stages, but as so many steps in the expansion of the rational competence of the individual.

How should we use the term "rational"? Rationality has less to do with knowledge as such, Habermas asserts, than with the manner in which knowledge is used. If we consider the circumstances in which we speak or something as "rational," we see it refers either to persons or to symbolic expressions which embody knowledge. To say that someone acts rationally, or that a statement is rational, is to say that the action or statement can be criticized or defended by the person or persons involved, so that they are able to justify or "ground" them. We cannot, as empiricism does, limit the grounds of rational acts or expressions to knowledge of the object-world. We must complement "cognitive-instrumental rationality" with a conception of "communicative rationality." "Dieser Begriff *kommunikativer Rationalität,*" Habermas says, "führt Konnotationen mit sich, die letztlich zurückgehen auf die zentrale Erfahrung der zwanglos einigenden, konsensstiftenden Kraft argumentativer Rede, in der veschiedene Teilnehmer ihre zunächst nur subjektiven Auffassugen überwinden und sich dank der Gemeinsamkeit vernünftig motivierter Überzeugungen gleichzeitig der Einheit der objektiven Welt und der Intersubjektivität ihres Lebenszusammenhangs vergewissern."[2] Rationality *presumes* communication, because something is rational only if it meets the conditions necessary to forge an understanding with at least one other person.

For those who know anything about Habermas's writings over the past few years it is easy to see where this line of thought leads him. He has often made the case that human language involves a number of "validity claims" that are ordinarily implicitly made by speakers, but which can be made explicit. When I say something to someone else, I implicitly make the following claims: that what I say is intelligible; that its propositional content is true; that I am justified in saying it; and that I speak sincerely, without intent to deceive. All of these claims are contingent or fallible, and all except the first can be criticized and grounded by the offering of reasons. When validity claims are rendered explicit, and when their grounding is assessed purely in terms of how far good reasons can be offered for them (rather than by constraint or force), there exists what Habermas calls a process of "argumentation." Argumentation, as he puts it, is a "court of appeal" of the rationality inherent in everyday communication: it makes possible the continuation of communicative action when disputes arise, without recourse to duress. It follows that the notion of communicative rationality can best be explicated through an examination of the general properties of argumentation. There is more than an echo of Popper in this – a mark, perhaps, of what Habermas has learned through argumentation. Reason, for Habermas as for Popper, becomes primarily a phenomenon of methodical criticism: "by identifying our mistakes," Habermas proposes, "we can correct our failed attempts."

The idea of communicative rationality is the basis upon which Habermas counters the tendencies towards relativism characteristic of much recent philosophical literature. In this context he discusses the nature of myths in traditional cultures and the relation between myth and science, in conjunction with the controversies to which Peter Winch's writings have given rise. Myths, Habermas argues, are concretized modes of thought, which integrate many different aspects of life within a single intellectual domain. They express the organization of societies which have not generated separate intellectual domains, or arenas of discourse, within which argumentation may be carried on. Here we reach one of Habermas's main –and, one might add, most questionable – proposals. The development of arenas of discourse, which he tries to trace through the emergence of the "world religions," and the subsequent differentiation of science, morality, and art in modern culture signifies a general evolution towards an expansion of rationality. The more we are able rationally to ground the conduct of our lives in the three main spheres of existence – relations with the material world, with others, and in the expressive realm of aesthetics – the more advanced our form of society can be said to be.

Enlightenment, obviously, is no joke. The modern world for Habermas *is* more enlightened than the primitive. In his evolutionary theory, Habermas tries to demonstrate that this still has some connection with Marx's materialist conception of history. Since in the more traditional cultures the productive forces are undeveloped, social life tends to be dominated by the hazards of nature. The need arises to check the "flood of contingencies." These cannot be checked in fact, so they are interpreted away, in myth. Myths merge the worlds of nature and culture and attribute to elements in nature powers superior to those of human beings. Myths are anthropomorphic, since they draw into the network of human relations features of nature; and they reify culture by treating it as the operation of autonomous forces. They suffer, Habermas avows, from a "double illusion." He says this "is certainly not well analyzed," referring presumably to pre-existing discussions. But the same judgement could be made of his own treatment of myth, which is cursory in the extreme given the length of the book as a whole.

He does, however, give some considerable attention to Winch's philosophical analysis of traditional cultures, which of course rests primarily upon Evans-Pritchard's celebrated portrayal of Zande sorcery. Habermas argues that the latter's own interpretation of the activities of the Zande is superior to that offered by Winch. For Evans-Pritchard shows that a hermeneutic sensitivity is necessary if Zande beliefs and practices are to be adequately understood. But this does not lead him towards relativism; on the contrary, he is at pains to point out that Zande thought is deficient as compared to the canons of the testing of validity claims embodies in Western science. We can compare different cultures, or world-views, in respect of their "cognitive adequacy" – which is to say, in terms of the defensible validity claims that they incorporate. Here Habermas leans rather heavily upon the views of Robin Horton. Traditional cultures, he accepts with Horton, usually involve closed world-views, refractory to change; modern culture, by contrast, is more open to modification in the light of learning experiences.

Piaget's conception of learning as stages of cognitive development can help us illuminate what such openness to learning consists in. The three main phases of social evolution – the mythical, religious–metaphysical, and modern (shades of Comte!) – correspond to the differentiation of cognitive capacities which Piaget identifies. Habermas is careful at this point to re-emphasize the significance of the procedure of rational reconstruction. The point, I take it, is not that each individual, in a modern culture, recapitulates the development of human societies as a whole. It is that there are several, increasingly extensive and intensive, modalities of the organization of rational thought and action. Cognitive development for Piaget is associated with a "decentering" process. The decentering of cognition leads the child away from primitive egocentrism, towards the differentiation of the capacity for coping with the external world, the social world, and the world of "inner subjectivity" – the three dimensions to which Habermas's types of validity claims correspond.

At this point, Habermas introduces the concept of the life-world (*Lebenswelt*). The life-world, as is suggested in phenomenology, is the taken-for-granted universe of daily social activity. It is the saturation of communicative action by tradition and established ways of doing things. The life-world is a pre-interpreted set of forms of life within which everyday conduct unfolds. It "stores up the interpretative work of many preceding generations." The weight of tradition in the life-world acts as a counterbalance to the intrinsic possibilities of disagreement which communication raises. The process of social evolution, involving the decentering of world-views and the consolidation of the three dimensions of discourse, alters the character of the life-world. The more advanced the decentering process, the less the achievement of consensus is guaranteed by pre-established beliefs or codes of behavior. The expansion of rationality thus presumes a diminution of the hold of the life-world. Looking to one of the sources of Piaget's own thought – the work of Durkheim – Habermas reinterprets the transition from mechanical to organic solidarity in these terms. The writings of Durkheim and G. H. Mead he sees as complementing one another in helping to distinguish the mechanisms of coordination of the life-world from the integration of social systems: "Ob man mit Mead von Grundbegriffen der sozialen Interaktion oder mit Durkheim von Grundbegriffen der kollektiven Repräsentation ausgeht, in beiden Fällen wird die Gesellschaft aus der Teilnehmerperspektive handelnder Subjekte als *Lebenswelt einer sozialen Gruppe* konzipiert. Demgegenüber kann die Gesellschaft aus der Beobachterperspektive eines Unbeteiligten nur als ein *System von Handlungen* begriffen werden, wobei diesen Handlungen, je nach ihrem Beitrag zur Erhaltung des Systembestandes, ein funktionaler Stellenwert zukommt."[3]

Habermas also seeks to forge here a direct connection with the writings of Max Weber. The formation of differentiated worldviews, as these become separate from the life-world, consolidates the rational conduct of life insofar as these meet certain conditions. They must make concepts available for formulating validity claims for the three dimensions of reality (which Habermas also explicitly connects with Popper's "three worlds"). Cultural traditions must allow reflective criticism which makes it possible to subject belief-claims embodied in customary ways of life to descriptive evaluation. There have to be institutional mechanisms which coordinate learning processes over time and feed back new knowledge into the life-world. This implies the differentiation of science, law, and art as the primary spheres relating to the "three worlds." Such a differentiation in turn presupposes the institutionalization of purposive-rational action, i.e., action which is oriented towards the achievement of specific goals, and which can hence be assessed in terms of its technical effectiveness. Max Weber, Habermas says, has helped us understand how important the differentiation of cultural spheres, and the formation of institutional forms geared to purposive-rational action, are to modernization. The two main spheres in which purposive-rational action becomes institutionalized, and the basis of system integration, are the economy and the state. Money is the dominant "circulating medium" (Parsons) in the former, power in the latter.

I shall pass over here the complicated typologies of action and modes of discourse which Habermas offers, as well as his attempt to connect these with speech-act theory. His typologies are as difficult to disentangle as ever, but I do not think they add much to what he has written before. More novel is his extensive critical analysis of Weber; his discussion of the relation between Weber's concept of rationalization and the notion of reification as employed by Lukács and others; plus the attempt to relate all this to features of Parson's social theory.

Weber helped to popularize the idea of *Verstehen* in the social sciences as well as connecting the rationality of action with the rationalization of culture. The notion of purposive-rational action plays a major role in Weber's characterization of the understanding of human conduct. Purposive-rational action can be assessed in terms of how far, given the goals an actor has, it meets criteria that are strategically "adequate." Although Weber used this form of assessment as the pre-eminent standard of rationality against which elements of irrationality of action can be discerned, for Habermas of course it is only one aspect of rational conduct. Normatively regulated action (corresponding to the social world) and expressive, or what Habermas also calls, following Goffman, "dramaturgical action" (corresponding to the "inner" world of subjectivity), also have standards of rationality. The notion of *Verstehen* as utilized by Weber needs to be modified in a twofold sense. Grasping these additional dimensions of the rationality of action is especially relevant to elucidating why people act as they do. But the "meaning" of action cannot be reduced to actors' intentions and reasons for the action. Here modern hermeneutics, and the philosophy of the later Wittgenstein, are much more important than the schools of thought from which Weber drew. To understand the meaning of action involves being able in principle to participate in the form of life in which that action is incorporated. However, Habermas emphasizes again, this cannot be done without, at least implicitly, assessing the validity claims raised within that form of life. Thus understanding cannot be severed off from the rational evaluation of action.

Discussion of metatheoretical and methodological problems of rationality, Habermas asserts, helps drive home that concern with rationality is intrinsic to the practice of the social sciences; it is not something imposed by philosophers from the outside. Since worldviews *already* embody validity-claims and, in differential degree, modes of their discursive redemption, these first two aspects of rationality are inherently bound up with the third: the rationalization of culture. In examining modes of approach to rationalization, Habermas attempts "a reconstruction of the history of theory" from Weber to Parsons, seeking to disclose how the social sciences have developed conceptual strategies for analyzing the nature of modernity. He acknowledges that this is at best an elliptical approach to the questions at issue, but seems to regard it as an important first step.

According to Habermas, Weber is particularly significant for the problems he wishes to analyze because, unlike the other classical social theorists, Weber broke both with the philosophy of history and with evolutionism in its orthodox, quasi-Darwinian, sense – while at the same time conceiving of Western modernization "as a result of a universal-historical process of rationalization." As in his conception of *Verstehen*, Weber allocated to the expansion of purposive-rationality the key part in the historical process of the rationalization of Western culture. He therefore did not capture other aspects in which learning processes have taken place; but his writings do nevertheless contain useful categories for describing them.

Weber mentions many phenomena as involved in the rationalization of Western culture, including science, law, political and economic administration, art, literature, and music. What gives a unity to the trends affecting this diverse array? Weber's own use of the term "rationalization" was rather confused. The main element underlying Weber's various discussions of rationalization, according to Habermas, is the convergence of modes of activity based upon universalistic principle. The rationalized ethics associated with modern law, for example, treat norms as conventions – not as binding imperatives of tradition – governed by decisions based upon generalizable principles rather than arbitrary assessments. In Habermas's interpretation of Weber (which is certainly questionable on this and other points) rationalization is also a process of differentiation – the emergence of three "value spheres," each with its own logic, corresponding once more to Habermas's "three worlds." These are the cognitive, moral, and expressive elements of cultural rationalization, and can be analyzed on an institutional level in terms of the threefold typology Parsons develops of society, culture, and personality.

One of Weber's most distinctive concerns, of course, was to contrast occidental rationalization with the directions of development of other civilizations. As Habermas points out, however, he did not formulate clearly in what ways the development of modernism in the West is more than one possible form of society among others. If "rationalization" means the ordering of life according to universalizable principles, in what sense are those principles universally valid? Weber's answer is ambiguous. We know Habermas's standpoint: there are indeed universally valid procedural forms of rationality. Insofar as the West has moved towards the "postconventional" stage of institutionalized learning processes, rationalization of the Western type equals increasing rationality of belief and conduct.

From Weber to Parsons . . . but of course Habermas does not seek to retrace the path of orthodox sociology. In between Weber and Parsons come Lukács and the Frankfurt School; and Habermas approaches his analysis of Parsonian thought via a "critique of functionalist reason." The connections between Weber's interpretation of rationalization, Lukács's discussion of reification, and the critique of instrumental reason formulated by Horkheimer and Adorno, are clear. They all agree that an expanding rationalization underlies the overall trend of development of Western society. In spite of placing different emphases upon the character of rationalization, these writers hold, like Weber, that the primacy accorded to purposive-rational action in modern culture produces both a loss of moral meaning in day-to-day life, and a diminution of freedom. Obviously Weber does not counterpose instrumental reason, as "subjective reason," to "objective reason" as Horkheimer and Adorno do; and he does not, like Lukács, equate rationalization with a reified social world which in principle can be radically transformed. But neither Lukács nor the Frankfurt School are able satisfactorily to free themselves from the limitations of Weber's standpoint. Lukács hoped to restore the missing philosophical dimension to Marxism by disclosing that rationalization, as described by Weber, involves an undialectical account of bourgeois culture. But this led him to relapse into an abstract "objective idealism" which was in fact something of a retrograde step in philosophy rather than an advance. Horkheimer and Adorno only partly avoided this tendency, and tended restlessly to shuffle back and forth between the poles of objective and subjective reason. Neither they nor Lukács were able to show how rationalization or reification are connected to the deformation of the communicative basis of interpersonal relationships. Thus, while retaining a necessary critical edge to social analysis, they lagged behind the advances already made by G. H. Mead on the other side of the Atlantic. For Mead made the transition from a philosophy of consciousness to a philosophy of language, centered upon symbolic interaction.

In Habermas's eyes there is something of an epistemological break between what he regards as the termination of the philosophy of consciousness – or of "the subject" – and the emergence of communicative analysis. The theory of communicative rationality does not posit a self-sufficient subject, confronting an object-world, but instead begins from the notion of a symbolically structured life-world, in which human reflexivity is constituted. To accept this, and to pursue its implications for social theory, demands however departing from some of Mead's emphases. Mead did not investigate the conditions of reproduction of the social world. As Parsons and other functionalist sociologists have consistently asserted, the conditions of societal reproduction involve imperatives over and beyond those directly involved in communicative interaction. The integration of the conduct of the participant members of societies also involves the coordination of divergent interest groups in the face of various specifiable system imperatives. This observation is essential for Habermas's reformulation of the concept of reification. The problematic of reification, he says, should not be associated, as it was by Lukács and the Frankfurt School, with the conception of rationalization (or purposive-rational action) as such. Instead, reification should be connected to ways in which the "functional conditions of system reproduction" in modern societies impinge upon and undermine the rational foundation of communicative action in the life-world. A critical appropriation of Parson's work, Habermas claims, allows us to formulate an approach to reification, thus understood, in terms of the mechanisms of social and system integration.

Many Anglo-American readers, who may have spent their formative sociological years struggling free from the influence of Parsonianism, are liable to receive this proposal with something of a sinking feeling. But for better or for worse, partly through the agency of Luhmann, Parsons's writings have today become influential in Germany, and Habermas accords them a sympathetic reading. As he recognizes, there is a certain parallel between the synthesis of classical social theory upon which Parsons built his own work and his own enterprise. Parsons indeed helped to make Weber and Durkheim two of the most influential figures in the development of sociology. More than this however, he directed attention to issues that have to remain of foremost concern of anyone interested in social theory today.

From his earliest writings, Habermas points out, Parsons was preoccupied with the relation between human action on the one side, and the constitution of social systems on the other. Although many interpreters of Parsons have tended to accentuate one of these at the expense of the other, Habermas insists that they are of equivalent importance. We can express them in terms of the social integration/system integration distinction. In the one instance, in the continuity of the life-world, we are concerned with the coordination of action orientations, in the other with functional conditions of system properties ordered along a broader scale of time and space. According to Parsons, norms and values are constitutive of social integration, but not of system integration, which depends upon more "impersonal" mechanisms. Habermas accepts this general standpoint, while profferring a range of criticisms of Parson's own formulation of it. Parson's conceptualization of action, he argues, is too restricted, and particularly in Parson's later writings tends to be swamped by a concentration upon system functions; and the account of modernity which Parsons developed paints too much of a consensual picture, neglecting the fundamental tensions which have come to exist in contemporary society. While these criticisms are not novel, the mode in which Habermas seeks to draw upon Parson's ideas is important (if still questionable).

According to Habermas, Parsons's concept of action – or, rather, the mode in which he sought to build such a concept into his theoretical scheme – represses the hermeneutic dimension of social analysis. Parsons failed to see that the social researcher must be able "to go on" in the forms of life involved in the everyday world in order to describe and to account for the nature of those forms of life in a satisfactory fashion. Recognizing this implies seeing that the differentiation of social and system integration has a methodological aspect to it. Social integration necessarily has reference to participants' own concepts, whereas system integration can be described in other terms; the "translation" from one to the other involves a shift in methodological orientation on the part of the social analyst. Of course, this view continues the line of argument Habermas has set out in previous writings in respect of systems theory. Systems analysis is certainly not illegitimate in social theory; but, on the other hand, it cannot lay claim to provide an overall framework for the explication of social conduct, as functionalists suppose. The integration of a society involves the constant renewal of a compromise between two forms of imperatives. The conditions for the integration of the life-world are bound up with the renewal of the validity claims (*Geltungsbasis*) underlying the structure of a definite world-view. The conditions for the functional integration of society have to do with the modes in which the life-world is related to a surrounding environment which is only partly controlled through the communicative action of human beings. Such a compromise can only be reached through the institutionalization and internalization of value-orientations (as Parsons also holds). If these do not conform to the functional demands of system reproduction, social cohesion is only preserved if such functional demands remain latent. In these circumstances the illusory nature of the validity claims on which the value-orientations are based may remain opaque. The result is systematically distorted communication.

For Parsons, language in common with power and money, is represented as a medium of societal integration. According to Habermas, however, language has to be excluded from this role since it is implicated in all social activity; Parsons is able to represent language as one medium of integration among others because he obscures the linguistic foundation of the hermeneutic properties of the life-world. However, we can make good use of the Parsonian treatment of power and money as the media of the extension and coordination of purposive-rational action. A high degree of rationalization, produced by the evolutionary movement towards modernity, is the necessary basis upon which money (in the economy) and power (in the polity) become differentiated as "steering media." Each presupposes the institutionalization of positive law and the separation of the household – which it is one of Weber's main achievements to have emphasized. As differentiated spheres of system integration, the economy and the polity remain grounded in the life-world, from which they draw normative support and value-commitment. At the same time, they presume the specialized development of processes of the formation of consensus through communicative action. This in turn involves not only institutional differentiation but the development of personality structures capable of participating in postconventional discursive will-formation.

From Parsons . . . back to Weber and to Marx. In the concluding sections of his analysis, Habermas tries to focus these ideas upon a diagnosis of the pathological aspects of modernity. If follows from Habermas's overall view that the rationalization of communicative action must be analytically separated from the formation of the purposive-rational institutional sectors of economy and polity. This in turn means revising key notions in both Weber and Marx, since neither recognizes this distinction in the mode Habermas formulates it. For Habermas, the disentangling of steering mechanisms from the life-world is not as such pathological, but intrinsic to modernization. Such differentiation therefore necessarily has to be distinguished from conditions – that Habermas thinks have come to the fore in recent times – under which the communicative basis of the life-world is drained of the very supports which the economy and polity demand. This can be described as a process of the "internal colonization" of the life-world, a destruction of tradition which threatens the very continuance of the reproduction of society as a whole.

The tensions and conflicts which dominate in modernized societies today have to be distinguished from those characteristic of earlier phases of development. The disembedding of steering processes from the life-world in postmedieval times provoked various kinds of protest movements, as the peasantry were forced into the towns and as the centralized state came into being. In the nineteenth and early twentieth centuries, the labor movement became the focus of resistance in the face of further economic and political differentiation. Marx showed how the transformation of concrete into abstract labor was the condition of the coordination of modern production. This was one of the very mechanisms distinguishing the economy as a separate institutional sphere. Labor movements may be seen as partially successful attempts to correct an imbalance between life-world and steering mechanisms deriving from the harsh dislocations effected by rapid capitalist development. But a parallel process of "abstraction" also occurs in political life with the further modernization of the state. This is in fact the type case of the colonization of the life-world, since the public sphere comes to be more and more "technicized" in the contemporary period.

Here we return to the question of reification. In Marx's writings, this notion is tied diffusely to the process of economic abstraction whereby "living labor" is subordinated to the rule of impersonal economic mechanisms. In some part this is again a necessary element of modernization, and cannot be regarded as pathological. The latter is the case, however, where monetary mechanisms have penetrated too far into the communicatively ordered life-world. The reification of "communicatively-structured spheres of action" is thus not first and foremost a phenomenon of class divisions. Here Habermas leans very definitely towards Weber and away from Marx. Against the hopes of revolutionary transformation which Marx anticipated would be achieved through class struggle,

hat Max Webers Prognose, "dass die Abschaffung des Privatkapitalismus . . . keineswegs ein Zerbrechen des stählernen Gehäuses der modernen gewerblichen Arbeit bedeuten würde," recht behalten. Der Marxische Irrtum geht letztlich auf jene dialektische Verklammerung von System– und Lebensweltanalyse zurück, die eine hinreichend scharfe Trennung zwischen dem in der Moderne ausgebildeten *Niveau der Systemdifferenzierung* und den *klassenspezifischen Formen siener Institutionalisierung* nicht zulässt. Marx hat den Versuchungen des Hegelschen Totalitätsdenkens nicht widerstanden und die Einheit von System und Lebenswelt dialektisch als ein "unwahres Ganzes" konstruiert. Sonst hätte er sich nicht darüber täuschen können, dass *jede* moderne Gesellschaft, gleichviel wie ihre Klassenstruktur beschaffen ist, einen hohen Grad an struktureller Differenzierung aufweisen muss . . . Marx fehlen Kriterien, anhand deren er die Zerstörung traditionaler Lebensformen von der Verdinglichung posttraditionaler Lebenswelten unterscheiden könnte.[4]

Marx's analysis, Habermas says, repeating a theme of his earlier writings, is most relevant to the early phases of the development of capitalist societies. In these phases, the economic mechanisms Marx identified do tend to be important. However, there is not one steering mechanism (the economy) in modern societies, but two; and the second, the administrative apparatus of power, was not satisfactorily grasped by Marx. Partly for this reason, orthodox Marxism is not able to illuminate some of the key phenomena of late capitalism, in which state intervention is increasingly extensive, and in which mass democracy and welfare reforms brook large.

The conjunction of these phenomena in late capitalism, Habermas affirms, produces a new type of "class non-specific reification" – although its effects are distributed unequally within the class system. His analysis of this is complex, and I shall not attempt to summarize it here. Basically, the theme is that the colonization of the life-world has destroyed traditional bases of communicative action, without replacing them with the forms of postconventional rationality that are required to couple the life-world to the range of activities controlled by expanding economic and political steering mechanisms. The colonization of the life-world has a double implication. Within the life-world itself, reification has the consequence of loss of meaning or anomie with the range of associated problems which this produces within personality structures. From the perspective of the steering mechanisms, the result is a set of motivational and legitimation deficits. Whereas in his previous work Habermas saw "motivation crises" as, in a certain sense at least, more deeply embedded than "legitimation crises," it now appears that these connect directly to each of the steering mechanisms, and are of equivalent potential importance. Lack of motivational input creates problems for the maintenance of economic organisation, while a diminution in legitimation threatens the stability of the political order.

The tasks of Critical Theory today, Habermas concludes, have to be integrated with this appraisal of the institutional form of, and the tensions inherent within, late capitalism. New conflicts, and new social movements, have developed which diverge from the older types of class struggle centered upon production relationships and the welfare state. Such conflicts no longer primarily concern the distribution of material goods, but rather cultural reproduction and socialization, and do not follow the established bargaining mechanisms associated with the unions or political parties. Since they are an expression of the reification of the communicative order of the life-world, it follows that these tensions cannot be alleviated through further economic development, or technical improvements in the administrative apparatus of government. The new conflicts, and associated social movements, derive from problems that can be resolved only through a reconquest of the life-world by communicative reason, and by concomitant transmutations in the normative order of daily life. How far do such tendencies contain an emancipatory promise which might in a significant way transform existing social institutions? Habermas hedges his bets; but he is inclined to see the new social movements as primarily defensive, concerned with protecting the life-world against further colonization. Ecological and anti-nuclear movements are of this kind, since they are characteristically linked with the impetus to defend the natural environment against despoliation, and to recreate communal relationships of various forms. Whatever the potential for specific movements, however, Habermas affirms strongly that the "stitching" between system and life-world is likely to continue in the near future to be their point of origin. The theory of communicative action, he contends, helps us to understand why this is so, and can be placed in the service of indicating the pressure-points at which real change might be achieved; it replaces the older type of critical theory, founded upon now – untenable philosophical positions.

It will take some time to digest the implications of a book such as this, written in the grand manner. As an initial reaction, however, I would say it displays the same mixture of appealing and frustrating features that marks most of Habermas's other writings. However much one might cavil at its length, it is impossible not to be impressed with the encyclopedic range of Habermas's discussion. Who else could one think of, among those writing on social theory today, who could cover – apparently without effort – such a diversity of classical and current traditions of thought, connecting these with abstract issues of philosophy on the one side, and contemporary political concerns on the other? As a synthesis of Habermas's own thought, this work brings out the unity of the theoretical standpoint which he has worked out over the past decade or so. It contains at the same time a veritable treasure-trove of critical commentary on the works of others. Yet it *is* much too long. Habermas's style does not become any more limpid over the years, and the reader has to do a lot of work trying to puzzle out the relation between some of the main arguments. Habermas has a passion for tables and classifications even where these seem to obscure the process of rational argumentation rather than further it. One table contains no fewer than thirty-two categories! A consequence of this taxonomic fervor is that Habermas's writing has something of a puritanical formalism. Often where one would like to see *evidence* presented to support a view that is proposed, a table is offered instead – as if the way to overcome potential objections is to pulverize them into conceptual fragments.

Habermas's writings have been so consistently subjected to scrutiny by friend and foe alike that it is probably hard to explore any aspects of them where the critical ground has not already been well dug over. Rather than attempting to raise any critical points that are especially new, I will indicate where to me some of the main interest of Habermas's ideas lies, and where it seems to be questionable or open to attack. In offering such an appraisal, however, I shall schizophrenically divide myself into two. Since Habermas's work has a systematic character, it invites the reader to be inside or outside: Habermas has many followers, who try to work within his system, offering relatively minor modifications of it; and just as many opponents, who reject much of his enterprise. My inclination, I suppose, is to side more with the second group than with the first, but for the rest of this article I shall try to throw out fodder to both. On the left hand side of the page I will mention the queries/problems/comments that are likely to occur to the sympathetic critic. On the right hand side, I shall list those which – to borrow Marx's term – a "critical critic" might ask of Habermas. (This tactic allows me both to have a table of my own, and to formalize a kind of discursive argumentation.)

Sympathetic Critic	*Critical Critic*
1. I have followed the course of your writings from your earliest work up to the present time. Early on, I was led to believe that knowledge is grounded in interest, and that three types of knowledge – constitutive interests could be distinguished. This was an attractive notion, which I adopted with some enthus-	1. There seem to me to be some quite radical, and unresolved, discrepancies between your earlier and your later work. The idea that knowledge is grounded in interest was a very bold claim, and the main basis upon which the distinctiveness of your views was founded. To give up this idea is surely to undermine

iasm. It seemed to help with the critique of hermeneutics and the critique of ideology. But having read your most recent work, I feel somewhat puzzled and even rather let down. Am I still to believe that knowledge is founded upon interest? And if so, how exactly do the three knowledge-constitutive interests relate to the three "worlds" and three types of validity-claims, which you now distinguish? You say that working through the theory of knowledge was a roundabout way of approaching the problems that most concern you, but what exactly is the implication of this? I can see how two of the knowledge-constitutive interests seem to correspond to two of the "worlds," but what of the third? This is a plea for enlightenment!

some of the major claims you made – about the "one-sided" character of hermeneutics, for example, in your debate with Gadamer.

(a) In your new work you seem clearly to admit the "claim to universality" of hermeneutics for which Gadamer argued. For you accept that there is a necessary hermeneutic moment in the description of social activity, involving the capability of the observer to "go on" in the form of life which is to be analyzed or accounted for.

(b) In your earlier writings you made space for nomological explanation, drawing upon some of the elements of logical empiricism. You made a distinction between various types of sciences: the "historical-hermeneutic" and the "empirical-analytical." What has happened to these sciences now? What role do nomological accounts play in the social sciences? These questions have become very obscure. Perhaps this is simply because you multiply classifications so much that it is difficult to see how they relate to one another. But I doubt that this is the only, or even the main, factor involved.

(c) If, as you now say, there are three "worlds" connecting types of validity-claim that can be discursively justified, surely you have moved towards a sort of neo-Kantian view which your earlier work was specifically concerned to avoid . . . or are you even flirting with some version of realism?

2. In treating "reason" as "rationality" you explicitly adopt the view that reason is wholly procedural – it refers to modes of justifying statements, or the belief-propositions that underlie action. I think I can discern the influence of your interchange with Albert and Popper in the formulation of this standpoint. Because for Popper also, rationality (in the shape of scientific rationality) is also purely procedural. What makes something "scientific" has nothing to do with its content, or its origins, but depends wholly upon the procedures that can be followed to test it. Popper's view, like yours, derives from the acknowledgement that there can no longer be a "first philosophy" – that all knowledge is built upon shifting foundations. But Popper does insist upon a clear criterion or criteria (falsifiability, and connected attributes) which can be put to use in seeking actually to differentiate among different theories or propositions. He also holds to a version of the correspondence theory of

2. You claim to be defending "reason" – as "rationality" – while disavowing the idea of a "first philosophy." But I do not find your mode of defense plausible; and even if it could be satisfactorily sustained, it is so empty of content that it seems to leave unresolved all the main problems raised by relativism.

(a) I do not see why your approach should be free of the self-destructive tendency of rationality. Once we admit the principle of the critical evaluation of beliefs, how can anything be exempt? The tactic followed by the logical empiricists in defence of the Verification Principle, by Popper, and by yourself – of declaring that your conception is procedural rather than substantive – is hardly convincing. Reason which concerns procedures of rational argumentation still needs to be defended by procedures of rational argumentation. Your approach therefore does not seem to cope with issues of relativism any more effectively than those based upon some kind of version of a "first philosophy."

truth, anchored in the notion of verisimilitude. I am not at all convinced by Popperianism, but it does seem to provide what you have not thus far developed, and what Popper does offer – a means of distinguishing among validity claims relevant to the object-world. It is one thing to say that there are modes of argumentation presumed in the use of language. This is an idea I find convincing. But how do such modes of argumentation work in respect of real issues? Nearly all the material you present is of a formal nature, categorizing "levels" of argumentation and so on. In discussing Winch, Evans-Pritchard, and poison oracles you show persuasively that relativism cannot be sustained. But you do not indicate – unless I have missed it – what criteria are to be used in assessing specific validity-claims. How exactly would we show that the Zande are wrong to believe in poison oracles?

This sort of problem relates to a feeling of disquiet I have about your theory of truth. Truth for you concerns the way in which statements about the object-world can be warranted. But what counts as the "evidence" that can warrant assertions? Since you say little about referential problems, we are left largely

(b) Truth cannot be identified with the warrantability of assertions. I take it that the aim of your discourse theory of truth is to show that specifying the truth-conditions of an assertion logically involves explaining what it means to justify, in argumentation, the claim that those truth-conditions are met. But the theory actually presumes this, it does not demonstrate it. No amount of warrants I – or an indefinite community of future observers – bring to bear upon a statement prevents the possibility that the statement is nonetheless false. Whatever the difficulties with Popper's position, it does have the merit of admitting this possibility, because Popper does distinguish between the modes of investigation we can develop, as rational enquirers, and "truth" as correspondence.

(c) Suppose your theory of truth were acceptable. It would still leave unresolved virtually all the major questions raised by the postpositivist philosophy of science and by the relativism debates. You distinguish between "truth," as a concept referring to modes of establishing consensus in argumentation, and statements having referential properties in respect to the object-world. But once "truth" has been made a in the dark about this. There seems to be a definite need for further development of your ideas here.

procedural notion, a theory of truth no longer copes with questions of *how* one generates "evidence," *what* counts as "evidence," and in what *sense* propositions are "testable."

(d) The same point could be made in regard to what you call "practical discourse." After all, whatever problems –and they of course are formidable enough – may exist concerning evidence about the material world, the difficulties involved in justifying normative claims are even harder to resolve. But your discussion of the character of practical discourse appears no less formal than that of theoretical-empirical discourse.

(e) You claim a connection between language, rationality, and a counter-factually posited ideal speech situation. I have never found this convincing. Is it anything other than the last gasp of a critical theory which, dissatisfied with the uncertainties of immanent critique, and suspicious of philosophical anthropology, pins its hopes upon the "linguistic turn"? Is not language more aptly regarded, with Wittgenstein, as *all* the things that can be done in and through language? "Our first sentence," you once wrote, "expresses unequivocally the intention of universal and unconstrained consensus." Why not say that our first gesture of recognition of another person promises a universal solidarity of human beings? Or perhaps the idea could be extended even further – to Lévi-Strauss's complicitous glance from a cat?

3. The conjunctions you draw between evolutionary theory, the psychology of cognitive development, and the method of rational reconstruction are evidently essential to your thesis that communicative reason is not just Western reason. I accept your contention that history has to be separated from evolutionary theory, just as empirical psychology is not the same as the reconstruction of levels of competence. At the same time, I am a bit worried by how much reliance you place upon Piaget and Kohlberg, both of whose views have, after all, been subject to serious critical attack. Some of the parallels you discern between the development of reasoning in the cognition of the individual and the social evolution of the species seem almost too neat and tidy. I was somewhat surprised to see that the section of your book concerned with myths in oral cultures amounts to only a few pages. If you are going

3. I have never understood how you are able to make such confident – and sweeping – use of Piaget and Kohlberg. Despite its brilliance, the empirical base of Piaget's work has always been weak, especially when generalized out of a Western context; and the studies on the basis of which Kohlberg claims that his stages of competence are universal are at best sketchy. Surely it is at least somewhat suspicious that the highest forms of human reason turn out to duplicate the ideals of the Western Enlightenment! If, again, you began with Lévi-Strauss rather than Piaget, you would surely have been led to very different conclusions. The fact that you discuss Lévi-Strauss only very cursorily reinforces the uncomfortable feeling I have that you tend to choose theories that *prima facie* fit with the general framework of your ideas – as if indicating how they can be fitted together is enough to validate them.

to demonstrate that oral cultures – and agrarian civilizations operate at a lower stage of rationality to Western or modernized culture, surely a more detailed treatment is called for?

On the whole I think it was a healthy shift when social theory turned against evolutionism. Evolutionary theories have always been difficult to disentangle from ethnocentrism, and especially from Europocentricism. Although you hedge the concept of evolution with numerous qualifications and you are very careful to consider the connotations of ethnocentrism, I am not at all convinced that you avoid them. Let us follow the proposal I mentioned above, and relate your arguments to Lévi-Strauss rather than Piaget. There are three respects in which you treat oral cultures as inferior to civilizations, and particularly to the modernized West. Oral cultures involved closed world-views; fail to distinguish the three "worlds" you see as integral to rationality; and are founded upon pre-conventional norms. A Lévi-Straussian viewpoint might agree, with some reservations, with such a categorization. But it would see these as involving forms of life that are every bit as "rational" as those introduced by the "hot" cultures of civilization. Oral cultures are not made up of individuals who have not yet undergone the "learning processes" that bring enlightenment. On the contrary, the introduction of writing and the other paraphernalia of civilization is an unlearning process – a process of cultural destruction. The division we make between nature and culture is one that dissolves the intimacy with nature which is one of the richest forms of human experience. Finally, norms which are founded upon debate and discussion, it might be argued, are not just new forms of tradition. They mark the undermining of tradition – the security of time-honored practices – as such.

4. One of your most important accomplishments, in my opinion, is in respect of the critical reception of systems theory. You have forcibly emphasized that systems theory is caught up in the technicization of politics, and have demonstrated that the seemingly neutral application of means–ends thinking may become ideological. Your analysis of "technique as ideology" is one of the most brilliant parts of your writings. At the same time, you have made it clear that systems theory, and the functionalist style of thought that tends to be associated with it, cannot be rejected out of hand. Thus you have adopted some systems-theoretical concepts into your own work, and in this book you have further clarified how

4. I am unhappy with your distinction between system and life-world – as I was with the differentiation between "labor" and "interaction" which appeared prominently in your earlier work. If, as you say, the separation between system and life-world is methodological, how can it also operate as a substantive distinction within modernized societies? Moreover, your use of systems theory, of notions such as "steering mechanisms" and so on, seems to do scant justice to the active struggles of individuals and groups out of which history is made. The sense of contingency in history, which is so strong in the writings of Max Weber, seems absent from your own work. You are critical of "functionalist reason," but not critical enough.

such concepts relate to phenomena of the life-world. I am particularly impressed by the manner in which you apply the notions of system and life-world to the elucidation of the nature of modernity. Some questions still puzzle me a little. One of these concerns the question of power. You now adopt a position, following Parsons, according to which the polity is the medium of the organization of political power. Since the polity is defined in terms of a specific institutional application of purposive-rational action, this seems to narrow down the concept of power rather considerably. How then would you connect the critique of ideology to the critique of domination today – since you seemingly previously employed "power" in a much broader way?

5. You have brought the ideas of Max Weber much more into the center of your work than was previously the case. I find your adaption and critique of Weber's concept of rationalization both intriguing and compelling. You have shown that Weber's work, in at least certain basic respects, is more important in diagnosing the traits of the type of society in which we live today than Marx's writings are. At the same time, by exposing some of the limitations of Weber's

5. Too much Weber! Too little Marx! Anyone who draws as heavily upon Weber as you do is likely to be also drawn into Weberian conclusions – whatever disclaimers they might make. You criticize Weber for confining rationalization primarily to the expansion of purposive-rationality, but you are forced to agree that this type of rationality does dominate modern culture. Your diagnosis of the origins, and likely future, of current social

own analysis of moderniz-ation, you make it clear how the type of critique Marx advocated can be kept alive. Your theory of the colonization of the life-world provides a new basis for analyzing the tensions, and the sources of opposition, characteristic of modern societies. All the same, I wonder if your analysis might lead to somewhat paradoxical conclusions. Aspects of the life-world have to be defended against the encroachments of political and economic steering-mechanisms. But how can such a defense be achieved without transforming those mechanisms themselves? I am not sure just what sort of transformations you think are possible, and how whatever possibilities you see might bear upon ideals of socialism as they have been conceived of in the past.

movements looks remarkably similar to that Weber might have made – except that you want to speak of "pathologies," and keep to a more optimistic outlook about the possibilities for social change. I cannot see what justifies your optimism. Weber did, after all, expect there to be protest movements directed against the prevalence of rationalization; and he expected that these would commonly take the form of religious revivalism or what have come to be called "countercultural" movements. But he did not believe that these could be successful in turning back the tide of rationalization, with its oppressive consequences. In spite of all you have to say about frustrated validity-claims, and about the colonization of the life-world, I cannot see that your analysis leads to a different substantive conclusion.

Let me at this stage put myself back together again. The fact that Habermas's work prompts so many questions – numerous others could of course also be raised – is indicative of its extraordinary intellectual power and scope. There is no doubt that this book represents a formidable achievement, and all of us working in social theory will be using it as a resource years after most of the current literature in the social sciences has been forgotten.

Part 2: Symposium

1

Habermas and Modernism

MARTIN JAY

In an important, but neglected, essay published in 1976, entitled "Aesthetic Experience and Self-Reflection as Emancipatory Processes: Two Complementary Aspects of Critical Theory,"[1] Shierry Weber located a fundamental, albeit often subterranean, tension in the Frankfurt School's work. Although emphasizing their potential complementarity, she singled out two impulses in Critical Theory that have been subtly at odds through much of its history: aesthetic experience as a prefigurative cipher of redemption and rational self-reflection as a critical tool in the struggle to achieve that utopian state. Recalling Critical Theory's debt to German Idealists like Schiller, she contended that it is the artistic representation of wholeness that explains the Frankfurt School's fascination for aesthetics which embodies "a nonalienated relationship between man and nature, subject and object, and reason and the senses."[2] In contrast, Weber contended, "the process of self-reflection is focused more on man conceived in his universal aspect as a rational member of a socio-historical species."[3] Rather than leading towards the reconciliation anticipated by aesthetic wholeness, rational self-reflection encourages humankind's increasing liberation from what Marx called his *Naturwüchsigkeit* or embeddedness in nature.[4]

The Critical Theorists who paid most attention to aesthetic experience are Walter Benjamin, Leo Lowenthal, Herbert Marcuse, and Theodor W. Adorno. The last works of the latter two were in fact called, respectively, *The Aesthetic Dimension* and *Aesthetic Theory*.[5] Although their work did not always adopt Weber's Schillerian characterization of the aesthetic as a model of reconciled wholeness – Adorno's defense of natural beauty as an embodiment of a nonidentical relationship between subject and object is a counterexample – art often did serve as a refuge for their never completely abandoned utopian aspirations. The same, however, has rarely been said of a more recent figure in the history of the Frankfurt School, Jürgen Habermas, who has stressed instead the process of rational self-reflection and explicitly abjured all hopes for a reconciliation of human beings and nature. As Weber notes, in his work "interest in the subjective or interactional components of domination has led to a more systematic return to the original problems of the nature of reason and its role in history, without, as yet, a similar reconsideration of the nature of the aesthetic and its relation to reason."[6]

Although Weber's cautious "as yet" has not become entirely outmoded in the years since she wrote her essay, Habermas has nonetheless come increasingly to dwell on aesthetic issues. If by no means at the actual center of his latest work, which has been devoted primarily to the development of a theory of communicative action and the reconstruction of historical materialism, art has found a modest place in his elaborate theoretical system. In particular, Habermas's recent attempt to formulate a theory of the modern has led him not only to reflect on modernization, understood in sociological terms, but on aesthetic modernism as well. He has thus, somewhat haltingly, returned to one of the fundamental themes of the classical Frankfurt School. But he has done so without abandoning his preference for rational self-reflection. Precisely what that return has meant for Habermas's reformulated version of Critical Theory has not, however, been widely discussed.[7] What follows is an attempt to rectify that omission, which has resulted in a failure to understand the full complexity of Habermas's exceptionally complicated undertaking.

Habermas's interest in aesthetic issues can in fact be detected even in his earliest works, such as his influential essay of 1963, "Between Science and Philosophy: Marxism as Critique."[8] But it was not until the early 1970s that he first seriously attempted to integrate his consideration of these issues with his more general theoretical position. In his 1972 essay on Walter Benjamin, and in the book published the following year entitled *Legitimation Crisis*, Habermas reflected on the importance of art in the process of emancipation.[9] To take the much briefer discussion in the latter first, Habermas upheld the traditional Frankfurt School position that art is an enclave of negation against the totalizing power of one-dimensional society:

Only bourgeois art, which has become autonomous in the face of demands for employment extrinsic to art, has taken up positions on behalf of the victims of bourgeois rationalization. Bourgeois art has become the refuge for a satisfaction, even if only virtual, of those needs that have become, as it were, illegal in the material life-process of bourgeois society. I refer here to the desire for a mimetic relation with nature; the need for living together in solidarity outside the group egoism of the immediate family; the longing for the happiness of a communicative experience exempt from imperatives of purposive rationality and giving scope to imagination as well as spontaneity . . . Thus, along with moral universalism, art and aesthetics (from Schiller to Marcuse) are explosive ingredients built into bourgeois ideology.[10]

Focusing more precisely on how aesthetic negation occurs in the modern world, Habermas then turned to the implications of what he called, borrowing Benjamin's term, "post-auratic art." Whereas traditional art was surrounded by a ritually induced aura that distanced it from everyday life, thus encouraging its cultic enjoyment as a beautiful illusion, modern art abandoned both its aura and the accompanying illusion of its autonomy from society.[11] The break between auratic and post-auratic art came where Benjamin had located it: "Surrealism marks the historical moment in which modern art destroyed the shell of the no-longer-beautiful illusion in order to pass desublimated over into life."[12]

Habermas, however, was enough of Adorno's student to challenge the essentially optimistic implications Benjamin drew from the de-auraticization of art. Not only did he call into question Benjamin's overemphasis on the technology of mass production as an explanation of the change, he also pointed out the costs of a premature integration of art and life. The surrender of artistic claims to autonomy, he warned, "can just as easily signify the degeneration of art into propagandistic mass art or into commercialized mass culture as, on the other hand, transform itself into a subversive counterculture."[13] Although he was not willing either to endorse Adorno's unequivocal defense of autonomous art without acknowledging its own limitations, most notably its *a priori* denial of the possibility of an exoteric art, he nonetheless concluded that

as long as avant-garde art is not completely deprived of its semantic content and does not share the fate of the more and more powerless religious tradition, it strengthens the divergence between the values offered by the socio-cultural system and those demanded by the political and economic systems.[14]

This conclusion, which drew on Daniel Bell's then widely discussed argument about the "cultural contradictions of capitalism,"[15] but reversed Bell's conservative application of it, was also based on the much more detailed analysis of aesthetic issues Habermas had made the year before in his remarkable essay on Walter Benjamin.

"Consciousness-Raising or Redemptive Criticism: the Contemporaneity of Walter Benjamin" began with a comparison of the aesthetic theories of Marcuse and Benjamin and stressed four central differences. First, whereas Marcuse employed the traditional Marxist critique of ideology to expose the contradiction between art's ideal essence, which transcends the current reality, and its consoling function as a means of helping persons endure that same reality, Benjamin sought to conserve and rescue the truth content of works of art themselves. His was, therefore, in the terms of Habermas's title, more a "redemptive" than "consciousness-raising" criticism, a theory of aesthetic experience rather than reflection.[16] Second, while Marcuse, in the tradition of idealist aesthetics, was biased towards classical works of art, whose essence appeared through symbols, Benjamin defended the nonaffirmative, nontotalizable works of art dependent more on allegory, which registered suffering rather than attempted to transfigure it. Third, whereas Marcuse only fleetingly contemplated the meaning of the avant-garde's destruction of auratic art, Benjamin emphasized the implications of that very destruction, which Surrealism in particular had carried out.[17] Fourth and finally, Marcuse differed from Benjamin in denying the responsibility of technological changes alone for the de-auraticization of modern art, its turn towards exoteric rather than esoteric forms.

Without immediately taking sides in this implicit debate, Habermas then turned to a similar comparison of Benjamin's aesthetics with those of Adorno, focusing on their celebrated dispute in the 1930s over the implications of the loss of the aura. Here, perhaps more than in *Legitimation Crisis*, he stressed the drawbacks of Adorno's faith in the critical power of autonomous, inaccessible, still auratic art which led, so Habermas argued, to a "strategy of hibernation, whose obvious weakness lies in its defensive character."[18] Adorno's dark vision of a totally controlled Culture Industry which allows no room for any negation outside of the most esoteric and incomprehensible works of art was, so Habermas argued, an unwarranted exaggeration. "A noticeable development of arts with a collective mode of reception," he optimistically insisted, ". . . points beyond mere culture industry and does not *a fortiori* refute Benjamin's hope for a universalized secular illumination."[19]

Adorno was also at fault in reducing Benjamin's position to an unnuanced celebration of modern art's loss of the aura, whose ambivalent implications Benjamin, in fact, had fully understood. Whereas Benjamin had not mourned the loss of the specifically cultic and irrational aspects of the aura, he was afraid that the experiential source of the aura's power, its derivation from a primitive moment of perfect plenitude, might also be entirely forgotten. As Habermas put it, "Since the historical experience of a past *Jetzt-zeit* needs to be recharged, and because this experience is locked within the aura of a work of art, the undialectical disintegration of the aura would mean the loss of this experience."[20] Morever, so Habermas argued, Benjamin had not been content with merely redeeming the experiential origin of the aura; he wanted to generalize it in the lived experience of everyone in the present. Benjamin's goal, Habermas insisted, is "a state of affairs in which the esoteric experience of happiness has become public and universal; for only in a context of communication into which nature has been included in a mutual way – as if once again stood up straight – can subjects return one another's gaze."[21]

Habermas's introduction of the theme of universal communication, which some commentators were to contend he illegitimately imposed onto Benjamin's actual argument,[22] shows the extent to which he identified with Benjamin's position. He was, however, unwilling to endorse all of its dimensions. On the question of technological determinism, for example, he sided with Marcuse and Adorno, whereas on the issue of preserving artistic autonomy in the contemporary world he remained ambivalent. Nor did he express an unequivocal preference for allegory over symbolism, although in the 1963 essay mentioned above he had claimed that Benjamin's concept of the allegorical "has proved its singular appropriateness especially for modern art, though it had first been formed in terms of the baroque."[23] But perhaps Habermas's most interesting uncertainty concerned the fundamental choice between consciousness-raising and redemptive criticism.

In important ways, he clearly felt attracted to the latter alternative. In order to explain what Benjamin had wanted to redeem, Habermas turned to his highly idiosyncratic theory of language which was based on a mimetic concept of meaning. In arguing that meaning was something to be preserved rather than created, Benjamin, so Habermas suggested, was probably "thinking of the semantic potential from which human beings draw and with which they invest the world with meaning, permitting it to be experienced. This semantic potential is deposited in myth to begin with and must be released from it – but it cannot be expanded, just continually transformed."[24] The original source of the semantic potential for

Benjamin was in fact mixed, simultaneously mimetic and expressive. Once again in Habermas's words, language for Benjamin "is merely a form of the animal instinct manifest in expressive gestures. Benjamin combines these in turn with the mimetic capacity (*Vermögen*) to perceive and reproduce similarities."[25] Thus what is actually expressed in language is not merely the subjective interiority of the speaker, but also an imitation of surrounding nature. Originally onomatopoetic, imitation is evidenced as well in the nonsensuous correspondences preserved in written script. What makes this type of combined expression and mimesis so attractive to Benjamin is its priority to the break between subject and object; in other words, that Schillerian motif of reconciliation which Shierry Weber identified in Critical Theory is evident here in Benjamin's linguistic speculations.

Now, in general, Habermas was sceptical of precisely such claims to reconcile man and nature through a new, nondominating science. His objections to Marcuse's faith in this possibility are well known. Yet, in this essay, he demonstrates a certain cautious approbation of the goal insofar as it is represented by art. "As odd as this mimetic theory of language sounds," he contended, "Benjamin is right in assuming that the oldest semantic stratum is that of expression. . . . One could speculate that a semantic store of original subhuman forms of communication has found a place in human language and represents a potential that cannot be augmented. With the meanings that comprise this potential, human beings interpret the world in terms of their own needs and create thereby a net of correspondences."[26] The mediated preservation of these primitive expressive-mimetic linguistic experiences is at the heart of the *promesse de bonheur* in art. According to Habermas, Benjamin understood that "we need those rescued semantic potentials if we are to interpret the world in terms of our own needs, and only if the source of these potentials does not run dry can the claim to happiness be fulfilled."[27] Insofar as Habermas himself shared Benjamin's anxiety over the loss of these potentials, he endorsed the redemptive impulse of the latter's criticism.

But Habermas drew back from accepting the nostalgic, and perhaps even conservative, implications of Benjamin's linguistic theory which "can but comprehend itself as identification and *repetition* of emphatic experiences and utopian contents – and not as reflection in a formative process.[28] Benjamin, to be sure had also recognized the regressive possibilities in his linguistics and had tried to counter it by adopting a materialist theory of history. But his attempt had failed, so Habermas concluded, because "the materialist theory of social development cannot be simply fitted into the anarchistic conception of *Jetztzeiten* which intermittently come crashing through fate as if from above. An anti-evolutionary concept of history cannot be tacked onto historical materialism as if it were a monk's cowl . . ."[29]

Habermas's own concept of history was anything but antievolutionary.[30] Without returning to an orthodox Marxist insistence on the inevitability of progress, he nonetheless combined the arguments of a wide range of thinkers, most notably Weber, Luhmann, Parsons, Piaget, and Kohlberg, to fashion a highly tentative rational reconstruction of the past as progressive from which the possibility of positive change in the future could be extrapolated. The species, Habermas hoped, might achieve what he called a "participatory remodeling of administrative structures"[31] which would approach the regulative, hitherto counterfactual ideal of the perfect speech situation latent in communicative action.

All of the implications and problems of Habermas's reconstruction of historical materialism need not concern us now. What is of interest is the role art might play in the process of emancipation as he reconceptualized it. For it was precisely to Benjamin's redemptive criticism that he turned for an account of the positive content that might be rationally discussed in the formal symmetry of the perfect speech situation. His essay on Benjamin concludes with the troubling question "Could an emancipated humanity one day confront itself in the expanded scope of discursive will-formation and nevertheless still be deprived of the terms in which it is able to interpret life as good life?"[32] The answer Habermas offers shows how seriously he took Benjamin's linguistic theory, despite all his reservations about its regressive implications: "Without the store of those semantic energies with which Benjamin's redemptive criticism was concerned, there would necessarily be a stagnation of the structure of practical discourse that had finally prevailed."[33] In short, communicative rationality is not enough to insure true emancipation; the experiential memories still contained, however faintly, in art are necessary to give humankind a motivational stimulus to the search for happiness.

In Habermas's more recent work on modernity, most notably his 1980 Adorno Prize address on *"Die Moderne: Ein unvollendetes Projekt,"* translated under the title "Modernity versus Postmodernity," and his mammoth two-volume *Theorie des kommunikativen Handelns,*[34] the implications of his reliance on art as a repository of endangered meanings have become clearer. Arguing once again against Daniel Bell's neoconservative attack on cultural modernism as the major source of our ills, he defended the ultimate value of modernization in which science, morality, and art are separated into autonomous spheres, each with its own internal logic. Based on institutionalization of professional expertise,

> there appear the structures of cognitive-instrumental, moral-practical, and of aesthetic-expressive rationality, each of these under the control of specialists who seem more adept at being logical in these particular ways than other people are. As a result, the distance has grown between the culture of the experts and that of the larger public.[35]

But if cultural modernization has implied differentiation and specialization, which for art was most clearly expressed in the *l'art pour l'art* movement of the nineteenth century, it has also produced a counter-move designed to reunite the increasingly autonomous spheres with the life-world out of which they emerged. The project of modernity, Habermas argued, "intended to release the cognitive potentials of each of these domains to set them free from their esoteric forms. The Enlightenment philosophers wanted to utilize this accumulation of specialized culture for the enrichment of everyday life, that is to say, for the rational organization of everyday social life."[36] In our own era, this same desire has been manifested in those modernist movements, most notably Surrealism, which attempted to de-auraticize art in the hope of revolutionizing life. This attempt, however, failed, so Habermas contended, for two essential reasons. The first, which Adorno had noted in his dispute with Benjamin, was that the destruction of autonomous art merely dispersed its contents without leading to a really emancipatory change in mass consciousness. The second, which Habermas called more important, followed from the fact that

> In everyday communication, cognitive meanings, moral expectations, subjective expressions and evaluations must relate to one another. Communication processes need a cultural tradition covering all spheres – cognitive, moral-practical and expressive. A rationalized everyday life, therefore, could hardly be saved from cultural improverishment through breaking open a single cultural sphere – art – and so providing access to just one of the specialized knowledge complexes. The surrealist revolt would have replaced only one abstraction.[37]

Like the aborted *Aufhebung* of philosophy in the Marxist attempt to realize it through the proletarian revolution, Surrealist and other anti-auratic movements have not really succeeded in reuniting their sphere of esoteric truth with everyday life. To do so, Habermas claimed, all three spheres of specialized knowledge would have to be made accessible at once. "A reified everyday praxis," he contended, "can be cured only by creating unconstrained interaction of the cognitive with the moral-practical and the aesthetic-expressive elements."[38]

Such an outcome is, needless to say, highly improbable, but Habermas claims that there is at least one example of something approaching it. In his book *The Aesthetics of Resistance*, Peter Weiss describes an incident in Berlin in 1937 when a group of politicized workers sought to reappropriate the cultural heritage of Europe, then being systematically distorted by the Nazis, for their own life experience.[39] This attempt to recapture the energies of the objective *Geist* for personal life, Habermas claims, shows that the Surrealists' dream can perhaps still be accounted viable, even if their own efforts to realize it foundered.

Whether or not this isolated example is really convincing, it shows Habermas's continued determination to redeem those semantic potentials that Benjamin had located in auratic art. But significantly, Habermas hopes to do so without aiming at the complete reversal of the process of differentiation which he identifies with the modern. What must be reversed, however, is the unbalanced relationship between the subsystems of rationality that characterize the types of modernization, capitalist and bureaucratic socialist, that have so far taken place. In particular, the domination of the subsystem of cognitive-instrumental (or what he calls in his new book, functional rationality) over both moral-practical and aesthetic-expressive rationality must be undone. What hitherto has been a relationship of colonization must be replaced by one of constructive mediation. Habermas admits that the prospects for this change to occur are very slim. But he warns against abandoning the unfulfilled project of modernity which, among other things, would mean a loss of hope in the creative reappropriation of aesthetic rationality into an increasingly rationalized everyday life. Thus, although Habermas must still be accounted a far less aesthetically inclined thinker than his mentors in the Frankfurt School, it will no longer do to claim that he gives no weight at all to the role of art in the process of emancipation.

That the way in which he does so is by no means without its problems has not escaped many of his commentators. Some, for example, have charged that he misconstrues Benjamin's theory of language by underestimating the extent to which it sees mimesis as a "*technical* act of human production."[40] By privileging human communication over representational construction, so these critics argue, Habermas has falsely emphasized the expressive moment of semantic potentiality in Benjamin's theory. This reading of Benjamin has, however, itself been called into question by Anson Rabinbach,[41] who claims that although Benjamin may have not understood language in communicative terms comparable to those, say, of Martin Buber's "I–Thou" relationship, he nonetheless was even more hostile to a purely technical or instrumental concept of language. As another commentator, Richard Wolin, has recently put it, Benjamin's essays on language "coincide in their rejection of an instrumentalist view of language and their emphasis on language as a privileged medium through which a 'flashing image' of reconciliation between man and nature can be glimpsed."[42] However much Benjamin may have admired and learned from Mallarmé's anticommunicative theory of language, he never embraced a purely technical alternative, as his critical response to the Soviet linguists Marr and Vigotsky demonstrates.[43] Still, it is clear that he did distinguish between the mimetic and communicative (or what he called "semiotic") dimensions of language. The latter may have been the "bearer"[44] of the former, but they lacked its utopian energies.

Yet Habermas himself, it should be noted, does not ignore the difference between the communicative and expressive-mimetic dimensions of language, as his refusal to collapse communicative and aesthetic rationality into one category makes clear. The belief that he wants to do so, however, motivates the work of several of his other critics, most notably the French poststructuralist philosopher Jean-François Lyotard. In a recent essay on postmodernism, Lyotard asks what sort of unity between spheres Habermas seeks.[45] Is it, he wonders, an organic unity of the type posited by Hegel or a synthetic unity of heterogeneities like that suggested in Kant's *Critique of Judgement*? Even if the latter, Lyotard contends, Habermas fails to address the severe criticisms recent postmodern thinkers have made of the Enlightenment ideas of a unified goal of history and a totalizing subject. In neglecting to confront these objections, Habermas thus shows himself to be less the partisan of cultural modernism than he claims. In fact, his implicit aesthetic ideal, Lyotard argues, is that of the beautiful as opposed to the sublime. Modernism, however, depends on the latter, even if it evinces some nostalgia for the allegedly lost wholeness and harmony captured in the traditional ideal of beauty.[46] Postmodernism, with which Lyotard more closely identifies, is equally dependent on an aesthetic of the sublime, although without the nostalgia for its beautiful opposite still apparent in modernism.

A similar accusation is made against Habermas by Andreas Huyssen, who claims that he

> ignores the fact that the very idea of wholistic (sic) modernity and of a totalizing view of history has become anathema in the 1970s, and precisely not on the conservative right. The critical deconstruction of Enlightenment rationalism and logocentrism by theoreticians of culture, the decentering of traditional notions of identity, the fight of women and gays for a legitimate social and sexual identity outside the parameters of male, heterosexual vision, the search for alternatives in our relationship with nature, including the nature of our own bodies – all these phenomena, which are key to the culture of the 1970s, make Habermas's proposition to complete the project of modernity questionable, if not undesirable.[47]

Huyssen, however, goes beyond Lyotard by arguing that Habermas's holistic impulse is shared by modernist art itself, which is no less universalistic and totalizing in its assumption about a positive future anticipated by an avant-garde in the present. There is thus a "secret bond between avant-garde and official culture in advanced industrial societies,"[48] which Habermas with his Adornoesque faith in the critical power of modernism fails to register.

An even more extensive critique of Habermas's position has been made by the German literary critic Peter Bürger, who nonetheless professes solidarity with many of his social and political goals.[49] According to Bürger, who worries, like Lyotard and Huyssen, about Habermas's smoothing over the ruptures of culture, there are three major problems in his theory of modernism. First, Habermas's assertion of a parallel development of the three spheres of science, morality, and art towards autonomy and specialization misconstrues the structural and social differences between each sphere. In particular, it underestimates the primacy of cognitive-instrumental rationalization in the modernization process. And perhaps even more significantly, it fails to acknowledge the fatal absence of an impulse in science to reintegrate itself with everyday life. "While autonomous art carries with it the idea of its self-transcendence," Bürger writes, "this cannot be said to be true of science in the same way."[50] Thus Habermas's hope for a simultaneous reintegration of the three spheres into a rationalized life-world seems highly unrealistic.

Secondly, there is a much greater contradiction between the two aspects of the modernization process – the growing differentiation of the separate spheres and the contrary desire for their reintegration with the life-world – than Habermas admits. "In fully developed bourgeois society 'autonomy' and 'use' of art have increasingly come to oppose each other. They will not be so easily reconciled as Habermas's construction of modernity suggests."[51]

And finally, the exaggerated tendency of art to proclaim its total autonomy creates a danger that Habermas fails to take seriously enough: the atrophy of that semantic potential in art derived from its original expressive-mimetic relation to nature. Habermas is thus wrong, Bürger contends, in so quickly dismissing the Surrealists' attempt to revitalize art. "Even the failure of the demand for sublation should not be regarded as a mistake without results. On the contrary. If it is possible today to think about free productivity for everyone, then it is certainly due to the fact that the avant-gardists questioned the legitimacy of the term 'great art work'."[52] Bürger, who elsewhere has made clear his opposition to Adorno's defense of autonomous modernist art for being no longer viable in the age of the post-avant-garde,[53] thus chastizes Habermas both for not abandoning that defense rigorously enough and for thinking that, should it be abandoned and art reintegrated with life, a genuinely emancipatory result would ensue!

Although Bürger's critique has these contradictory implications, it does point to certain unresolved difficulties in Habermas's treatment of modernism. In conjunction with the others mentioned above, it suggests two major ambiguities that require clarification before Habermas's attempt to include cultural modernism, despite the qualms of neoconservatives like Daniel Bell, in his general defense of modernity can be accounted a success. First, he must clarify the extent to which his vision of a mediated rather than colonizing relation between the subsystems he posits as inevitable differentiations in the modernization process is qualitatively superior to the old and largely discredited idealist dream of a perfectly harmonious and rational totality. That he has not expressed himself with complete clarity on this issue is demonstrated by the fact that whereas Lyotard, Huyssen, and Bürger, as well as other recent deconstructionist critics, fault him for still dreaming this dream, others like Thomas McCarthy and Henning Ottmann attack him precisely for having abandoned it.[54] Against the former, Habermas has explicitly written,

> Nothing makes me more nervous than the imputation – repeated in a number of different versions and in the most peculiar contexts – that because the theory of communicative action focuses attention on the

social facticity of recognized validity-claims, it proposes, or at least suggests, a rationalistic utopian society. I do not regard the fully transparent society as an ideal, nor do I wish to suggest *any* other ideal – Marx was not the only one frightened by vestiges of utopian socialism.[55]

Against the latter, who are particularly hostile to his refusal to countenance the overthrow of humanity's instrumental relationship to nature and its replacement by an entirely aesthetic one, he has replied that both are necessary aspects of an emancipated society. Not only is it impossible to extend a communicative ethic based on full reciprocity to inorganic nature or even plant life, it is difficult to know how to ground such a naturalistic ethic without regressing to discredited religious or metaphysical world views. Science, therefore, must be instrumental. Still, "the discussion from Kant to Adorno concerning natural and artistic beauty could provide grounds for the thesis that the *expressive attitude* to external nature opens up a domain of experience that can be exploited for *artistic production*."[56] The best that can be hoped for between these separate spheres is the noncolonizing interpenetration that may be reestablished on the level of everyday experience.

But precisely what that mediated relationship might look like, especially when the cognitive and aesthetic attitudes towards nature may be more contradictory than complementary, is not really clear. Nor is it easy to grasp how the return to the life-world as the arena of cooperation can be reconciled with the continued differentiation of the separate cultural spheres. Here Habermas's ambivalence about the implications of the debate between Adorno and Benjamin over the de-auraticization of art reveals a larger tension in his work which needs to be more explicitly addressed. As Bürger contends, it may be much harder to reconcile the autonomy of art with its usefulness in the life-world than Habermas imagines.

The second major issue which needs clarification concerns the status of the artistic sphere itself. With that partiality for reason demonstrated throughout his work, Habermas contends that alongside cognitive-instrumental and moral-practical rationality, there is also a kind of "aesthetic-practical rationality."[57] What he seems to mean by this term is that the aesthetic sphere has come "under the control of specialists who seem more adept at being logical"[58] in artistic terms than are laymen. Here certain remarks of Adorno in his *Aesthetic Theory* about the way in which increased technical virtuosity in art combines the mimesis of nature with non-instrumental rationality are tacitly assumed.[59] But precisely how this type of increased mastery of technique can be seen as rational in the same evolutionary sense that Habermas attributes to the other types of rationality is not clear. For there are certainly many other standards of judgment in aesthetic matters besides technical virtuosity which makes the idea of artistic progress highly problematic.

Nor are we nearer to an understanding of aesthetic rationality if we remember Habermas's Benjaminian identification in his 1963 essay "Between Science and Philosophy: Marxism as Critique" of modernist art with allegory rather than classical symbolism. Although this argument gives the lie to Lyotard's contention that Habermas's aesthetics is closer to the beautiful than the sublime, it makes it difficult to see the rationality in modernist art, except insofar as it provides a critique of the false wholeness of affirmative culture. It may do so in order to redeem the semantic potentials that Benjamin saw preserved in art as a residue of its original mimetic-expressive relationship with nature, but it does not seem clear why the non-sensuous correspondences that allegedly underlie art can be said to be *rational* in any normal sense of that term.[60] Indeed, Habermas very explicitly warns against attributing to mimesis "the role of representative of an original Reason, whose place has been usurped by instrumental rationality."[61] Moreover, if Bürger is right about the atrophy of the original semantic potential of art as a result of too much autonomous technical virtuosity, there may even be a contradictory relationship between increased artistic rationalization and its redemptive function.

One possible way in which Habermas might turn for help in resolving these problems is to draw on the work of a theorist whose concepts of rational development have been useful for him in other contexts: Jean Piaget. Following the art historian Suzi Gablik in her controversial analysis of *Progress in Art*,[62] he might then argue that increasingly nonrepresentational modern art expresses a cognitive advance from Piaget's concrete-operational to formal-operational stages. But the difficulties of this solution are not hard to discern. Aside from the limited applicability of this schema to the visual arts and its blissful unawareness of the social underpinnings of too much abstraction in reification, it fails to provide a place for that reintegration of artistic rationality into everyday life which Habermas wants to defend. Nor is it in any way compatible with his Benjamian stress on mimesis as a source of art's ultimate value. In fact, it would lead to the very collapse of aesthetic into cognitive and moral rationality that Habermas's critics accuse him of fostering and which he has been at such pains to refute.

In short, although I would not want to ally myself with those deconstructionists who reach for their gun every time they hear the word *reason*, I do think Habermas owes us a more explicit explanation of the nature of the aesthetic-practical rationality he wants to defend in modernism. It is difficult enough to grasp what a mediated relationship among cognitive-instrumental, moral-practical, and aesthetic-expressive rationalities would look like, even if they all might be simultaneously reintegrated with the life-world. It is even harder if the rational status of the third remains somewhat of a mystery. Habermas has devoted an enormous amount of intellectual energy in the effort to define and defend a communicative concept of rational action. But he has recognized, although many of his critics have been slow to acknowledge it, that its full realization alone cannot provide us with the substantive visions of the good life which will make discussion worthwhile. If the aesthetic is to come to the rescue, without, however, leading to an Adornoesque strategy of hibernation, Habermas will need to expand his still rudimentary treatment of it. Not only is modernity an uncompleted project, so, too, is Habermas's enormously ambitious attempt to salvage its still emancipatory potential.

2

Reason and Happiness: Some Psychoanalytic Themes in Critical Theory*

JOEL WHITEBOOK

If it is appropriate to speak of the perennial problems of Critical Theory after approximately a half a century of its existence, then the entire complex of questions raised by the appropriation of Freud would certainly have to be counted among them. Psychoanalysis not only provided the Frankfurt School with a means of empirically investigating subjects which therefore could be approached only "philosophically," it also opened a new dimension for social theory. Of the four pillars on which the theory of the Frankfurt School was constructed, Freud was the most heterogeneous. Hegel, Marx, and Weber came from the tradition of classical nineteenth-century social theory and were all primarily concerned with understanding the great transformation from premodern to modern society. While he was also interested in the question of modernity in an indirect way, Freud's major concern lay elsewhere, namely, in the exploration of the unconscious and of the instinctual substratum of human culture. And it was the integration and elaboration of this so-called subjective dimension, opened up by Freud, which marked the real innovation of the Frankfurt School in contrast to the other contemporary Marxian and non-Marxian schools of social theory.

The impact of Freud is apparent in Marcuse's 1938 article "On Hedonism."[1] In the article, Marcuse provides perhaps the best general formulation of the problematic that arose from the appropriation of Freud – albeit in philosophical terms. Marcuse outlined

* An earlier version of this paper was given at the 1982 Dubrovnik seminar on Philosophy and Social Sciences.

what he saw as the central antinomy in the history of ethics: the conflict between rationalism, on the one hand, and hedonism and eudaimonism on the other. The truth of rationalism derives from its defense of the social moment of human existence. It asserts the claim of collectivity for objectivity, universality, and truth against the contingency and transience of individual existence. Hedonism and eudaimonism, in comparison, assert the claim of the biologically embodied individual to gratification and happiness against the sacrifices the collectivity inevitably imposes on him/her. Marcuse argues that, as the antinomy reflects a deep-seated historical reality, it cannot be dissolved at the level of philosophical reflection. Rather, the reconciliation of the collective's claim to reason with the individual's claim to happiness will become possible only after the abolition of class society and the radical dimunition of scarcity. To soften the opposition *now* would be to falsify the realities of an unfree society.

Whatever the merits of Marcuse's "solution," he has articulated the desideratum which Critical Theory has set for itself, i.e. to do justice to both sides of the antinomy. Any scheme that fails to fulfill that goal would fall short of Critical Theory's own self-defined project. With these considerations in mind, I shall examine several of the psychonanalytic themes in Critical Theory. In Section I, I will reconsider the critique of ego psychology with respect to some of that critique's unexamined presuppositions. Section II will discuss "the end of the individual" and attempt to link it with the current discussion of narcissism. And Section III will be concerned with Habermas's reworking of these "perennial" themes within the framework of his communication theory.

I

We know that Adorno and Marcuse embraced the "biological" Freud as the truly revolutionary Freud. At the same time as this stance of theirs accounts for much of the penetration of their social critique, it also determines the ultimate limitations of their position. Given the historical and political context within which they were theorizing, we can appreciate how attractive Freud the id psychologist must have been to them. If one's theoretical-political intention is to bring into sharp relief the price society – perceived as tending toward total domination on both sides of the political spectrum – exacts from the individual, the id psychology provides an effective framework for critique. Above all, it is a theory of uneliminable conflict between the biologically embodied individual and society which can be used as a heuristic to decipher domination in every nook and cranny of social existence. All development, if we rightfully speak of development, occurs through conflict: first between the biological organism and the social environment; later, intrapsychically, between the internalized agencies of society and the individual's biological substratum.

It is understandable, then, that Adorno and Marcuse would view any revising of the biological Freud as backsliding from the revolutionary potential of psychoanalysis. Thus in their well known attacks, they criticize the ego psychologists for trying to turn psychoanalysis to an ameliorist and conformist science – of trying to clean it up, in short. And, there can be no denying that was the actual role ego psychology played historically. I believe the uncertainties of their new situation in New York prompted the emigré analysts who founded ego psychology to try to make psychoanalysis socially and scientifically respectable in the American context. This was especially unfortunate, given the conservative cultural mood and the dominance of positivism in the post-war American scene. And the success of the ego psychologists did indeed have a deadening effect on the development of psychoanalysis as a cultural institution. Nevertheless, independent of the political intentions of its founders, there were compelling theoretical and clinical reasons for the introduction of ego psychology. For, in some sense, drive theory by itself is *aporetic*. And, while Adorno and Marcuse's critique of ego psychology may have hit the mark politically, they inherited the *aporia* of the id psychology to which they continued to adhere.

The controversy between id psychology and ego psychology centers on the amount of genetic and functional independence that ought to be ascribed to the ego. The drive theorists maintain that the ego has no independent sources of its own. It is simply the byproduct of the conflict between external reality, which obeys the logic of the reality principle, and the instinctual makeup of the individual, which operates according to the logic of the pleasure principle. As Freud put it:

> It is easy to see the ego is the part of the id which has been modified by the direct influence of the external world through the medium of Pepts.-Cs.; in a sense it is an extension of the surface differentiation. Moreover, the ego seeks to bring the influence of the external world to bear on in the id and its tendencies and endeavors to substitute the reality principle for the pleasure principle which reigns unrestrictedly in the id.[2]

Likewise, the id psychologists tended to view the ego almost exclusively from the point of view of its defensive functions: as the opponent of the drives. A consequence of this way of seeing things is a low estimate of the possible role of the ego, and therefore rationality, in human affairs. Indeed, it is difficult to see how reason can be conceptualized as anything other than "repressive." It was in this context that Freud introduced the famous metaphor of the ego as "a man on horseback, who has to hold in check the superior strength of the horse." He later tried to recant that metaphor because of the gloomy *Weltanschauung* it was encouraging among some of his followers – a *Weltanschauung* not dissimilar from that of the early Frankfurt School.[3]

The ego psychologists, on the other hand, argued that, rather than the ego growing out of the id, both psychic institutions develop out of a prior undifferentiated phase. But, more importantly, they maintained that there is an independent source or inborn *Anlage* for ego development. Somewhere in the course of human evolution the species acquired the capacity for individual ego development so that each newborn is not faced with the task of developing an ego from scratch. Hartmann called the functions that correspond to these innate capacities, such as mobility, perception etc., primary autonomous ego functions. They constitute the minimal core functions – the transcendental preconditions, if you will – that organize human experience and activity, and make higher-level achievements possible. The primary functions, that is, can become the basis for establishing secondary autonomous ego functions, such as the capacity to work. It is usually these latter, secondary capacities that we have in mind when we speak of autonomy as a life achievement.[4]

Hartmann is careful to point out that this conception does not eliminate conflict as a major factor in psychic life. While it is not their only source, conflict can stimulate the development of the ego *Anlage* in much the same way that experience stimulates the development of innate structures in Chomsky. Likewise, secondary autonomous functions can be born out of conflict, but through a process of automatization and structuralization can achieve functional autonomy vis-à-vis the conflicts that gave rise to them. This is not to say that the autonomous functions cannot become re-embroiled in conflict at any time. Regression is possible with respect to primary and secondary autonomous structures, and the relationship between conflicted and conflict-free areas of psychic functioning is always an important clinical indicator. What we are talking about is relative stability and "resistivity" to regression over time.

An important implication follows from these theoretical innovations, namely, the relationship between the biological and the social spheres changes. Somewhat unexpectedly, as the conception of the ego becomes more independent, it also becomes biological. Id psychology identified the drives with biology and the ego with internalized society and set up an insurmountable antagonism between biological inheritance and sociability. Ego psychology, by identifying the biological sources of the ego, actually locates some of the biological roots of sociation. A similar transformation can be traced in the relationship of the reality principle to the pleasure principle. Whereas before this has been conceived of as the logics of two incommensurable and antagonistic realms, now they could be brought into relation so that, at least in part, the reality principle serves the pleasure principle. At any rate, the earlier view presupposed the rather primitive concept of pleasure as nothing but the autistic discharge of tension, and it is difficult to see how anything like "higher pleasures" could be adequately conceptualized.

Id psychology, in a manner analogous to Hobbes, begins with an assumption of constitutional unsociability and then unsuccessfully tries to account for the facts of society. Social norms must be brought in from the outside, "grafted up on the genetically asocial individual by 'discipline and socialization'." Ego psychology, on the other hand, explains "the individual's social development by tracing the unfolding of *the genetically social character of the human individual* in the course of his encounter with the social environment at each phase of epigenisis."[5] While Adorno's and Marcuse's wholesale appropriation of id psychology allowed them to dramatize the conflict between the individual and society, and demonstrate the depth psychological consequences of social oppression in a way that was unique in Marxism, it also prevented them from conceiving the condition of the possibility of a free society. This forced them to posit an eschatological rupture as the only means to emancipation. The ego psychologists have no difficulty in accounting for the possibilities of sociation. The danger with their position lies in the opposite direction, namely, of becoming too harmonistic. What was an account of human genetic sociability at the level of theory often became conformism and a disregard for the social origins of psychopathology at the level of practice.

Habermas has made the following observation concerning the early Frankfurt School's relationship to the idea of autonomous ego:

> But even the melancholy farewell to psychoanalysis appeals to an uncoerced ego that is identical with itself; how else would the form of

total socialization be recognized, if not in the fact it neither produces nor tolerates upright individuals.[6]

While the observation is true, it requires further elaboration. That is to say, it is true that Adorno and Marcuse must make implicit reference to an idea of an autonomous ego simply to make the concept of a totally socialized world intelligible. However, it is questionable whether they possessed the conceptual terms to have explicated the concept of the ego adequately. To be sure, Adorno, on theoretical grounds, systematically refrained from grounding basic concepts. Thus, in a discussion of the Kantian idea of freedom, he refuses to come down either on the side of the unity of the subject or the diffuseness of inner nature.

> According to the Kantian model subjects are free to the extent that they are conscious of themselves, are identical with themselves; and in such identity they are also unfree to the extent they stand under and perpetuate its compulsion. As non-identical, as diffuse nature they are unfree; and yet they are free, because in the impulses that overpower them they also become free of the compulsive character of identity.[7]

Habermas interprets this passage "as an aporetic development of the determinations of an ego identity that makes freedom possible without demanding for it the price of unhappiness, violation of one's inner nature."

But we can say more than this, for the aporetic character of this passage results from a specific assumption, namely, that the unity of the self can only be achieved and maintained through compulsion. To put it psychoanalytically, because he takes the ego only in its defensive aspect, as the opponent of the drives, and does not sufficiently appreciate its synthetic function, Adorno can only think unity as compulsion:

> Men had to do fearful things to themselves before the self, the identical, purposive and virile nature of man, was formed, and something of that recurs in every childhood. The strain of holding the "I" together adheres to the "I" in all stages.[8]

Adorno elevated the pathological character structure of the obsessive-compulsive into the only possible outcome of identity formation. While we are indeed accustomed to thinking of the ego as anti-instinctual, I would like to suggest that, insofar as the ego possesses a synthetic function, and insofar as *Eros* is defined as the drive to establish and preserve "ever greater unities,"[9] we can locate something like *Eros* in the ego itself.

I do not mean to imply that the relationship between society and the drives, or the ego and the drives, is devoid of conflict, object loss, or the "domination of inner nature." My point is only that, because the early Frankfurt School clung so militantly to drive theory, with is limited conceptual resources, they could not think themselves out of the dialectic of enlightenment. All development is, *a priori*, self-defeating:

> Man's domination over himself, which grounds his selfhood, is almost always the destruction of the subject in whose service it is undertaken.[10]

This alluring proposition, which is the main thesis of the Odysseus chapter, and which is the unstated assumption of much neoromantic politics, is based on the fallacy that there is a subject worth saving that exists prior to the inception of development.

II

The psychoanalytic doctrine that ideal individuation lies between the extremes of merger, on the one hand, and isolation, on the other, can be used to elucidate the early Critical Theorists' view of high bourgeois society.[11] For them, the "brief intermezzo of liberalism" constituted a short, self-liquidating phase of historical development in which autonomous individuality was articulated as a social norm, partially realized, and finally undermined. The same market which, in the first instance, had served to differentiate the individual from the precapitalist collectivity, in the long run destroys the conditions of individuality. Thus, insofar as psychology is the science that investigates the inner life of a differentiated individual, Adorno wrote that "the prebourgeois order does not yet know psychology, the oversocialized one knows it no longer."[12] Their ambivalence towards liberalism – an ambivalence which, on their account, corresponds to ambiguities in the object – determined one of the central dilemmas of early Critical Theory. Despite the repressiveness of its socialization process, the largely ideological character of its professed norms, and the highly sublimated character of its *"promesse de bonheur,"* the relative individuation achieved under liberalism appears preferable to the totally socialized world toward which late capitalism was tending.

Thus, if the early Frankfurt School criticized the notion of the autonomous ego with respect to the instinctual cost of its attainment, they nevertheless defended it when confronted with the prospect of a totally socialized world. This brings us to another way of formulating the central *aporia* of early Critical Theory: they sought an individual who could rationally and autonomously oppose the authoritarianism of the existing order, but the only way they knew to achieve rational autonomy was through the internalization of paternal authority. Thus, strangely enough, with the transition from the patriarchal family of the liberal phase to the more permissive one of the post-liberal period, they were forced to mourn the passing of the authoritarian father. Jessica Benjamin has put the dilemma well:

> Yet, at the center of critical theory's analysis of modern capitalism is a paradox about the nature of resistance to domination. Those aspects of consciousness where this resistance might be located – critical reason, individuation, integrity and ultimately resistance itself – are tied to the process of internalizing authority. As a result, the rejection of authority can only take place through its acceptance. Even though the subjective dimension of domination is found to be in the way authority is internalized, the only possible resistance to authority is located in the same process of internalization. If reason, reflection and individuation are historically tied to the process of internalizing authority, is not the result that authority is in some sense seen as necessary or even vindicated? [13]

The difficulty arises as a difficulty because of the Frankfurt School's ambivalent use of Freud. While they employed him to diagnose the changes in family structure, socialization, and character formation accompanying the transition from liberal to organized capitalism, they were unwilling to accept the political consequence he drew from the theory they were employing. For the liberal, thoroughly unutopian Freud, who dismissed the claim to unfettered instinctual expression, the fact that autonomy results from the internalization and depersonification of authority figures is only one of the countless paradoxes psychoanalysis discovers in the socialization of finite-beings.

It should be pointed out that, in the passage I quoted, Jessica Benjamin fails to distinguish between legitimate and illegitimate authority. This is a tendency she shares with the Old Frankfurt School and much of the antiauthoritarian Left; to simply subsume this distinction under the undifferentiated concept of domination. Be that as it may, given the dilemma as she poses it, two alternatives present themselves for its dissolution. On the one hand, one can reject "autonomy, rationality and individuation" as the proper goals of social development. This is the path followed by some of our better known avant-garde cultural critics, feminist theoreticians, and postmodernist antihumanists.[14] In this case, it is typically argued that these categories represent particularistic prejudices – Western, male, modern or what have you – and, far from representing emancipatory norms, are idealogical illusions which are constitutive of the crisis of modernity is the first place. They are, in short, part of the problem, not of the solution.

On the other hand, one can contest the thesis that authoritarian socialization is the only path, or even a path to autonomy. Piaget offers an interesting suggestion in this context. He maintains that the "struggle with the father" can in fact never produce autonomy – "respect for the law" in Kant's sense – but only compliance to the law, motivated by fearful submissiveness.[15] In his analysis of the game of marbles, Piaget seeks to show that true autonomy can only be learned in reciprocal interaction between peers. He argues, further, that autonomy, which is a potential for the species as such, only became an explicit norm in modern Western society because only in the West has an extended period of adolescence emerged where one could have this extended peer interaction. From a psychoanalytic perspective, adolescence – while it does indeed constitute a chance for a new beginning[16]– represents a relatively late stage of development. Therefore, along with more information about the psychodynamics of the situation, one would want to know more about the transformations that occurred in the earlier stages of socialization with the emergence of the modern family that lay the groundwork for this adolescent experience.

Piaget's point about submissiveness, however, is in part well taken. Even within psychoanalysis, it was necessary to modify Freud's views on the civilizing function of castration anxiety. Edith Jacobson, for example, has argued that, while still an important factor, castration anxiety *by itself* is too early and too primitive an affect to account for the formation of so sophisticated a structure as the superego or for sophisticated moral judgement.[17] The difficulty with the more benign monsieur Piaget is that he is in danger of losing sight altogether of the moment of fear that has informed the "realism" of bourgeois social thought from Hobbes through Freud. It does not follow from the fact that an overly severe upbringing will most likely produce submissiveness, constriction, and timidity rather than autonomy that permissiveness is without difficulties. Clinically, it has been recognized for some time that a superego formed in permissive socialization can actually be unduly harsh, even paranoid, precisely because it has not been tested in an encounter with a real, rather than a fantasized, father.

For the Old Frankfurt School, then, the thesis of the "end of the individual" and the thesis of the "fatherless society" go together. Habermas, on the other hand, who does not share their analysis of the self-negating character of liberalism, and who wants to defend the "project of modernity" against the dialectic of enlightenment, must necessarily offer a different interpretation of the transformation the modern family has undergone. And, although he does not deny the dangers of a "fatherless society," he also sees new possibilities for development *in the very things* Horkheimer and Adorno saw as nothing but sources of regression. Following a direction closer to Piaget's, he focuses on the adolescent phase of development, maintaining that a new constellation of factors – i.e. extended adolescence, egalitarian families, increased education, and so on – promotes the likelihood of a nonconventional resolution of the adolescent crisis. While that outcome can result in alienation and apolitical withdrawal, it can also result in the true autonomy of postconventional morality. As in all these cases, the passing of institutionalized forms of traditional authority opens up new possibilities for autonomy and self-development at the same time as they create new dangers for regression and *anomie*.[18] Empirically, however, Habermas's estimate of the potential for a positive outcome would have to be reconsidered in the light of recent economic and educational retrenchment and the decline of student activism and countercultural activities, at least in the United States.

If we turn to clinical material for data on the "end of the individual," we find considerable evidence for the thesis in a form similar to the way the early Frankfurt School posed it. Indeed, recent clinical experience suggests that it is not even the Oedipal phase, but the pre-Oedipal period, which is assuming increasing importance in this context. While, to be sure, there is no universal agreement concerning the interpretation of these phenomena, I believe there exists a broad consensus among analysts that a new type of patient is presenting himself or herself for treatment with increasing regularity. The "classical neurotic," for whom "classical psychoanalysis" was specifically designed, typically suffered from painful symptoms lodged, as it were, in a self that was otherwise basically intact. Their present problems generally centered around inhibitions in love and work, ego-alien obsessions and compulsions, a sense of guilt, and high-level social and sexual anxieties. Genetically, this type of pathology, which more or less presupposes the accomplishments of the separation-individuation phase during the first three years of life, centers on the Oedipal phase of development. A sufficiently individuated and coherent self is a precondition for the child's entering into and passing through the Oedipus crisis in a relatively undistorted form.

The "new patient," in contrast, tends to suffer from disorders in that very sense of self. While he or she has developed beyond the elemental deficiencies of the psychotic, development has not progressed to the point where a stable identity structure has coalesced. They have not, in short, sufficiently traversed the requirements of the pre-Oedipal period. Typically he or she suffers from feelings of emptiness, isolation and futility, pre-Oedipal rage and primitive separation, annihilation, and fragmentation anxieties concerning the intactness of the self. All of this can be masked by grandiose, narcissistic fantasies, which in many instances prove socially adaptive. As the self has failed to adequately coalesce, it cannot be taken for granted in psychoanalytic treatment. Rather, the consolidation of the self itself becomes a primary goal of that treatment. I might point out that the experience of working with these new patients has, in part, been responsible for the controversy over metapsychology which is currently raging in psychoanalysis. The old metapsychology has simply proven inadequate – theoretically and clinically – for dealing with these new phenomena.

A connection is often pointed to between the recent increase in narcissism as a clinical syndrome and as a sociological phenomenon, e.g., the marked intensification of the pursuit of material success, power, and status; an increased preoccupation with youth, health, and glamour and a concomitant dread of sickness, aging, and weakness in any form; and a "repressive desublimitation" of sexuality accompanied by difficulty in forming ongoing relationships with emotional depth. Once again – while it is difficult to specify the exact relationship between narcissism as a psychopathological entity and as a sociological trend – I believe there is a consensus that such a connection must exist. One does not have to defend the notion of the "fatherless society" *per se* to maintain that the disruptions caused in the life-world by capitalist development have had a profound impact on the family. To cite one example, P. Aries has shown how the dissolution of urban neighborhoods tends to overburden the family with functions it is not equipped to perform. Hartmann's "average expectable environment" is becoming progressively less expectable.

It has been recognized since Hegel at least that modern subjectivity rests on a particular combination of intimacy, affective conflict, and insulation from civil society found in the modern family so that we should expect changes in the family structure to have consequences for that subjectivity. Kohut has gone so far as to assert that narcissism is to our time as hysteria was to Freud's. Just as the investigation of the hysteric led Freud to a critique of the sexual repressiveness of Victorian society, so the study of narcissism leads to the pathogenic core of ours. Whether these developments prove dysfunctional for social integration remains to be seen. Unfortunately, some varieties of narcissism seem perfectly adapted to the privitized success-oriented existence required by the system, despite their psychic costs.

III

In an earlier article I attempted to show how the strategy Habermas adopts to overcome the theoretical impasse of early Critical Theory causes him to violate the spirit of the old Frankfurt School on certain key issues.[19] The most notable of these is, of course, the question of external nature. For the old Frankfurt School, nothing short of a reconciliation with external nature could dissolve the *aporia* of enlightenment, however unlikely such a reconciliation might be. Through the introduction of his dualistic framework, however, Habermas is able to conceive a solution to the dialectic of enlightenment which does not require the reconciliation with external nature. Indeed, not only is such a notion not required for Habermas, but the very idea of a reconciliation with external nature becomes meaningless within his theory. External nature is unalterably constituted as an object of instrumental rationality, and it is incorrect to think otherwise. Habermas is therefore perfectly content to concede it *in toto* to the natural sciences.

The situation is somewhat different with respect to the question of the reconciliation with inner nature, which is to say, with respect to the question of happiness. There Habermas seems to feel the pull of the older generation of critical theorists more strongly and attempts to meet the concerns of their more substantive form of theorizing within the confines of his approach. Habermas pursues a strategy which, while not formulated within the philosophy of consciousness, is nevertheless Kantian insofar as it is formal and dualistic. However, he is less content with a Kantian outcome in his ethics than he is in his philosopy of science. Whereas Habermas is willing, with Kant, to concede external nature to the Galilean sciences, he is unwilling to allow his ethics to remain arrested at the opposition of understanding and inclination or reason and happiness. Therefore, after attempting to meet Kant's formal requirements for the discursive justification of basic norms – something the old Frankfurt School was not particularly interested in – Habermas reintroduces the questions of inclination, inner nature, and happiness into his ethics. He thus tries to do justice to the psychoanalytically informed eudaemonism and hedonism of early Critical Theory within a rationalist framework.

Is the integration of a robust conception of happiness into an intentionally formalistic ethics possible, or is this a makeshift on Habermas's part to avoid losing one half of the original project of Critical Theory? I will point to certain tensions and ambiguities in his analysis that suggest the demand for happiness cannot be adequately accommodated within a formalistic approach as he conceives it. Indeed, the concern for happiness does not appear to be a central theoretical impulse for Habermas as it was for Benjamin, Adorno, Marcuse, and the Left Counter-Enlightenment in general; his passion is for justice. Rather, it is more of a secondary concern – sometimes almost an afterthought – which is introduced into a theory that is basically external to it.

The basic problematic results from Habermas's strict separation of formal from substantive issues and comes into sharp relief with his treatment of "the end of the individual." We know that Habermas is eager to combat the Weberian anti-modernism of the early critical theorists and to develop a view of modernity which is more differentiated than the "iron cage." Without such a view, we are condemned to utopianism in the bad sense, for the only conceivable pathway to a socialist society lies through an eschatological rupture of the historical process. As no immanent roots for socialism can be located within modern society, a utopian conclusion can ironically be drawn from "iron cage." Thus, against a totalized logic of decline, Habermas must point to at least one important area where it can be claimed progress has occurred. This area is, of course, moral development. Where Adorno, in accordance with his antipositivist principle of not grounding basic concepts, never explicitly spelled out the criteria by which he was judging "the end of the individual," Habermas supplies an explicit criterion for evaluating the thesis: "the end of the individual" would occur, for Habermas, when the process of socialization became detached from a system of norms that require justification.

Habermas's use of this criterion not only allows him to challenge "the end of the individual" thesis, as Adorno and Horkheimer had posed it, it also allows him to make the even stronger claim that, with respect to moral judgement, there has in fact been progress. Earlier in his career Habermas has reversed the positions of Adorno and Marcuse and argued that the possibilities for critique are greater in modern societies because those societies must attempt to legitimate themselves through appeal to rational, as opposed to traditional, norms. Now he can argue that moral progress has occurred for similar reasons. Not only does socialization still take place with reference to norms that require justification, but the standard for justifying those norms has itself improved.[20] The learning process of the species has progressed to the point (at least in the West) where mythical, religious, or even ontological justification of those norms is no longer acceptable. Instead, the species has discovered, so he argues, the formal principles for discursive justification as such, and they provide the procedural standards for the legitimation of basic norms. If we take Kant's rationality of the moral will or Freud's depersonalization of the superego as measures of moral maturity, then the morality of an individual socialized under these conditions is (potentially) mature indeed. Postconventional morality, according to its concept, has been purged of all elements of tradition, charisma, paternalism, etc., and rests on nothing, as it were, but the intersubjectively conceived principles of pure practical reason.

I have indicated some of the ambiguities surrounding the decline of traditional forms of authority above – i.e. how the very developments which offer the promise of new forms of autonomy and individual development also hold the threat of new experiences of anomie and estrangement. Here I would like to approach the question of postconventional socialization and morality from a different perspective, namely, from the perspective of happiness. Let us assume, for the sake of argument, that Habermas is correct in his appropriation of Kohlberg, and that new modes of moral learning are in fact operative in modern society which correspond to Stage 6 in Kohlberg's scheme. If this were established, then two things would have been accomplished. First, in the important area of morality, it would have been shown that there has been progress with modernity and a totalized dialectic of enlightenment would have been avoided. Secondly, the formal requirements for ethics, which were laid down by Kant, would have been met in the Kohlberg–Habermas account of moral development.

Habermas, however, is not content to let his moral theory rest with the fulfillment of the requirement for formal validity. Rather, in an attempt to reintroduce the demand for happiness, Habermas criticizes Kohlberg for taking Stage 6, the stage of autonomy, as the culmination of moral development. In so doing, Kohlberg, like Kant, absolutizes the conflict between inclination and understanding. He takes needs "that are current at any contingent stage of development" as immutably given, with the result that any need which is incompatible with the demands of the understanding must be suppressed as it cannot be transformed. Habermas maintains that only a seventh stage of communicative ethics can solve the problem. He envisions a situation where "drive potentials" could be inserted into the "communicative structure of action" and needs could become the object of rational transformation. Were such a stage possible, it would indeed reconcile the demands of reason with the claims of happiness.[21]

How, then, does Habermas account for the "mutability of the instincts" that would make this degree of "communicative fluidity" and transparency of inner nature possible?[22] As we saw, the ego psychologists were compelled to introduce a second dimension, as it were, to correct the instinctual monism of drive theory. Habermas, for similar reasons, introduced the dualistic framework of communicative and instrumental reason to overcome the implicit monism of the early Frankfurt School. Habermas's fundamental insight that took him beyond early Critical Theory is that the domination of outer nature and the domination of inner nature follow different logics. Whereas the domination of outer nature proceeds through the application of nomological laws to an heterogeneous object, the mastery of inner nature takes place through the internalization of intersubjective norms. While this allows him to conceptualize simultaneous progress in both dimensions, so that he does not have to posit socialism as a utopian rupture of history, curiously enough, a certain utopian specter enters his own theory as a result of the very theoretical innovations he made to correct the utopianism of early Critical Theory.

The question becomes: how strong are the conclusions that can be drawn from the linguisticality of the socialization process? To be sure, it is true that "language functions as a kind of transformer"[23] that draws private inner nature into the web of intersubjectivity. And, it is also true that the extent to which inner nature can be socialized remains an historically open question. It does not follow, however, from the linguisticality of society and the linguisticality of the socialization process that a pre-established harmony exists between society and inner nature. It does not follow, in other words, from the fact that inner nature is amenable to linguistic mediation that it is linguistic *an sich*. The possibility of a completely public language is not entailed by the demonstration of the impossibility of a totally private language. While the "linguistic turn" certainly dissolved the impasse of early Critical Theory, it is not clear that it will carry the quasi-utopian load Habermas suggests here.

The implicit linguistic idealism that allows Habermas to make these quasi-utopian assertions was already apparent in his reconstruction of Freud in terms of communication theory. The method of immanent critique is meant to rescue a thinker's theoretical intentions from a framework in which they cannot be realized. However, I am afraid that Habermas's linguistic reinterpretation of Freud has the effect of, as it were, destroying certain of Freud's central intentions in order to save them. The agendas of Habermas the methodologist, who wants to critique objectivism and provide a transcendental foundation for the human sciences, and of Freud the *"Stoffdenker"*[24] and practicing analyst, who wants to forge a new science, do not always coincide. And the requirements of his communicatively conceived methodological program cause Habermas to violate a cardinal tenet of Freudian psychoanalysis, namely, the reality and independence of the body as formulated in the theory of the drives. The transcendental turn of the methodologist, which is supposed to ground the science, does not allow the practicing scientist to say what prephilosophically he knows must be the case.

The problem is exactly parallel to the one I pointed to in the earlier article on Habermas's theory of external nature. It stems from Habermas's attempt to be a materialist – in the sense of taking nature to be the independent ground of mind – and epistemologically sophisticated, i.e., nonobjectivistic, at the same time.[25] Where the philosophers of the consciousness has difficulty reaching extramental existence from within the closed circle of subjectivity, Habermas has difficulty contacting extralinguistic reality from within the equally closed circle of intersubjectivity. The linguistic-transcendental turn does not allow him to grant the fully independent status to extralinguistic existence that his materialism requires. Thus with respect to external nature, the simple, uncontroversial fact that external, prehuman nature produces speaking, human nature – which is known by the layman and the evolutionary scientist alike – must necessarily remain an inexplicable mystery to the transcendental philosopher.[26] Habermas is forced to introduce the notion of privative reasoning as a theoretical expedient to account for the precursors of human subjectivity that exist among the higher species of animals. And with respect to inner nature (which is always the sore point for a dualistic scheme), Habermas must likewise privately derive the drives from the distortions of communication in the analytic setting rather than grant them an independent status in their own right.

While it is true that "in the order of knowing" the drives can be deciphered only from their derivatives, Freud never doubted that "in the order of being" they have a somatically based existence whose status is at least equal to, if not determinative of, the mental: "Although instincts are wholly determined by their origins in somatic sources, in mental life we know them only by their aim."[27] However, because of the priorities of his theoretical program, Habermas must deny the drives the status Freud ascribed to them. Just as he cannot account for the fact that prehuman nature produced human nature in the course of evolution, so here Habermas cannot account for the fact – which was no less obvious to Freud – that the body has a more or less independent existence that makes "demands" on the psyche for "work." And, just as the transition from prehuman to human nature was precluded *a priori* from the domain of legitimate theoretical investigation by transcendental dualism, so here the transition from *soma* to *psyche* must likewise be excluded; both transitions fall between the categories. And in both instances Habermas introduces the notion of privative reasoning in an attempt to make up the deficit. But it was precisely this nether region of the "frontier between the mental and the somatic"[28] which Freud sought so hard to colonize theoretically with his *Trieblehre*. Methodological sophistication must not be achieved in a way which precludes so many of the most interesting questions.

Habermas adopts different strategies for treating extralinguistic existence within and outside of the person. With external nature, after conceding it completely to the domain of the nonlinguistic, he formulates a theory of reference to account for the mediation between the web of intersubjectivity and *res extensa*. With respect to inner nature, on the other hand, he attempts not so much to solve the problem as to dissolve it. He tries to assimilate as much of inner nature as possible to the category of the linguistic by construing it as protolinguistic. This would have the effect of blunting the categorial distinction between the linguistic and the nonlinguistic within humans. Habermas wants to argue that, as inner nature is susceptible of socialization, i.e. "linguisticalization," it must in some sense already be protolinguistic; thus, he must deny the existence of the unconscious as a "nonlinguistic substratum."[29] He is forced to make this assumption because he cannot conceive of any transition across the great categorial divide. Ironically, Habermas's argument could be turned against him. It could be maintained that, as prehuman nature produces speaking human nature, prehuman nature must also be protolinguistic. But this would lead down the path of philosophy of nature, a path Habermas assiduously wants to avoid.

We can now appreciate why Marcuse and Habermas both reach utopian conclusions but from different directions. Marcuse drawing on id psychology, presupposes an absolute opposition – a pre-established disharmony – between the instinctual substratum, which is the seat of happiness, and the repressive ego. He calls for a revolt of the instincts as the only way of meeting the demands of happiness. But, as he does not want to ignore the claims of reason either, and as the ego is presumed to be inherently repressive, he must resort to a conception of aesthetic rationality that would do the job. Only the utopian combination of the emancipation of the instincts and aesthetic rationality can solve the riddle of history as Marcuse formulates it with the help of Freud. For Habermas, however, the riddle is not so extreme. The utopianism of Stage 7 of his moral scheme can be asserted in an almost glib manner because he does not assume the absolute disharmony between reason and the instincts that Marcuse does. On the contrary, like the ego psychologists, he errs in the opposite direction. Because of the thrust of his linguistic approach, he fails to capture the sense of an "inner foreign territory" which is a hallmark of Freudian thought; in principle, everything is potentially transparent. As a result, he is in danger of losing sight of the opposition between reason and the drives altogether. With both Marcuse and Habermas, utopianism results from the failure to grasp theoretically the dialectic of harmony and disharmony between human rationality and its instinctual substratum.

Habermas had explicitly addressed the question of happiness at one other point in his career, and that was in his article on Benjamin. There, however, the conclusions had been anything but utopian; in fact, the implications were rather unsettling. In that article Habermas sought to clarify his position with respect to Benjamin and the Left Counter-Enlightenment in general. He argued that, by judging history only in terms of an emphatic notion of happiness, they missed what "modest progess" had in fact occurred historically and necessarily became entangled in a dialectic of enlightenment:

> By remembering in melancholy what was unsuccessful and in invoking moments of happiness that are in the process of becoming obliterated the historical sense of secular progress threatens to become stunted.[30]

To correct this situation and avoid a dialectic of enlightenment, Habermas wants to introduce a more differentiated framework that is capable of detecting progress. More specifically, he reintroduces the old distinction between happiness, which was the goal of the utopian tradition, on the one hand, and social justice, which was the goal of the natural law tradition, on the other. This allows him to maintain there has been progress in the later dimension insofar as there has been progress in the discursive justification of moral and legal norms.

Habermas, as we have seen, also separates the hedonic and normative lines of development in his theory of moral development. But, where he tries to reunify them with Stage 7 in his moral theory, in the Benjamin article no such attempt at reunification was even undertaken. Moreover, not only does he not link progress in the realm of happiness to progress in the realm of morality, but, as the lines of development are left so utterly unrelated, he is forced to entertain the possibility that a future society may be emancipated with respect to morality and justice, and, at the same time, not be happy, as it were. Given his line of reasoning, it is entirely possible that a society may be moral and just and not have the content available to it to provide a good life for its members: "Could an emancipated humanity one day confront itself in the expanded scope of discursive will formation and nevertheless still be deprived of the terms in which it is able to interpret life as a good life?"[31] *Logically*, this outcome must arise as a possibility for Habermas once he has separated the questions of form from content, and morality from happiness. This possibility follows, in other words, from the fact that his defense of the project of modernity against the antimodernism of the Counter-Enlightenment pertains to the development of formal rationality and to it alone.

Furthermore, when we turn to Habermas's analysis of the dynamics of late capitalism, we find that there is much *empirical* evidence to support the eventuality of a just, but ungratified, social order. With the thinkers of the Counter-Enlightenment, Habermas shares a basically Weberian analysis of the progressive expansion of administrative rationality into the life-world and of the resulting destruction of historically sedimented meaning. He argues that, whereas until recently capitalism had exploited the residue of meaning of more traditional forms of society to legitimize itself, it is now in the process of "non-renewably dismant[ling]"[32] resources of meaning. The culmination of this process would be a society which had been emptied of its content.

A culture which for thousands of years was exploited for the purpose of legitimizing domination would take its revenge just at the moment when age old repression could be overcome: not only would it be free of violence, it would no longer have any content.[33]

Even if one does not assume that *bourgeois* moral and legal norms are simply epiphenomena of the capitalist economy as the Counter-Enlightenment tended to do, it still appears that progress in morality and justice do not preclude the reification of the life-world.

Habermas gives a surprisingly sympathetic reading of Benjamin's rather speculative semantic theory, but fails to explore its consequences for the questions we are examining. Benjamin maintains that human meaning derives from the expressive gestures of animals, and that, at the point of its emergence, the human species was endowed with as specific quantum of meaning which cannot be expanded nor regenerated. The history of cultures represents so many transformations of that initial semantic endowment. What is occurring now, however, with the reification of the life-world, is the destruction of that nonrenewable resource of meaning. *The suggestive thing here is the link between meaning and the natural substratum of human existence.* If we take the disembedding from nature as the *telos* of the Enlightenment, and if we take our natural substratum as intrinsically linked with our capacity for meaning, then there would indeed be a connection between enlightenment and reification as the Counter-Enlightenment argued.

Habermas is absolutely correct, against the Counter-Enlightenment, in defending the real advances of the modern age to which they remained blind. At the same time, however, he fails to deal adequately with the realm of problems with which they were most concerned – as if demonstrating historical advancement in reflexivity were enough to refute the dialectic of enlightenment. The shift in the center of gravity in Critical Theory is apparent in the different uses that are made of Freud. Where Adorno, Horkheimer, and Marcuse used Freud to introduce the subterranian dimension of the unconscious, the drives, and the demand for happiness into Marxian social theory, Habermas essentially uses him to discuss methodological problems in philosophy of the social sciences. And he leaves the dynamic unconscious behind completely when he moves to Piaget and Kohlberg. This is not to say that one should mystify the unconscious or the drives as the special repository of truth against the established order, or advocate the "resurrection of the body" as much of the so-called Freudian Left has done. Nor does it mean that one should pursue a return to more "organic" *gemeinschaftliche* modes of life as a solution to the problems of modernity as many of the participants in the New Social Movements suggest. It is to say, however, that we cannot defend the project of modernity – which must be defended – at the price of sacrificing the naturalistic tradition that runs from Feuerbach through the young Marx and Freud to the early Frankfurt School.

3

Habermas and Lyotard on Postmodernity

RICHARD RORTY

In *Knowledge and Human Interests* Habermas tried to generalize what Marx and Freud had accomplished by grounding their projects of "unmasking" in a more comprehensive theory. The strand in contemporary French thought which Habermas criticizes as "neo-conservative" starts off from suspicion of Marx and Freud, suspicion of the masters of suspicion, suspicion of "unmasking." Lyotard, for example, says that he will

> use the term "modern" to designate any science that legitimates itself with reference to a metadiscourse of this kind [i.e., "a discourse of legitimation with respect to its own status, a discourse called philosophy"] making an explicit appeal to some grand narrative, such as the dialectics of the Spirit, the hermeneutics of meaning, the emancipation of the rational or working subject, or the creation of wealth.[1]

He goes on to define "postmodern" as "incredulous towards metanarratives," and to ask "Where, after the metanarratives, can legitimacy reside"?[2] From Lyotard's point of view, Habermas is offering one more metanarrative, a more general and abstract "narrative of emancipation"[3] than the Freudian and Marxian metanarratives.

For Habermas, the problem posed by "incredulity towards metanarratives" is that unmasking only makes sense if we "preserve at least one standard for [the] explanation of the corruption of *all* reasonable standards."[4] If we have no such standard, one which escapes a "totalizing self-referential critique," then distinctions between the naked and the masked, or between theory and ideology, lose their force. If we do not have these distinctions, then we have

to give up the Enlightenment notion of "rational criticism of existing institutions," for "rational" drops out. We can still, of course,
have criticism, but it will be of the sort which Habermas ascribes
to Horkheimer and Adorno: "they abandoned any theoretical
approach and practiced ad hoc determinate negation . . . The praxis
of negation is what remains of the 'spirit of . . . unremitting
theory'."[5] Anything that Habermas will count as retaining a "theoretical approach" will be counted by an incredulous Lyotard as a
"metanarrative." Anything that abandons such an approach will be
counted by Habermas as "neoconservative," because it drops the
notions which have been used to justify the various reforms which
have marked the history of the Western democracies since the
Enlightenment, and which are still being used to criticize the socio-
economic institutions of both the Free and the Communist worlds.
Abandoning a standpoint which is, if not transcendental, at least
"universalistic," seems to Habermas to betray the social hopes
which have been central to liberal politics.

So we find French critics of Habermas ready to abandon liberal
politics in order to avoid universalistic philosophy, and Habermas
trying to hang on to universalistic philosophy, with all its problems, in order to support liberal politics. To put the opposition in
another way, the French writers whom Habermas criticizes are willing to drop the opposition between "true consensus" and "false
consensus," or between "validity" and "power," in order not to
have to tell a metanarrative in order to explicate "true" or "valid."
But Habermas thinks that if we drop the idea of "the better argument" as opposed to "the argument which convinces a given audience at a given time," we shall have only a "context-dependent"
sort of social criticism. He thinks that falling back on such criticism
will betray "the elements of reason in cultural modernity which are
contained in . . . bourgeois ideals'" e.g., "the internal theoretical
dynamic which constantly propels the sciences – and the self-
reflexion of the sciences as well – *beyond* the creation of merely
technologically exploitable knowledge."[6]

Lyotard would respond to this last point by saying that Habermas
misunderstands the character of modern science. The discussion of
"the pragmatics of science" in *The Postmodern Condition* is intended to "destroy a belief that still underlies Habermas's research,
namely that humanity as a collective (universal) subject seeks its
common emancipation through the regularization of the 'moves'
permitted in all language games, and that the legitimacy of any
statement resides in its contribution to that emancipation."
Lyotard claims to have shown that "consensus is only a particular

state of discussion [in the sciences], not its end. Its end, on the contrary, is paralogy."[7] Part of his argument for this odd suggestion is that "Postmodern science – by concerning itself with such things as undecidables, the limits of precise control, conflicts characterized by incomplete information, '*fracta*', catastrophes, and pragmatic paradoxes – is theorizing its own evolution as discontinuous, catastrophic, non-rectifiable and paradoxical."[8]

I do not think that such examples of matters of current scientific concern do anything to support the claim that "consensus is not the end of discussion." Lyotard argues invalidly from the current concerns of various scientific disciplines to the claim that science is somehow discovering that it should aim at permanent revolution, rather than at the alternation between normality and revolution made familiar by Kuhn. To say that "science aims" at piling paralogy on paralogy is like saying that "politics aims" at piling revolution on revolution. No inspection of the concerns of contemporary science or contemporary politics could show anything of the sort. The most that could be shown is that talk of the aims of either is not particularly useful.

On the other hand, Lyotard does have a point, the point he shares with Mary Hesse's criticism of Habermas's Diltheyan account of the distinction between natural science and hermeneutic inquiry. Hesse thinks that "It has been sufficiently demonstrated [by what she calls 'post-empiricist' Anglo-American philosophy of science] that the language of theoretical science is irreducibly metaphorical and unformalizable, and that the logic of science is circular interpretation, re-interpretation, and self-correction of data in terms of theory, theory in terms of data."[9] This kind of debunking of empiricist philosophy of science is happily appropriated by Lyotard. Unfortunately, however, he does not think of it as a repudiation of a bad account of science but as indicating a recent change in the nature of science. He thinks that science used to be what empiricism described it as being. This lets him accuse Habermas of not being up to date.

If one ignores this notion of a recent change in the nature of science (which Lyotard makes only casual and anecdotal attempts to justify), and focuses instead on Lyotard's contrast between "scientific knowledge" and "narrative," that turns out to be pretty much the traditional positivist contrast between "applying the scientific method" and "unscientific" political or religious or common-sensical discourse. Thus Lyotard says that a "scientific statement is subject to the rule that a statement must fulfill a given set of conditions in order to be accepted as scientific."[10] He contrasts this with "narrative knowledge" as the sort which "does not give priority to the question of its own legitimation, and . . . certifies itself in the pragmatics of its own transmission without having recourse to argumentation and proof." He describes "the scientist" as classifying narrative knowledge as "a different mentality: savage, primitive, under-developed, backward, alienated, composed of opinions, customs, authority, prejudice, ignorance, ideology."[11] Lyotard, like Hesse, wants to soften this contrast and to assert the rights of "narrative knowledge." In particular, he wants to answer his initial question by saying that once we get rid of the *meta*narratives, legitimacy resides where it always has, in the first-order narratives:

> There is, then, an incommensurability between popular narrative pragmatics, which provides immediate legitimation, and the language game known as the question of legitimacy . . . . Narratives . . . determine criteria of competence and/or illustrate how they are to be applied. They thus define what has the right to be said and done in the culture in question, and since they are themselves a part of that culture, they are legitimated by the simple fact that they do what they do.[12]

This last quotation suggests that we read Lyotard as saying: the trouble with Habermas is not so much that he provides a metanarrative of emancipation as that he feels the need to legitimize, that he is not content to let the narratives which hold our culture together do their stuff. He is scratching where it does not itch. On this reading, Lyotard's criticism would chime with the Hesse-Feyerabend line of criticism of empiricist philosophy of science, and in particular with Feyerabend's attempt to see scientific and political discourse as continuous. It would also chime with the criticisms offered by many of Habermas's sympathetic American critics, such as Bernstein, Geuss, and McCarthy. These critics doubt that studies of communicative competence can do what transcendental philosophy failed to do in the way of providing "universalistic" criteria.[13] They also doubt that universalism is as vital to the needs of liberal social thought as Habermas thinks it. Thus Geuss, arguing that the notion of an "ideal speech situation" is a wheel which plays no part in the mechanism of social criticism, and suggesting that we reintroduce a position "closer to Adorno's historicism," says:

If rational argumentation can lead to the conclusion that a critical theory [defined as "the 'self-consciousness' of a successful process of emancipation and enlightenment"] represents the most advanced position of consciousness available to us in our given historical situation, why the obsession with whether or not we may call it 'true'?[14]

Presumably by "rational argumentation" Geuss means not "rational by reference to an extra-historical, universalistic set of criteria" but something like "uncoerced except in the ways in which all discourse everywhere is inevitably coerced – by being conducted in the terms and according to the practices of a given community at a given time." He is dubious that we need a theoretical account which gets behind that vocabulary and those conventions to something "natural" by reference to which they can be criticized. As Geuss says, the "nightmare which haunts the Frankfurt School" is something like Huxley's *Brave New World*, in which

agents are actually content, but only because they have been prevented from developing certain desires which in the 'normal' course of things they would have developed, and which cannot be satisfied within the framework of the present social order.[15]

To take the scare-quotes out from around "normal," one would have to have just the sort of metanarrative which Lyotard thinks we cannot get. But we think we need this only because an overzealous philosophy of science has created an impossible ideal of ahistorical legitimation.

The picture of social progress which Geuss's more historical line of thought offers is of theory as emerging at dusk, the belated "self-consciousness" of emancipation rather than a condition for producing it. It thus has links with the antirationalist tradition of Burke and Oakeshott, as well as with Deweyan pragmatism. It departs from the notion that the intellectuals can form a revolutionary vanguard, a notion cherished even by French writers who claim to have dispensed with Marx's metanarrative. On this account of social change, there is no way for the citizens of *Brave New World* to work their way out from their happy slavery by theory, and, in particular, by studies of communicative competence. For the narratives which go to make up their sense of what counts as "rational" will see to it that such studies produce a conception of undistorted communication which accords with the desires they presently have. There is no way for us to prove to ourselves that we are not happy slaves of this sort, any more than to prove that our life is not a dream. So whereas Habermas compliments "bourgeois ideals" by reference to the "elements of reason" contained in them, it would be better just to compliment those untheoretical sorts of narrative discourse which make up the political speech of the Western democracies. It would be better to be frankly ethnocentric.

If one is ethnocentric in this sense, one will see what Habermas calls "the internal theoretical dynamic which constantly propels the sciences . . . beyond the creation of technologically exploitable knowledge" not as a *theoretical* dynamic, but as a social practice. One will see the reason why modern science is more than engineering not as an ahistorical teleology – e.g., an evolutionary drive towards correspondence with reality, or the nature of language – but as a particularly good example of the social virtues of the European bourgeoisie. The reason will simply be the increasing self-confidence of a community dedicated to (in Blumenberg's phrase) "theoretical curiosity." Modern science will look like something which a certain group of human beings invented in the same sense in which these same people can be said to have invented Protestantism, parliamentary government, and Romantic poetry. What Habermas calls the "self-reflection of the sciences" will thus consist not in the attempt to "ground" scientists' practices (e.g., free exchange of information, normal problem-solving, and revolutionary paradigm-creation) in something larger or broader, but rather of attempts to show how these practices link up with, or contrast with, other practices of the same group or of other groups. When such attempts have a critical function, they will take the form of what Habermas calls "ad hoc determinate negation."

Habermas thinks that we need not be restricted, as Horkheimer and Adorno were, to such merely socio-historical forms of social criticism. He views Horkheimer, Adorno, Heidegger, and Foucault as working out new versions of "the end of philosophy":

> no matter what name it [philosophy] appears under now – whether as fundamental ontology, as critique, as negative dialectic, or genealogy – these pseudonyms are by no means disguises under which the traditional [i.e., Hegelian] form of philosophy lies hidden; the drapery of philosophical concepts more likely serves as the cloak for a scantily concealed end of philosophy.[16]

Habermas's account of such "end of philosophy" movements is offered as part of a more sweeping history of philosophy since Kant. He thinks that Kant was right to split high culture up into science, morality, and art and that Hegel was right in accepting this as "the standard (*massgeblich*) interpretation of modernity."[17] He thinks that "The dignity specific to cultural modernism consists in what Max Weber has called the stubborn differentiation of value-spheres."[18] He also thinks that Hegel was right in believing that

"Kant does not perceive the . . . formal divisions within culture . . . as diremptions. Hence he ignores the need for unification that emerges with the separations evoked by the principle of subjectivity."[19] He takes as seriously as Hegel did the question "How can an intrinsic ideal form be constructed from the spirit of modernity, that neither just imitates the historical forms of modernity nor is imposed upon them from the outside?"[20]

From the historicist point of view I share with Geuss, there is no reason to look for an intrinsic ideal that avoids "just imitating the historical forms of modernity." All that social thought can hope to do is to play the various historical forms of modernity off against one another in the way in which, e.g., Blumenberg plays "self-assertion" off against "self-grounding."[21] But because Habermas agrees with Hegel that there is a "need for unification" in order to "regenerate the devastated power of religion in the medium of reason,"[22] he wants to go back to Hegel and start again. He thinks that in order to avoid the disillusionment with "the philosophy of subjectivity" which produced Nietzsche and the two strands of post-Nietzschean thought which he distinguishes and dislikes (the one leading to Foucault, and the other to Heidegger), we need to go back to the place where the young Hegel took the wrong turn.[23] That was the place where he still "held open the option of using the idea of uncoerced will formation in a communication community existing under constraints of cooperation as a model for the reconciliation of a bifurcated civil society."[24] He thus suggests that it was the lack of a sense of rationality as *social* that was missing from "the philosophy of the subject" which the older Hegel exemplified (and from which he believes the "end-of-philosophy" thinkers have never really escaped).

But whereas Habermas thinks that the cultural need which "the philosophy of the subject" gratified was and is real, and can perhaps be fulfilled by his own focus on a "communication community," I would urge that it is an artificial problem created by taking Kant too seriously. On this view, the wrong turn was taken when Kant's split between science, morals, and art was accepted as a *donnée*, as *die massgebliche Selbstauslegung der Moderne*. Once that split is taken seriously, then the *Selbstvergewisserung der Moderne*, which Hegel and Habermas both take to be the "fundamental philosophical problem" will indeed seem urgent. For once the philosophers swallow Kant's "stubborn differentiation," then they are condemned to an endless series of reductionist and anti-reductionist moves. Reductionists will try to make everything scientific, or political (Lenin), or aesthetic (Baudelaire, Nietzsche).

Antireductionists will show what such attempts leave out. To be a philosopher of the "modern" sort is precisely to be unwilling either to let these spheres simply coexist uncompetitively, or to reduce the other two to the remaining one. Modern philosophy has consisted in forever realigning them, squeezing them together, and forcing them apart again. But it is not clear that these efforts have done the modern age much good (or, for that matter, harm).

Habermas thinks that the older Hegel "solves the problem of the self-reassurance of modernity too well," because the philosophy of Absolute Spirit "removes all importance from its own present age . . . and deprives it of its calling to self-critical renewal."[25] He sees the popularity of "end-of-philosophy" thought as an over-reaction to this over-success. But surely part of the motivation for this kind of thought is the belief that Hegel too was scratching where it did not really itch. Whereas Habermas thinks that it is with Hegel's own over-success that philosophy becomes what Hegel himself called "an isolated sanctuary" whose ministers "from an isolated order of priests . . . untroubled by how it goes with the word," it is surely possible to see this development as having been Kant's fault, if anybody's, and precisely the fault of his "three-sphere" picture of culture. On this latter view, Kant's attempt to deny knowledge to make room for faith (by inventing "transcendental subjectivity" to serve as a fulcrum for the Copernican revolution) was provoked by an unneccessary worry about the spiritual significance, or insignificance, of modern science. Like Habermas, Kant thinks that modern science has a "theoretical dynamic," one which can be identified with (at least a portion of) "the nature of rationality." Both think that by isolating and exhibiting this dynamic, but distinguishing it from other dynamics (e.g., "practical reason" or "the emancipatory interest"), one can keep the results of science without thereby disenchanting the world. Kant suggested that we need not let our knowledge of the world *qua* matter in motion get in the way of our moral sense. The same suggestion was also made by Hume and Reid, but unlike these pragmatical Scotchmen, Kant thought that he had to back up this suggestion with a story which would differentiate and "place" the three great spheres into which culture must be divided. From the point of view common to Hume and Reid (who disagreed on so much else) no such metanarrative is needed. What is needed is a sort of intellectual analogue of civic virtue – tolerance, irony, and a willingness to let spheres of culture flourish without worrying too much about their "common ground," their unification, the "intrinsic ideals" they suggest, or what picture of man they "presuppose."

In short, by telling a story about Kant as the beginning of modern philosophy (and by emphasizing the difference between modern and premodern philosophy) one might make the kind of fervent end-of-philosophy writing Habermas deplores look both more plausible and less interesting. What links Habermas to the French thinkers he criticizes is the conviction that the story of modern philosophy (as successive reactions to Kant's diremptions) is an important part of the story of the democratic societies' attempts at self-reassurance. But it may be that most of the latter story could be told as the history of reformist politics, without much reference to the kinds of theoretical backup which philosophers have provided for such politics. It is, after all, things like the formation of trade unions, the meritocratization of education, the expansion of the franchise, and cheap newspapers, which have figured most largely in the willingness of the citizens of the democracies to see themselves as part of a "communicative community" – their continued willingness to say "us" rather than "them" when they speak of their respective countries. This sort of willingness has made religion progressively less important in the self-image of that citizenry. One's sense of relation to a power beyond the community becomes less important as one becomes able to think of oneself as part of a body of public opinion, capable of making a difference to the public fate. That ability has been substantially increased by the various "progressive" changes I have listed.

Weber was of course right in saying that some of these changes have also worked the other way (to increase our sense of being controlled by "them"). But Habermas is so preoccupied with the "alienating" effects of such changes that he allows himself to be distracted from the concomitant increase in people's sense of themselves as free citizens of free countries. The typical German story of the self-consciousness of the modern age (the one which runs from Hegel through Marx, Weber, and Nietzsche) focuses on figures who were preoccupied with the world we lost when we lost the religion of our ancestors. But this story may be both too pessimistic and too exclusively German. If so, then a story about the history of modern thought which took Kant and Hegel less seriously and, for example, the relatively untheoretical socialists more seriously, might lead us to a kind of "end-of-philosophy" thinking which would escape Habermas's strictures on Deleuze and Foucault. For these French writers buy in on the usual German story, and thus tend to share Habermas's assumption that the story of the realignment, assimilation, and expansion of the three "value-spheres" is essential to the story of the *Selbstvergewis-*

serung of modern society, and not just to that of the modern intellectuals.

In order to interpret this problem of the three spheres as a problem only for an increasingly "isolated order of priests," one has to see the "principle of the modern" as something other than that famous "subjectivity" which post-Kantian historians of philosophy, anxious to link Kant with Descartes, took as their guiding thread. One can instead attribute Descartes' role as "founder of modern philosophy" to his development of what I earlier called "an overzealous philosophy of science" – the sort of philosophy of science which saw Galilean mechanics, analytic geometry, mathematical optics, and the like, as having more spiritual significance than they in fact have. By taking the ability to do such science as a mark of something deep and essential to human nature, as the place where we got closest to our true selves, Descartes preserved just those themes in ancient thought which Bacon had tried to obliterate. The preservation of the Platonic idea that our most distinctively human faculty was our ability to manipulate "clear and distinct ideas," rather than to accomplish feats of social engineering, was Descartes' most important and most unfortunate contribution to what we now think of as "modern philosophy." Had Bacon – the prophet of self-assertion, as opposed to self-grounding – been taken more seriously, we might not have been stuck with a canon of "great modern philosophers" who took "subjectivity" as their theme. We might, as J. B. Schneewind puts it, have been less inclined to assume that epistemology (i.e., reflection on the nature and status of natural science) was the "independent variable" in philosophical thought and moral and social philosophy the "dependent variable." We might thereby see what Blumenberg calls "self-assertion" – the willingness to center our hopes on the future of the race, on the unpredictable successes of our descendants – as the "principle of the modern." Such a principle would let us think of the modern age as defined by successive attempts to shake off the sort of ahistorical structure exemplified by Kant's division of culture into three "value-spheres."

On this sort of account, the point I claimed Lyotard shared with Feyerabend and Hesse – the point that there are no interesting epistemological differences between the aims and procedures of scientists and those of politicians – is absolutely fundamental. The recovery of a Baconian, non-Cartesian attitude towards science would permit us to dispense with the idea of "an internal theoretical dynamic" in science, a dynamic which is something more than the "anything goes that works" spirit which unites Bacon and

Feyerabend. It would break down the opposition between what Habermas calls "merely technologically exploitable knowledge" and "emancipation," by seeing both as manifestations of what Blumenberg calls "theoretical curiosity." It would free us from pre-occupation with the purported tensions between the three "value-spheres" distinguished by Kant and Weber, and between the three sorts of "interests" distinguished by Habermas.

In the present space, I cannot do more than gesture towards the various rosy prospects which appear once one suggests that working through "the principle of subjectivity" (and out the other side) was just a side-show, something which an isolated order of priests devoted themselves to for a few hundred years, something which did not make much difference to the successes and failures of the European countries in realizing the hopes formulated by the Enlightenment. So I shall conclude by turning from the one issue on which I think Lyotard has a point against Habermas to the many issues about which Habermas seems to me in the right.

The thrust of Habermas's claim that thinkers like Foucault, Deleuze, and Lyotard are "neoconservative" is that they offer us no "theoretical" reason to move in one social direction rather than another. They take away the dynamic which liberal social thought (of the sort represented by Rawls in America and Habermas himself in Germany) has traditionally relied upon, viz., the need to be in touch with a reality obscured by "ideology" and disclosed by "theory." Habermas says of Foucault's later work that it

> replaced the model of repression and emancipation developed by Marx and Freud with a pluralism of power/discourse formations. These formations intersect and succeed one another and can be differentiated according to their style and intensity. They cannot, however, be judged in terms of validity, which was possible in the case of the repression and emancipation of conscious as opposed to unconscious conflict resolutions.[26]

This description is, I think, quite accurate, as is his remark that "the shock" which Foucault's books produce "is not caused by the flash of *insight* into a confusion which threatens identity" but instead by "the affirmed de-differentiation and by the affirmed collapse of those categories which alone can account for category mistakes of existential relevance." Foucault affects to write from a point of view light-years away from the problems of contemporary society. His own efforts at social reform (e.g., of prisons) seem to have no connection with his exhibition of the way in which the "humane" approach to penal reform tied in with the needs of the modern state. It takes no more than a squint of the inner eye to read Foucault as a stoic, a dispassionate observer of the present social order, rather than its concerned critic. Because the rhetoric of emancipation – the notion of a kind of truth which is *not* one more production of power – is absent from his work, he can easily be thought of reinventing American "functionalist" sociology. The extraordinary *dryness* of Foucault's work is a counterpart of the dryness which Iris Murdoch once objected to in the writing of British analytic philosophers.[27] It is a dryness produced by a lack of identification with any social context, any communication. Foucault once said that he would like to write "so as to have no face." He forbids himself the tone of the liberal sort of thinker who says to his fellow-citizens: "*We* know that there must be a better way to do things than this; let us look for it together." There is no "we" to be found in Foucault's writings, nor in those of many of his French contemporaries.

It is this remoteness which reminds one of the conservative who pours cold water on hopes for reform, who affects to look at the problems of his fellow-citizens with the eye of the future historian. Writing "the history of the present," rather than suggestions about how our children might inhabit a better world in the future, gives up not just on the notion of a common human nature, and on that of "the subject," but on our untheoretical sense of social solidarity. It is as if thinkers like Foucault and Lyotard were so afraid of being caught up in one more metanarrative about the fortunes of "the subject" that they cannot bring themselves to say "we" long enough to identify with the culture of the generation to which they belong. Lyotard's contempt for "the philosophy of subjectivity" is such as to make him abstain from anything that smacks of the "metanarrative of emancipation" which Habermas shares with Blumenberg and Bacon. Habermas's socialization of subjectivity, his philosophy of consensus, seems to Lyotard just one more pointless variation on a theme which has been heard too often.

But although disconnecting "philosophy" from social reform – a disconnection previously performed by analytic philosophers who were "emotivist" in metaethics while being fiercely partisan in politics – is one way of expressing exasperation with the philosophical tradition, it is not the only way. Another would be to minimize the importance of that tradition, rather than seeing it as something which urgently needs to be overcome, unmasked, or genealogized. Suppose, as I suggested above, one sees the wrong turn as having been taken with Kant (or better yet, with Descartes) rather than (like Habermas) with the young Hegel or the young Marx. Then one might see the canonical sequence of philosophers from Descartes to Nietzsche as a distraction from the history of concrete social engineering which made the contemporary North Atlantic culture what it is now, with all its glories and all its dangers. One could try to create a new canon – one in which the mark of a "great philosopher" was awareness of new social and religious and institutional possibilities, as opposed to developing a new dialectical twist in metaphysics or epistemology. That would be a way of splitting the difference between Habermas and Lyotard, of having things both ways. We could agree with Lyotard that we need no more metanarratives, but with Habermas that we need less dryness. We could agree with Lyotard that studies of the communicative competence of a transhistorical subject are of little use in reinforcing our sense of identification with our community, while still insisting on the importance of that sense.

If one had such a de-theoreticized sense of community, one could accept the claim that valuing "undistorted communication" was of the essence of liberal politics without needing a theory of communicative competence as backup. Attention would be turned instead to some concrete examples of what was presently distorting our communication – e.g., to the sort of "shock" we get when, reading Foucault, we realize that the jargon we liberal intellectuals developed has played into the hands of the bureaucrats. Detailed historical narratives of the sort Foucault offers us would take the place of philosophical metanarratives. Such narratives would not unmask something created by power called "ideology" in the name of something not created by power called "validity" or "emancipation." They would just explain who was currently getting and using power for what purposes, and then (unlike Foucault) suggest how some other people might get it and use it for other purposes. The resulting attitude would be neither incredulous and horrified realization that truth and power are inseparable nor Nietzschean *Schadenfreude*, but rather a recognition that it was only the false lead which Descartes gave us (and the resulting over valuation of scientific theory which, in Kant, produce "the philosophy of subjectivity") that made us think truth and power *were* separable. We could thus take the Baconian maxim that "knowledge is power" with redoubled seriousness. We might also be made to take seriously Dewey's suggestion that the way to re-enchant the world, to bring back what religion gave our forefathers, is to stick to the concrete. Much of what I have been saying is an attempt to follow up on the following passage from Dewey:

We are weak today in ideal matters because intelligence is divorced from aspiration . . . When philosophy shall have cooperated with the force of events and made clear and coherent the meaning of the daily detail, science and emotion will interpenetrate, practice and imagination will embrace. Poetry and religious feeling will be the unforced flowers of life.[28]

I can summarize my attempt to split the difference between Lyotard and Habermas by saying that this Deweyan attempt to make concrete concerns with the daily problems of one's community – social engineering – the substitute for traditional religion seems to me to embody Lyotard's postmodernist "incredulity towards metanarratives" while dispensing with the assumption that the intellectual has a mission to be avant-garde, to escape the rules and practices and institutions which have been transmitted to him in favor of something which will make possible – "authentic criticism." Lyotard unfortunately retains one of the Left's silliest ideas – that escaping from such institutions is automatically a good thing, because it insures that one will not be "used" by the evil forces which have "co-opted" these institutions. Leftism of this sort necessarily devalues consensus and communication, for in so far as the intellectual remains able to talk to people outside the avant-garde he "compromises" himself. Lyotard exalts the "sublime," and argues that Habermas's hope that the arts might serve to "explore a living historical situation" and to "bridge the gap between cognitive, ethical and political discourses,"[29] shows that Habermas has only an "aesthetic of the beautiful."[30] On the view I am suggesting, one should see the quest for the sublime, the attempt (in Lyotard's words) to "present the fact that the unpresentable exists," as one of the prettier unforced blue flowers of bourgeois culture. But this quest is wildly irrelevant to the attempt at communicative consensus which is the vital force which drives that culture.

More generally, one should see the intellectual *qua* intellectual as having a special, idiosyncratic need – a need for the ineffable, the sublime, a need to go beyond the limits, a need to use words which are not part of anybody's language-game, any social institution. But one should not see the intellectual as serving a *social* purpose when he fulfills this need. Social purposes are served, just as Habermas says, by finding beautiful ways of harmonizing interests, rather than sublime ways of detaching oneself from others' interests. The attempt of leftist intellectuals to pretend that the avant-garde is serving the wretched of the earth by fighting free of the merely beautiful is a hopeless attempt to make the special needs of the intellectual and the social needs of his community coincide. Such an attempt goes back to the Romantic period, when the urge to think the unthinkable, to grasp the unconditioned, to sail strange seas of thought alone, was mingled with enthusiasm for the French Revolution. These two, equally laudable, motives should be distinguished.

If we do distinguish them, then we can see each as a distinct motive for the kind of "end of philosophy" thinking Habermas deplores. The desire for the sublime makes one want to bring the philosophical tradition to an end because it makes one want to cut free from the words of the tribe. Giving these words a purer sense is not enough; they must be abjured altogether, for they are contaminated with the needs of a repudiated community. Such a Nietzschean line of thought leads to the kind of avant-garde philosophy which Lyotard admires in Deleuze. The desire for communication, harmony, interchange, conversation, social solidarity, and the "merely" beautiful wants to bring the philosophical tradition to an end because it sees the attempt to provide metanarratives, even metanarratives of emancipation, as an unhelpful distraction from what Dewey calls "the meaning of the daily detail." Whereas the first sort of end-of-philosophy thinking sees the philosophical tradition as an extremely important failure, the second sort sees it as rather unimportant excursus.[31] Those who want sublimity are aiming at a postmodernist form of intellectual life. Those who want beautiful social harmonies want a postmodernist form of social life, in which society as a whole asserts itself without bothering to ground itself.[32]

4

Reflections on Rationalization in
The Theory of Communicative Action

THOMAS McCARTHY

Max Weber viewed the process of societal rationalization as a growing hegemony of *Zweckrationalität*, of technique and calculation, of organization and administration. The triumph of Reason brought with it not a Realm of Freedom but the dominion of impersonal economic forces and bureaucratically organized administrations, not a Kingdom of God on Earth but an "iron cage" in which we were henceforth condemned to live. In the *Dialectic of Enlightenment*, written in the darkness of the early 1940s, Max Horkheimer and Theodor Adorno acknowledged the force of Weber's diagnosis. Critical theory became resignative; it could at most unmask the unreason at the heart of what passed for reason, without offering any positive account of its own. In his *Theory of Communicative Action*,[1] Jürgen Habermas argues that the dead end in which critical social theory thus found itself is by no means unavoidable. Because Weber construed rationalization in terms of the spread of *Zweckrationalität*, he was unable, according to Habermas, adequately to grasp the *selectivity* of capitalist modernization; and because they followed him in this respect, Horkheimer and Adorno were led to deny any trace of reason to the structures and institutions of modern life. In opposition to the dialectic of enlightenment standpoint, Habermas argues that the discontents of modernity are rooted not in rationalization as such but in the failure to develop and institutionalize in a balanced way all the different dimensions of reason opened up by the modern understanding of the world. As he puts it:

> If we start from the view that modern structures of consciousness condense to the three complexes of rationality mentioned above

rationality of authentic interpretations of needs in eroticism and art. These relations are represented in figure 1 (238).

The X's in the areas 1.3, 2.1 and 3.2 express Habermas's hypothesis that these three relations are not susceptible of rationalization in the way that the other six are. To examine this hypothesis we have to get a clearer idea of the criterion of rationalizability to which he appeals, viz. "suitable for the accumulation of knowledge." This is spelled out in somewhat more detail in the following passage: "If cultural value spheres are distinguished by a

Worlds / Basic Attitudes	1 Objective	2 Social	3 Subjective	1 Objective
3 Expressive	Art			
1 Objectivating	Cognitive-instrumental rationality — Science Technology	Social technologies	X	
2 Norm-Conformative	X	Moral-practical rationality — Law	Morality	
3 Expressive		X	Aesthetic-practical rationality — Eroticism	Art

Figure 1 Rationalization Complexes

[cognitive-instrumental, moral-practical, aesthetic-practical, TMc], then we can think of the structurally possible rationalization of society as a combination of the corresponding ideas (from the domains of science and technology, law and morality, art and eroticism) with interests, and their embodiment in correspondingly differentiated orders of life. This (rather risky) model would enable us to state the necessary conditions for a non-selective pattern of rationalization: The three cultural value spheres have to be connected with corresponding action systems in such a way that the production and transmission of knowledge that is specialized according to validity claims is secured; the cognitive potential developed by expert cultures has, in turn, to be passed on to the communicative practice of everyday life and to be made fruitful for social action systems; finally, the cultural value spheres have to be institutionalized in such a balanced way that the life-orders corresponding to them are sufficiently autonomous to avoid being subordinated to laws intrinsic to heterogeneous orders of life. (240)

Though he repeatedly emphasizes its "intuitive," "nonsystematic," merely "provisional" character, this model of three complexes of rationality with their corresponding action systems plays a central role in Habermas's diagnosis of the ills of modernity and in his general prescription for their cure. Thus it merits a closer look, even if one that is itself only intuitive and non-systematic.

The basic idea behind Habermas's schema of the structurally possible dimensions of rationalization is that the growing decentration of consciousness in the modern age enables us to adopt different basic attitudes – objectivating, norm-conformative, and expressive – toward the elements of different (formally conceived) worlds – objective, social, and subjective. Combining the three basic attitudes with the three formal world concepts, we get nine fundamental "formal-pragmatic relations" between actors and their worlds (see figure 1) and the question arises as to which of these relations permit of rationalization. Habermas advances the provisional thesis that only six of them are "suitable for the accumulation of knowledge," that is, are "sufficiently productive from the standpoint of acquiring knowledge to permit, in Weber's terms, a development of cultural value spheres with their own inner logics" (237). These six relations fall into three "complexes of rationality," each of which reflects one of the basic attitudes. Thus the objectivating attitude to the objective and social worlds yields the "cognitive-instrumental rationality" of science and technology, including social technology; the norm-conformative attitude toward the social and subjective worlds yields the "moral-practical rationality" of the systematic treatment of law and morality; and the expressive attitude toward the subjective and objective worlds yields the "aesthetic-practical" production of knowledge that is differentiated according to validity claims and rendered cumulative, and if the continuity of this knowledge can be guaranteed only by learning processes becoming reflective – that is, being coupled in feedback relations with specialized and institutionalized forms of argumentation – then we should be able to demonstrate for each historically articulated value sphere . . . the existence of plausible relations to a typical form of argumentation specialized in accord with a universal validity claim" (239). If the weight of the argument is not to fall exclusively on the identification of universal validity claims, the test of the hypothesis becomes: Is it the case that the six relations (three complexes) singled out by Habermas permit a continuous and cumulative production of knowledge connected to specialized forms of argumentation in ways that the remaining three do not?

When the question is posed in this form, the hypothesis presents a number of obvious difficulties. To begin with: in what sense is there a continuous and cumulative production of knowledge in the domains of art and morality? In science and technology – despite the serious problems raised by postempiricist philosophers of science concerning the continuous and cumulative character of *theory* change – there seems to be little question about the accumulation of knowledge of phenomenal regularities and instrumental connections. On the other hand, even if we grant Habermas his developmental-logical account of the formal structures of consciousness in general, and of the formal structures of moral and aesthetic consciousness in particular, there is no clear counterpart to this accumulation of "content" across paradigm shifts. To put this in another way, even at the "highest" stage of aesthetic-practical consciousness "authentic interpretations of needs . . . have to be renewed in each historically changed set of circumstances" (238);[2] and even at the "highest" stage of moral-practical consciousness, the rightness of norms has to be examined and re-examined in each historically changed set of circumstances.[3] That is, advances at the structural level do not seem to entail an accumulation of knowledge at the content level. This suggests that we cannot put too much weight on the "continuous" and "cumulative" character of the production of knowledge in Habermas's schema of rationalizable actor-world relations. Let us then shift the burden to the idea of "learning processes becoming reflective" by being linked with "specialized and institutionalized forms of argumentation." But this immediately raises the question: In what ways is moral-practical rationality institutionalized or institutionalizable? If we grant for the sake of argument that cognitive-instrumental rationality is institutionalized in the "scientific enterprise" (240), and that aesthetic-practical rationality is institutionalized in the "artistic-enterprise" (240), that is, in the institutions for the production, dissemination, reception, and criticism of art, and if we grant the institutionalization of legal rationality, where do we look for "institutionalized forms of (moral) argumentation" which serve "the production and transmission of (moral) knowledge" in "expert (moral) cultures"? Weber assigned this role historically to the religious community; but in a secularized world this is no longer a plausible option. Habermas elsewhere advances the "practical hypothesis" of a democratic organization of society in which moral-practical discourse is institutionally secured in the cultural and political public spheres. Be that as it may, the point remains that a communicative ethic detached from its religious foundations has not yet gained much of an institutional foothold, either in cultural or societal institutions. This loosens the ties between rationalizability and de facto institutionalization enough to warrant our construing the question: To what extent are actor-world relations, other than those singled out by Habermas, or by modern Western society, rationalizable in the following sense: To what extent *can* they be linked to forms of argumentation in reflective learning processes so as to develop a "cognitive potential" that *can* be "made fruitful for social action systems"?

In the schema above, the fact that the area 1.3 is empty stands, Habermas tells us, for the assumption that "nothing can be learned in an objectivating attitude about inner nature qua subjectivity" (237). This assumption seems rather implausible at first glance. There is evidently quite a bit that can be learned about emotions and feelings, desires and inclinations, beliefs and intentions, and the like in an "objectivating attitude"– in the attitude, for instance, of the physiologist or experimental psychologist; and this type of knowledge can certainly be "made fruitful" for social life – in psychopharmacology, for instance, or in techniques for attitude change. Thus it must be the phrase "qua subjectivity" that carries the burden of the assumption: in an objectivating attitude inner nature is not knowable *qua* subjective experience. On one reading this threatens to become a tautology; on another it takes us to the heart of the problem of "adopting different attitudes to elements of the same world." For reasons that will become evident, it is more fruitful to tackle this problem first in connection with the other objectivating attitude toward a non-objective world, namely the objectivating attitude towards the social world (2.2), which *is* characterized as suitable for the accumulation of knowledge.

Knowledge here takes the form of "social technologies" for rationalizing "cognitive-strategic" relations. What is striking here is that there is no mention of social *science*. "Science" appears (along with "Technology") only in area 1.1 which marks out the objectivating attitude toward the objective world. Correspondingly, "assertions" and "observations" are said to be "characteristic forms of expression" only for this relation, while "social actions of the purposive-rational type" are mentioned as characteristic of the objectivating attitude toward the social world (236). There seem to be two possibilities here. Habermas might be denying that there can be any objectivating social science. Since social inquiry appears in no other area of the schema, this would leave it completely out of a purported classification of the structurally possible dimensions in which knowledge can be accumulated! And it would not square with Habermas's frequently stated view that we can in fact adopt a theoretically objectivating attitude toward society. Thus it appears that another reading is called for.

For Habermas the different worlds are conceived *formally* and not materially. Thus the distinction between the objective and the social worlds is *not* the usual distinction between the *object domains* of nature and culture. Rather it is derived from a distinction between basic attitudes: "We have to go beyond differentiating object domains to differentiating between a basic attitude toward the objective world of what is the case and a basic attitude toward the social world of what can legitimately be expected, what is commanded or ought to be" (49). If I read it correctly, this formal distinction between worlds cuts across the usual material distinction between object domains. That is, the objective world of existing states of affairs (51) which can be observed or manipulated (49), the one objective world identical for all observers (50), the inter-subjective validity of which is actualized in claims to truth or efficacy, includes elements of what is usually regarded (materially) as "society" as well as of "nature." Defined formally, the objective world is what is "presupposed in common as the totality of facts, whereby 'fact' signifies that a statement about the existence of a corresponding state of affairs can count as true" (52). On this definition, elements of both nature and culture "belong to the world of facts about which true statements are possible" and in which effective interventions are possible. On the other hand, "our social world" of legitimately regulated interpersonal relations, of norms that can be followed or violated (49), the intersubjectively shared social world, whose commonality is actualized in claims to normative rightness, is, on Habermas's definition, a normative reality to which our basic relation is one of obligation and not observation. Defined formally in this way, the social world contains elements of what is normally regarded (materially) as society, but not, according to Habermas, of nature.

If this is the correct reading of these "formal world concepts" we have a possible explanation of why "science" appears only under the column headed "objective world": scientific inquiry is a search for true statements about what is the case in a world of existing states of affairs. But this leaves us in the dark as to why "social technologies" appears under the column headed "society"; for on this reading claims to efficacy also relate to a world of existing states of affairs, of objective situations that can be intervened in and manipulated in a goal-directed fashion (48). If Habermas's social world is defined formally, on the basis of a norm-conformative attitude toward legitimately regulated interpersonal relations, toward norms and values claiming validity, then wouldn't it "drop from sight" when the actor adopted the perspective of goal-directed intervention in objectively given situations? It seems, in other words, that we could not at all relate to Habermas's social world in an objectivating attitude, for it is defined formally as the correlate of a norm-conformative attitude. And this raises the general question: If Habermas's three worlds are defined *formally*, in relation to three different basic attitudes, how is it all possible to adopt different attitudes toward one and the same (attitudinally specified) world? Unless this question can be answered, the entire schema that serves as the backdrop against which the "jagged profile" of capitalist modernization stands out is in danger of collapsing.

The formula behind the construction of the schema is that "the acting and knowing subject is able to assume different basic attitudes toward *elements* of the same world" (236, my emphasis). I can see only one way of interpreting this that is in line with (if not the letter, at least the spirit) of Habermas's explanation of the schema. It is a reading suggested by an earlier account of how communication involves taking up a relation to different "domains of reality," of how different "regions" or "segments of reality" come to appearance in communication.[4] A key passage reads:

> One can, of course, adopt an objectivating attitude not only toward inanimate nature but toward all objects and states of affairs that are directly or indirectly accessible to sensory experience. *Society* designates that symbolically prestructured segment of reality that the adult subject can understand in a normconformative attitude, that is, as one acting communicatively (as a participant in a system of com-

munication). Legitimate interpersonal relations belong here, as do institutions, traditions, cultural values, etc. We can replace this conformative attitude with an objectivating attitude toward society.[5]

The underlying idea here seems to be that elements which belong properly to one world, which are basically conceived (or "constituted") in one attitude, which originally "appear" from one point of view, can also be conceived or appear from other points of view – that is, that the "reality" of the elements in question is not exhausted by their "appearance" from one or another point of view. But I do not wish to pursue this epistemological (phenomenological? transcendental?) line of inquiry here;[6] in the present context it is the methodological consequences of this view that are of interest. We have to understand how it is that certain transformations of attitude toward elements of domains constituted in different attitudes can be fruitful for the production of knowledge, how it is, for instance, that we can adopt an objectivating attitude toward such socially constructed realities as "interpersonal relations, institutions, traditions, cultural values" and the like.

In his discussion of the logic of *Verstehen* in chapter one of *The Theory of Communicative Action*, Habermas attempts to establish the very strong thesis that meaning intelligibility, and understanding are in the final analysis inseparable from validity, rationality, and assessment, that "access to the object domain of social action through understanding meaning of itself makes the rationality problematic unavoidable. Communicative actions always require an interpretation that is rational in approach" (106). The central passage in the argument supporting this thesis runs as follows:

In order to understand an utterance in the paradigm case of a speech act oriented to reaching understanding, the interpreter has to be familiar with the conditions of its validity; he has to know under what conditions the validity claim linked with it is acceptable or would have to be acknowledged by a hearer. But where could the interpreter obtain this knowledge if not from the context of the observed communication or from comparable contexts? . . . Thus the interpreter cannot become clear about the semantic content of an expression independently of the action contexts in which participants react to the expression with a "yes" or "no" or an abstention. And he does not understand these yes/no positions if he cannot make clear to himself the implicit reasons that move the participants to take the positions they do . . . But if, in order to understand an expression, the interpreter must bring to mind the reasons with which a speaker would, if necessary and under suitable conditions, defend its validity, he is himself drawn into the process of assessing validity claims. For reasons are of such a nature that they cannot be described in the attitude of a third person . . . One can understand reasons only to the extent that one understands why they are or are not sound. (115-116)

Because the object domain of social inquiry is the "symbolically prestructured" reality produced and reproduced by speaking and acting subjects, the social scientist can gain access to it only by way of understanding the meaning of the objects he studies. This he cannot do, Habermas argues, solely in the "third-person" attitude of a disengaged observer: "If the interpreter confines himself to observations in the strict sense, he perceives only the physical substrata of utterances without understanding them. In order to have communicative experience he must adopt a performative attitude and participate, be it only virtually, in the original process of reaching understanding" (114). In contrast to the perceptual experience of physical objects, the communicative experience of symbolic objects requires a performative orientation to validity claims.[7] One cannot grasp what is being said or done without some idea of the reasons underlying the utterance or action; and in trying to understand reasons, Habermas argues, the interpreter is forced to relinquish any claim to an extramundane position and to assume, at least virtually, the mundane status of the layperson. For reasons are of such a nature that they cannot be grasped in the purely objectivating attitude of a third person. "The interpreter would not have understood what a reason was if he did not reconstruct it with its claim to provide grounds . . . The description of reasons demands eo ipso an evaluation" (115–116). To understand reasons *as* reasons, we have to draw (at least implicitly) upon our own (intuitively mastered) competence as members of a lifeworld to assess the internal connections between ideas, to evaluate evidence and arguments, to distinguish the valid from the invalid, the sound from the unsound, the cogent from the weak, the persuasive from the unpersuasive.

Habermas understands this as an argument for the *very* strong thesis that an interpreter cannot understand symbolic expressions "without taking a position on them" (116), without "reacting to the validity claim raised," without involving "his judgment of the validity" of the claims. This conclusion, it seems to me, is stronger than is warranted by the argument.[8] If the argument works, it demonstrates the unavoidability of something like what Weber called the *Wertbezogenheit*, the value-relatedness, of our interpretations; it does not suffice to exclude the *Werturteilsfreiheit*, freedom from value *judgments*, that he combined with it. That is, from the fact that we cannot understand reasons as reasons without relying on our own competence to judge validity, cogency, soundness and the like, it does not follow that we have to actually or implicitly "take a position" on reasons in order to understand them. Interpreters raised in pluralistic cultures and schooled in cultural and historical differences are quite capable, it seems, of understanding symbolic expressions without taking a position on their validity – not, to be sure, as ideally neutral observers, not as interpreters without a language, and standards of their own to serve as a hermeneutic starting point, but as individuals whose primary and professional socialization have schooled them in appreciating differences of belief and practice, in "bringing (other people's) reasons to mind" while suspending judgment on them.[9] Habermas does, constantly and repeatedly, allow for a reaction of "abstention," of leaving the validity claim "to one side as not yet decided." One can "understand reasons only to the extent that one understands why they are or are not sound, or why in a given case a decision as to whether reasons are good or bad is not (yet) possible" (116). It might appear that this type of suspension of judgment is nothing else than Weber's *Werturteilsfreiheit*; but this appearance is deceiving. Weber thought that questions of value were ultimately undecidable in any rationally binding sense and thus that the social scientist ought to avoid taking a position on them (*qua* social scientist). Habermas is not a sceptic in such matters. For him normative validity claims, no less than truth claims, admit of rationally motivated consensus. They are in this sense rationally decidable, and the social scientist must, at least implicitly, decide "yes" or "no" or "still open." But even if one grants Habermas's version of cognitivism in matters ethical, and even if one agrees that the social scientist can, may, and even should adopt a critical stance toward validity claims, the question remains: Must he or she? The considerations adduced above indicate, I think, that the answer is no, that an objectivating, hypothetical attitude in which judgment is simply bracketed is a structural possibility as well. Rational interpretations, while possible, are not necessary.

This would account for the palpable implausibility of Habermas's position on the necessity for rationally interpreting normatively regulated action.

According to the presuppositions of this model of action, an actor can comply with (or violate) only norms that he subjectively regards as valid or justified; and with this recognition of normative validity claims he exposes himself to an objective judgment. He challenges the interpreter to examine not only the actual norm-conformity of his action, or the de facto currency of the norm in question, but the rightness of this norm itself. The interpreter can in turn accept the challenge or, from a standpoint sceptical of values, dismiss it as senseless. If the interpreter adopts such a sceptical standpoint, he will explain, with the help of a non-cognitive variety of ethics, that the actor is deceiving himself in regard to the possibility of justifying norms, and that instead of reasons he could at best adduce empirical motives for the recognition of norms . . . He will try to replace a description initially drawn in concepts of normatively regulated action with another one given, for example, in causal-behavioristic terms. (104)

This argument strikes me as doubly flawed. There is, to begin with, a third alternative to "accepting the challenge" or "dismissing it as senseless" – namely, simply ignoring it, bracketing the question altogether without "calling for enlightenment" in any way.[10] And even if, secondly, one is a sceptic in ethical matters, this does not force one in any obvious way to give one's description of the *actor's* behavior in causal-behavioristic terms or some equivalent thereto. I can point out that the subjects believe the norms in question to be capable of objective grounding in this or that metaphysical, religious or theoretical framework; and because I know what it is to act on reasons in general, I can comprehend their *reasons* for acting as *they* do, even if I do not share them.

These reflections seem to point in the following direction: While our ability to understand a symbolically prestructured reality at all is based upon our own competences as social actors and thus is originally acquired in a performative attitude, we do have the ability (also socially acquired) to adopt an objectivating, hypothetical attitude toward the reality so understood, that is, to treat it as an object of scientific inquiry and technical control. Of course, *social facts* do not thereby lose their characteristic differences from purely physical facts.[11] What I want now to suggest, very briefly to be sure, is that a similar *complementarity* of attitudes is possible in the three areas left empty in Habermas's schema of rationalizable relations to reality.

(1.3), *Objectivating Attitude toward the Subjective World*. As I mentioned above, Habermas explains that the empty area "stands for the assumption that nothing can be learned in an objectivating attitude about inner nature qua subjectivity." He uses the term "inner nature" to refer to subjective experiences – beliefs and intentions, feelings and desires, etc. – to which each actor has privileged access and which he or she can express as his or her experiences before a public. The paradigm cases for the expressive use of language are first-person utterances of the form "I long for . . .," "I wish that . . .," and the like (and, at another level, avowals such as "I must confess to you that . . ., "I don't want to conceal from you that . . ."). Of course, such first-person utterances are connected to corresponding third-person utterances of the form "He longs for . . .," "She wishes that . . .," in such a way that the truth of the latter is internally related to the truthfulness of the former. This suggests to Habermas that learning the meaning of terms referring to subjective experiences is inextricably tied to mastering the expressive use of language, that is, learning how to express one's experiences in the first-person. But even if we grant that understanding third-person reports concerning someone's inner nature depends in the final analysis on one's ability, in a performative attitude, to express one's own inner nature (and to serve as a thou for the self-presentations of others), this does not of itself rule out the possibility of adopting the objectivating attitude of an observer reporting on the "facts" of other people's feelings and desires, beliefs and intentions.[12] And as a matter of fact Habermas explicitly allows that the attitude of the empirical psychologist is the attitude of the observer oriented exclusively to truth claims.[13] As noted earlier, then, the operative phrase in his explanation of the empty field 1.3 must be "qua subjectivity." But can this mean anything more than that first-person experiences and their expression are fundamental to our understanding of subjectivity, so that no *purely* third-person access to inner nature is possible? If this is what is meant, I could just as well argue – in line with Habermas's own views – that "nothing can be learned about society *qua society* in an objectivating attitude"; for, as noted above, social reality as a symbolically prestructured normative reality is "hermetically sealed" to the view of observers incapable of adopting the performative attitude of acting in conformity with or violation of norms. But, as we also saw above, the truth of this claim does not exclude the possibility of adopting the complementary attitude of an observer toward the interpersonal relations that one understands as normatively regulated. A similar complementarity and integration of points of view, or attitudes, seems to be involved in some of the theories, techniques, and even therapies developed to deal with inner nature. This world-relation thus seems to be no less rationalizable than art or morality – indeed, it has become evident in our dawning brave new world that it is more readily so.

(3.2) *Expressive Attitude Toward the Social World.* On Habermas's account, the empty area signifies that "expressively determined forms of interaction (for example, countercultural forms of life) do not form structures that are rationalizable in and of themselves" (238). On the other hand, the schema does allow that expressively determined relations to nature – in the form of art – are rationalizable. But why are aesthetic relations to society any less rationalizable? Is art that takes nature as its theme fundamentally different in some crucial way from that which takes the human world as its theme? There appears to be a shift in the specification of what is at stake in the adoption of the expressive attitude: In relation to nature it seems to be a question of the possibility of expressive representation; in relation to society it becomes a question of "expressively determined forms of interaction" – that is of structuring social reality itself in an expressive attitude. But even if we accept some such shift – on the grounds, say, that social reality is actually structured by the attitudes and relations we adopt to it – we might well come to a different conclusion on the matter at issue if we approach it from the standpoint of a complementarity of attitudes, instead of as an either/or. In the norm-comformative attitude we view society as a nexus of legitimately regulated interpersonal relations, the commonality of which is actualized in claims to normative rightness – in plainer English, we view society from the standpoint of the right. It requires only a glance at our tradition of social and political thought to make plausible the suggestion that this has to be complemented by a view of society from the standpoint of the good. Habermas seems to recognize this in other contexts. In his discussion of Walter Benjamin, for instance, he recalls Bloch's distinction between overcoming hunger and overcoming oppression, between an improvement in the standard of living and an increase in freedom, and he notes that:

> In the tradition that reaches back to Marx, Benjamin was one of the first to emphasize a further moment in the concepts of exploitation and progress: besides hunger and oppression, failure; besides prosperity and liberty, happiness . . . The claim to happiness can be made good only if the sources of that semantic potential we need for interpreting the world in the light of our needs are not exhausted. Cultural goods are spoils that the ruling elite carries in its triumphal parade, and so the process of tradition has to be disentangled from myth. The liberation of culture is certainly not possible without overcoming the oppression anchored in institutions. Yet, for a moment the suspicion cannot help but arise that an emancipation without happiness and lacking in fulfillment might be just as possible as relative prosperity without the elimination of repression.[14]

Though Habermas disagrees with Benjamin in certain respects, and though he takes this insight in another direction than Benjamin, he seems to agree that freedom without happiness is not freedom, and that the marriage of the two depends also on keeping alive and renewing the utopian contents of tradition, images of the good life, of human fulfillment. From this perspective, there appears to be a clear place for expressive as well as obligatory relations to society, or better, for some form of integration of the two. But is this expressive relation to society "suitable for the production of knowledge"? No more or less, it seems to me, than the expressive relation to inner nature, that is, than the authentic interpretation of our needs generally.

(2.1) *Norm-Conformative Attitude toward the Objective World.* The fact that this area is empty signifies, in Habermas's words, "a scepticism concerning the possibility of giving a rational form to fraternal relations with a non-objectivated nature – for instance, in the form of a philosophy of nature that could compete with the modern sciences of nature" (238). In a reply to earlier counterarguments advanced by myself and others, he spells out his position as follows: "While we can indeed adopt a performative attitude to external nature, enter into communicative relations with it, have aesthetic experiences and feelings analogous to morality with respect to it, there is for this domain of reality only one *theoretically fruitful* attitude, namely the objectivating attitude of the natural-scientific, experimenting observer."[15] And he goes on to add that

It does not make sense to demand of a reason separated into its moments a reconciliation at the level of the scientific system, or at the level of the cultural tradition generally. We cannot expect to use the experiential potential gathered in non-objectivating dealings with external nature for purposes of knowledge and to make them theoretically fruitful. Precisely from the perspective of the theory of knowledge, which has to orient itself to successful examples of theory formation, the internal obstacles become visible which modern science places in the way of all attempts to reestablish the unity of reason in the theoretical dimension. Such attempts would have to lead back to metaphysics, and thus behind the levels of learning reached in the modern age into a reenchanted world.[16]

There are two important assumptions underlying this argument: first, that any theoretical attempt to rethink the unity of nature and morality would inevitably lead back to metaphysics; and second, that any philosophy of nature that re-established this unity would have to compete with the modern sciences of nature – in vain. However, we do have models for reconceptualizing nature in this way that do neither. Most prominent among them, perhaps, is Kant's *Critique of Judgment*. On this model, teleological explanation of nature does not compete with causal explanation but is complementary to it; nor are teleological judgments of purpose in nature "metaphysical" in any pre-Kantian sense, for the principles governing them are maxims only of reflective judgment. I do not wish to go into the details of Kant's model here, nor to hold it up as an adequate model for contemporary attempts to rethink the unity of theoretical and practical reason. My only point is that there is no *conceptual necessity* for the philosophy of nature to take on the form of a metaphysics of nature claiming a validity independent of and prior to science, that is, the form of an *Ursprungsphilosophie*. It is possible to envision a philosophy of nature constructed after the transcendental turn as a non-foundationalist, falliblist attempt to conceive of nature as a *natura naturans* that gave rise to, among other things, a species capable of communicating in language and thereby of giving its intraspecific relations the form of a moral order. Of course, this attempt would have constantly to be renewed in light of our historically changing scientific and moral experience.[17]

While this approach remains fundamentally anthropocentric – and thus unsuited for the restoration of a cosmological ethic based on a teleology of nature-in-itself – it might provide a view of our place in nature that could complement and relativize the objectivating view of a nature to be dominated. Habermas does not deny that we can take up a non-objectivating attitude toward nature, but that knowledge can be gained in this attitude "at the same level . . . that Newton attained in his objectivating knowledge of nature."[18] But it seems rather arbitrary to judge the rationalizability of one actor-world relation by the standards of another.[19] If we were to ask instead whether specialized forms of argumentation could take shape which were sufficiently productive from the standpoint of acquiring knowledge to permit the development of a cognitive potential that could be made fruitful for social action systems, it is not at all clear that the answer would be negative. The view of the human species as in-and-of-nature that we would get from a non-objectivating perspective would be quite different from the view of the human species as set over-against-nature that lies behind the objectivating sciences, which, on Habermas's own account, are structured by a cognitive interest in prediction and control. And this change in viewpoint might well have consequences for our sense of obligation to nature and for the norms governing our interaction with nature that we regard as justifiable.

My purpose in assembling these somewhat scattered reflections on the schema of rationality and rationalization in Habermas's *The Theory of Communicative Action* is not to replace it with another one. I want only to show, primarily by way of raising rather than answering questions, how very problematic that schema is, and thus to head off any unwarranted abridgement of possibilities of rationalization at the analytical level. Habermas acknowledges that his schema singles out "just those three cultural value spheres that were differentiated out in modern Europe" (239); but he insists that "this is not in itself an objection against the systematic status of the schema." True enough. On the other hand, the more problematic that status becomes, the more the privileging of just those three complexes does appear to reflect "idiosyncratic traits of Western culture." At all events, the point is to avoid conceptually screening out utopian – or, for that matter, dystopian – possibilities of social development, to be extremely wary of erecting analytical barriers to the "attempt to test the limits of the realizability of the utopian contents of cultural tradition."[20]

5

Questions and Counterquestions

JÜRGEN HABERMAS

I am happy to accept the editors' invitation to respond to the articles by Richard Rorty, Martin Jay, Thomas McCarthy, and Joel Whitebook.* Though critical, their friendly spirit reveals that we are all concerned if not with the same problems, then at least with the same themes. At the same time, it is immediately apparent that there is some distance between us, for instance, between Rorty and myself. The gaps between the different universes of discourse become so wide at times that the mixture of reciprocal interpretations, suppositions, and misunderstandings suddenly also serves to reveal residual unconscious presuppositions, implications, and background assumptions. All this amounts to the quite normal confusion in conversation among friends who have sufficiently different points of view.

The confusion of lines of argument is much more drastic in controversies among adversaries who, feeling that their identity is threatened by the others' fundamental convictions, struggle with rhetorical weapons. Scarcely anyone would disagree that such distances and oppositions have increased and intensified in the modern age, which has itself become a philosophical theme of the first rank since the eighteenth century. Individuals, groups, and nations have drifted far apart in their backgrounds of biographical and social-cultural experience. This pluralization of diverging universes of discourse belongs to specifically modern experience; the shattering of naive consensus is the impetus for what Hegel calls "the experience of reflection." We cannot now simply wish this experience away; we can only negate it. In the framework of our

* At the time of writing this essay, I had not yet read the careful chapter on my work by Martin Jay in his *Marxism and Totality* (Polity Press, Cambridge; University of California Press, Berkeley: 1984), 423–460.

culture, invested as it is with reflection, the thrust of this experience had to be worked through not only politically but also philosophically. Today we can survey the spectrum of answers given by philosophers: roughly speaking, it extends all the way from historicism to transcendentalism.

On the one side, Dilthey, Weber, Jaspers, and Kolakowski take an affirmative position on the growing pluralism of "gods and demons" (*Glaubensmächte*), existential modes of being, myths, value attitudes, and metaphysical or religious world-views. A philosophy that treats forms of truth in the plural is supposed to leave to the sciences the job of providing an adequate reserve of consensual knowledge. On the other side, philosophers such as Husserl, the early Wittgenstein, Popper, and Apel, all attempt to maintain, at a higher level of abstraction, the unity of reason, even if only in a procedural sense. They distill the common characteristics of rational activity that *must* be implicitly presupposed in the pluralism of "gods and demons" and in the argumentative collisions between universes of discourse. In this way, there arise what Rorty calls "metanarratives," that is, the theories of rationality that are supposed to account for why and in what sense we can still connect our convictions and our descriptive, normative, and evaluative statements, with a transcending validity claim that goes beyond merely local contexts.

These are philosophical answers to the *unavoidable* experience of modernity; when they are sharpened into the opposition between relativism and absolutism, an *unmediated* confrontation emerges between pure historicism and pure transcendentalism. At that point the failures of both positions become clear: the one side carries the burden of self-referential, pragmatic contradictions and paradoxes that violate our need for consistency; the other side is burdened with a foundationalism that conflicts with our consciousness of the fallibility of human knowledge. No one who gives this situation much thought would want to be left in this bind.

In the context of our discussion here, this reading of the present situation is not really in dispute, although Rorty, Bernstein, and I react to it in different ways. Forcefully freeing himself from the straight-jacket of analytic philosophy, Richard Rorty has undertaken the most ambitious project: he wants to destroy the tradition of the philosophy of consciousness, from its Cartesian beginnings, with the aim of showing the pointlessness of the entire discussion of the foundations and limits of knowledge. He concludes that philosophers need only recognize the hybrid character of their controversies and give the field over to the practitioners of science, politics, and daily life to be rid of the problem. Like the later Wittgenstein, Rorty sees philosophy itself as the sickness whose symptoms it previously and unsuccessfully tried to cure. But Rorty is still enough of a philosopher to give a reason for his recommendation that we avoid the *Holzweg* of philosophical justification: one shouldn't scratch where it doesn't itch. It is just this assumption that "it doesn't itch" that I find problematic.

Forms of life are totalities which always emerge in the plural. Their coexistence may cause friction, but this *difference* does not automatically result in their *incompatibility*. Something similar is the case for the pluralism of values and belief systems. The closer the proximity in which competing "gods and demons" have to live with each other in political communities, the more tolerance they demand; but they are not incompatible. Convictions can contradict one other only when those who are concerned with problems define them in a similar way, believe them to need resolution, and want to decide issues on the basis of good reasons.

To be sure, it is also a characteristic of modernity that we have grown accustomed to living with dissent in the realm of questions that admit of "truth"; we simply put controversial validity claims to one side "for the time being." Nonetheless, we perceive *this* pluralism of contradictory convictions as an incentive for learning processes; we live in the expectation of *future* resolutions. As long as we take part and do not merely look over our own shoulders as historians and ethnographers, we maintain precisely the distinctions that Rorty wants to retract: between valid and socially accepted views, between good arguments and those which are merely successful for a certain audience at a certain time.

In believing that he can consistently replace the implicitly normative conception of "valid arguments" with the descriptive concept of "arguments held to be true for us at this time," Rorty commits an objectivistic fallacy. We could not even understand the meaning of what we describe from a third-person perspective as argumentative conduct if we had not already learned the performative attitude of a participant in argumentation; that is, what it means from the perspective of the first person to raise a validity claim that points beyond the provincial agreements of the specific local context. Only this capacity gives our *opinions* the character of *convictions*. (This is no less true for the practice of everyday communication than for argumentative disputes about the hypothetical validity of statements.) Any mutual understanding produced in communication and reproduced in the life-world is based on a potential reserve of reasons that may be challenged, reasons that force us to take a rationally motivated position of yes or no. This calls for a *different* type of attitude from that which we bring to the claims of merely influential ideas. From the perspective of the participant, a moment of *unconditionedness* is built into the *conditions* of action oriented toward reaching understanding. From the perspective of the first person, the question of which beliefs are justified is a question of which beliefs are based on good reasons; it is not a function of life-habits that enjoy social currency in some places and not in others.

And because in the modern age the gaps between competing convictions reach deep into the domain of questions that "admit of truth," there exists, contrary to Rorty, a philosophical interest "to see social practices of justification as more than just such practices."[1] The stubbornness with which philosophy clings to the role of the "guardian of reason" can hardly be dismissed as an idiosyncrasy of self-absorbed intellectuals, especially in a period in which basic irrationalist undercurrents are transmuted once again into a dubious form of politics. In my opinion, it is precisely the neoconservatives who articulate, intensify, and spread this mood of the times via the mass media – with such an effect that "it itches."

II

In his latest book Richard Bernstein gives us another answer: instead of bidding farewell to philosophy from an artificially alienated viewpoint of an ethnologist, he turns it toward the practical. While Rorty absolutizes the perspective of the observer, Bernstein remains within the perspective of the participant and enters into a debate which today leads beyond the mistaken alternatives of historicism and trancendentalism, a debate going on between Gadamer, Arendt, Rorty, and myself, among others.[2] Bernstein does not end his splendid reconstruction of the diverse paths of this discussion – a discussion that has not yet come to a close – with a proposal for a theoretical solution, but with a practical recommendation: we ought to *act* under the presupposition of the unifying power of communicative reason. In order to make this argumentative move intelligible, let me cite a thesis of Herbert Schnädelbach with which Bernstein would probably agree: "that the difference between what we always claim for our rationality and what we are actually able to explicate as rational can in principle never be eliminated."[3] If I understand the conclusion of his book correctly, it is for this reason that Bernstein from the start locates the moment of unconditionedness built into the universalistic validity *claims* of our communicative practices in the horizon of *practical* reason; he finds in the communicative infrastructure of the life-world a practical postulate, one that is dictated by reason itself. He refuses to regard the procedural unity of rationality within the historical and cultural multiplicity of standards of rationality as a question that is accessible to *theoretical* treatment.

I suspect that behind Bernstein's argumentative strategy there lies an absolutizing of the perspective of the participant which is complementary to Rorty's absolutizing of that of the observer. I don't see why one could not, at least in a preliminary way, explore a *third path*, which I have embarked upon with my "theory of communicative action." In this approach, philosophy surrenders its claim to be the sole representative in matters of rationality and enters into a nonexclusive division of labor with the reconstructive sciences. It has the aim of clarifying the presuppositions of the rationality of processes of reaching understanding, which may be presumed to be universal because they are unavoidable. Then philosophy shares with the sciences a falliblistic consciousness, in that its strong universalistic suppositions require confirmation in an interplay with empirical theories of competence.[4] This revisionary self-understanding of the role of philosophy marks a break with the aspirations of first philosophy (*Ursprungsphilosophie*) in any form, even that of the theory of knowledge; but it does not mean that philosophy abandons its role as the guardian of rationality. With its self-imposed modesty of method, a philosophy starting from formal pragmatics preserves the possibility of speaking of rationality in the singular. Unlike the sciences, it has to account reflectively for its own context of emergence and thus its own place in history.[5] Thus, "metanarratives," in the sense of foundational "ultimate groundings" or totalizing philosophies of history, could never even arise.

The most important achievement of such an approach is the possibility of clarifying a concept of communicative rationality that escapes the snares of Western logocentrism. Instead of following Nietzsche's path of a totalizing and self-referential critique of reason, whether it be via Heidegger to Derrida, or via Bataille to Foucault,[6] and throwing the baby out with the bathwater, it is more promising to seek this end through the analysis of the *already* operative potential for rationality contained in the everyday practices of communication. Here the validity dimensions of propositional truth, normative rightness, and subjective truthfulness or authenticity are intermeshed with each other. From this network of a bodily and interactively shaped, historically situated reason, our philosophical tradition selected out only the single thread of propositional truth and theoretical reason and stylized it into the monopoly of humanity. The common ground that unites both von Humboldt and pragmatism with the later Wittgenstein and Austin is the opposition to the *ontological* privileging of the world of beings, the *epistemological* privileging of contact with objects or existing states of affairs, and the *semantic* privileging of assertoric sentences and propositional truth. Logocentrism means neglecting the complexity of reason effectively operating in the life-world, and restricting reason to its cognitive-instrumental dimension (a dimension, we might add, that has been noticeably privileged and selectively utilized in processes of capitalist modernization).

Rorty takes Western logocentrism as an indication of the exhaustion of our philosophical discourse and a reason to bid adieu to philosophy as such. This way of reading the tradition can not be maintained if philosophy can be transformed so as to enable it to cope with the entire spectrum of aspects of rationality – and with the historical fate of a reason that has been arrested again and again, ideologically misused and distorted, but that also stubbornly raises its voice in every inconspicuous act of successful communication. Such a transformation is possible only if philosophy does not remain fixated on the natural sciences. Had Rorty not shared this fixation, he might have entertained a more flexible and accepting relationship to the philosophical tradition. Fortunately, not all philosophizing can be subsumed under the paradigm of the philosophy of consciousness.

Rorty believes that the need in the modern age for self-reassurance is a capricious problem created by intellectuals – indeed, even a typically German problem. In his view, it arises from the esoteric *Weltschmerz* of small intellectual circles, from their preoccupation with a world that was lost along with the religious beliefs of their fathers. But does it not remain an open question whether or not the social integrative powers of the religious tradition shaken by enlightenment can find an equivalent in the unifying, consensus-creating power of reason? This was indeed the motivation behind German Idealism; this type of idealism has found equally influential proponents in the tradition of Peirce, Royce, Mead, and Dewey, in which Rorty prefers to place himself. What is perhaps specifically German is the philosophical concept of alienation, both in the Hegelian – Marxist version and the early Romantic version taken up by Nietzsche. This same theme resonates not only in post structuralist France; since the sixties, and I need not remind Rorty of this, the discussion of modernity in conflict with itself had been nowhere so lively as in the USA – admittedly, more so among social scientists and psychologists than among analytic philosophers. Carl Schorske even thought he could see intellectual affinities between the contemporary American scene and Weimar Germany. While the expression "postmodern" was not invented by American neoconservatives, they at least popularized it.

Do not these and similar signs indicate that intellectuals articulate shifts in mood, which they in no way invent, but which have instead palpable social and often economic causes? As a good pragmatist, I hold the view that a philosopher's capacity to create problems through intentionally inciting doubt is quite limited. I share Peirce's doubt about any type of Cartesian doubt. Problems emerge in situations over which we are not in control; they are something which objectively happens to us. The slogan that leftist intellectuals are the cause of the misery they analyze has already been bandied about for too long among rightist intellectuals in Germany to be credible. It is no more credible in the attractive packaging of a theory of the new class.

To me, the notion of intellectual "value elites" is absolutely worthless. Like Rorty, I have for a long time identified myself with that radical democratic mentality which is present in the best American traditions and articulated in American pragmatism. This mentality takes seriously what appears to so-called radical thinkers as so much reformist naïveté. Dewey's "attempt to make concrete concerns with the daily problems of one's community" expresses both a practice and an attitude. It is a maxim of action about which it is in fact superfluous to philosophize.

Rorty puts in question the entire undertaking of the theory of communicative action. As opposed to this form of questioning, the reservations of Martin Jay, Thomas McCarthy, and Joel Whitebook are directed toward particular steps in its execution. These authors direct their attention to complications in my attempt to work out the concept of communicative rationality. Jay points out an underilluminated aspect; McCarthy touches upon a central difficulty; Whitebook deals with a problem which emerges as a consequence of the theory. In the framework of a short reply, I can only respond in such a way as to allude to how I have dealt with some of these problems in the past, and how I would like to work on others in the future. An added difficulty here is that only McCarthy directs his remarks to my more recent works.

III

With a great deal of hermeneutic sensitivity, Martin Jay has collected and interpreted my scattered remarks on the question of aesthetic modernity. In every case these remarks had a secondary character, to the extent that they arose only in the context of other themes and always in relation to the discussions among Adorno, Benjamin, and Marcuse. In *The Theory of Communicative Action*, my discussion of Max Weber's theory of culture and his diagnosis of the times required understanding the autonomous art that emerged in modern Europe (together with art criticism institutionalized since the eighteenth century) as the product of a disintegration and the result of a process of rationalization. Weber describes the rationalization of world-views as a process of decomposition and differentiation. On the one hand, the basic substantial concepts with which the world-orders of "salvation history" and cosmology were constructed have been dissolved; with this dissolution, ontic, moral, and expressive aspects are no longer fused into one and the same concept. Without the possibility of recourse to God and the cosmic order as an origin, theological and metaphysical forms of grounding lose their credibility. On the other hand, along side a subjectivized "faith," there arose profane forms of "knowledge" which are relatively independent of one another. Philosophy, forced into the position of mediator, becomes dependent on them. As documented in the division of Kant's three *Critiques*, questions of truth are differentiated from questions of justice, and these in turn from questions of taste.

Originating in the eighteenth century, idealistic aesthetics strictly distinguished aesthetic pleasure from other "empirical" forms of satisfaction; that is, it separated the beautiful and the sublime on the one hand from the useful and the desirable on the other. Art emerges with its own proper claim, *along with* science and technology, law and morality. Max Weber speaks of the inner logic or intrinsic meaning (*Eigensinn*) of these three cultural value spheres, which are also separated from each other institutionally in the form of functionally specified systems of action. Since the investigations of Arnold Hauser into the social history of modern art, this *institutional* differentiation of art has often been analyzed.[7]

There is no need here to go into the external aspects of the transformation of the forms of the production of art, the purposes to which it was put, or the modes of its reception in the transition from sacrally bound art, through the art of the court and patron, to bourgeois commercialized art.[8] What is in dispute are the internal aspects of the "inner logic" of autonomous art since the eighteenth century. One of the two questions raised by Martin Jay is the extent to which one can speak of an aesthetic-practical *rationality*, or even of a *learning* process, in this sphere.

There is an unmistakable indicator for the fact that a certain type of "knowing" is objectified in art works, albeit in a different way than in theoretical discourse or in legal or moral representations: these objectivations of mind are also fallible and hence criticizable. Art criticism arose at the same time as the autonomous work of art; and since then the insight has established itself that the work of art calls for interpretation, evaluation and even "linguistification" (*Versprachlichung*) of its semantic content. Art criticism has developed forms of argumentation that specifically differentiate it from the forms of theoretical and moral-practical discourse.[9] As distinct from merely subjective preference, the fact that we link judgments of taste to a criticizable claim presupposes non-arbitrary standards for the judgment of art. As the philosophical discussion of "artistic truth" reveals, works of art raise claims with regard to their unity (harmony: *Stimmigkeit*), their authenticity, and the success of their expressions by which they can be measured and in terms of which they may fail. For that reason I believe that a pragmatic logic of argumentation is the most appropriate guiding thread through which the "aesthetic-practical" type of rationality can be differentiated over and against other types of rationality.

If we speak about "learning processes," it is the works of art themselves, and not the discourses about them, that are the locus of directed and cumulative transformations. As McCarthy correctly notes, what accumulates are not epistemic contents, but rather the effects of the inner logical differentiation of a special sort of experience: precisely those aesthetic experiences of which only a decentered, unbound subjectivity is capable. Authentic experiences of this type are possible only to the extent that the categories of the patterned expectations of organized daily experience collapse, that the routines of daily action and conventions of ordinary life are destroyed, and the normality of foreseeable and accountable certainties are suspended. The ever more radical uncoupling of this potential for experience, the purification of the aesthetic from admixtures of the cognitive, the useful, and the moral is mirrored in the reflections of the early Romantic period (especially in Friedrich Schlegel), in the aestheticism of Baudelaire and the Symbolists, in the program of *l'art pour l'art*, in the surrealistic celebration of illumination through shock effects, with its ambivalence of attraction and repulsion, of broken continuity, of the shudder of profanization, of agitated disgust: in short, in the reflection of those moments in which the bewildered subject "transgresses his boundaries," as Bataille puts it. What is reflected in these interpretations and declarations is a transformation of the form of aesthetic experience, induced by avant-garde art itself, in the direction of the decentering and unbounding of subjectivity. At the same time, this decentering indicates an increased sensitivity to what remains unassimilated in the interpretive achievements of pragmatic, epistemic, and moral mastery of the demands and challenges of everyday situations; it effects an openness to the expurgated elements of the unconscious, the fantastic, and the mad, the material and the bodily – thus to everything in our speechless contact with reality which is so fleeting, so contingent, so immediate, so individualized, simultaneously so far and so near that it escapes our normal categorical grasp.

Benjamin called this style of experience "concentrated distraction" and set it off from the contemplative style of experience. It is in this direction that the characteristics and tendencies of the development of avant-garde art, analyzed repeatedly since Benjamin and Adorno, point. The loss of aura and the importance of allegory are continuous with the destruction of the organically unified work of art and its pretended totality of meaning; one can think here of the incorporation of the ugly, of the negative as such. By treating materials, methods, and techniques reflectively, the artist opens up a space for experiment and play and transfers the activity of the genius to "free construction" (*freie Arbeit*).[10] Forced novelty, dependence on the latest trends, the accelerated pace of fads, perpetuate the creative break with the tradition and serve to make all stylistic means equally accessible. Art becomes a laboratory, the critic an expert, the development of art the medium of a learning process – here, naturally, not in the sense of an accumulation of epistemic *contents*, of an aesthetic "progress" – which is possible only in individual dimensions – but nonetheless in the sense of a concentrically expanding, advancing exploration of a realm of possibilities structurally opened up with the autonomization of art. (I do not know whether or not the results of Piaget's genetic psychology are as appropriate for the analysis of this "level of learning" as they are for the analysis of the stages of postconventional conceptions of law and morality. I tend to be rather skeptical.)

Martin Jay's other question concerns the relation between the independence of art in a culture of experts and the cultural impoverishment of the life-world. Jay asks why I do not unambiguously decide between Adorno and Benjamin – between the esotericism of the exclusive, often hermetically sealed avant-garde work of art, and the hope for profane illumination in exoteric mass art. He notes, that I seem to find some truth in both positions.

Peter Bürger takes an unambiguous position. In his view, the impulse of several avant-garde movements to rebel against the institutionalization of art, against its being split off from the life-world, was correct despite the failure of the surrealistic revolt.[11] I do not differ with this judgment per se. The intention of redeeming a promise of happiness, whose superabundance radiates beyond art, is part of art itself. But this intention cannot be realized in the way in which the surrealists wanted, through the liquidation of appearance as the medium of artistic representation. This false *Aufhebung* of art into life certainly does not preclude the possibility of a correct mediation of art with the life-world. An aesthetic experience that is not simply to be transposed into judgments of taste by the professional arbiters, that is not merely to circulate in the realm of art alone, would entail a change in the status of an, as it were, experimentally unbound subjectivity.

If aesthetic experience is incorporated into the context of individual life-histories, if it is utilized to illuminate a situation and to throw light on individual life-problems – if it at all communicates its impulses to a collective form of life – then art enters into a language game which is no longer that of aesthetic criticism, but belongs, rather, to everyday communicative practice. It then no longer affects only our evaluative language or only renews the interpretation of needs that color our perceptions; rather, it reaches into our cognitive interpretations and normative expectations and transforms the totality in which these moments are related to each other. In this respect, modern art harbors a utopia that becomes a reality to the degree that the mimetic powers sublimated in the work of art find resonance in the mimetic relations of a balanced and undistorted intersubjectivity of everyday life. However, this does not require the *liquidation* of an art set off from life in the medium of *appearance*, but rather a *changed constellation* of art and the life-world.

I developed these ideas earlier at the suggestion of Albrecht Wellmer.[12] In the meantime, Wellmer has elaborated them in such an ingenious way that I can here be content simply to refer to his treatment.[13] I do not wish to retrace Wellmer's subtle line of argument but only to repeat his main thesis, in order to offer it as an answer to Martin Jay's question. The fact that we can dispute the reasons for evaluating a work of art in aesthetic discourse is, as we said, an unmistakable indication for a validity claim inherent in works of art. The aesthetic "validity" or "unity" that we attribute to a work refers to its singularly illuminating power to open our eyes to what is seemingly familiar, to disclose anew an apparently familiar reality. This validity claim admittedly stands for a *potential* for "truth" that can be released only in the whole complexity of life-experience; therefore, this "truth potential" may not be connected to (or even identified with) just one of the three validity claims constitutive for communicative action, as I have been previously inclined to maintain. The one-to-one relationship which exists between the prescriptive validity of a norm and the normative validity claims raised in regulative speech acts is not a proper model for the relation between the potential for truth of works of art, and the transformed relations between self and world stimulated by aesthetic experience. "Neither truth nor truthfulness may be attributed unmetaphorically to works of art, if one understands 'truth' and 'truthfulness' in the sense of a pragmatically differentiated, everyday concept of truth. We can explain the way in which truth and truthfulness – and even normative correctness – are metaphorically interlaced in works of art only by appealing to the fact that the work of art, as a symbolic formation with an aesthetic validity claim, is at the same time an object of the life-world experience, in which the three validity domains are unmetaphorically intermeshed."[14]

IV

Thomas McCarthy raises two sorts of objections: first, against my systematic interpretation of Weber's diagnosis of the times; and second, against my analysis of interpretative understanding. Since I believe that the relationship between the two problems established by McCarthy is artificial, I will first deal separately with the problem of the objectivity of understanding.

In the field of meaning theory I hold the view that we understand a literally meant speech act when we know the conditions under which it could be accepted as valid by a hearer. This pragmatically extended version of truth conditional semantics is supported by the fact that we connect the execution of speech acts to various validity claims: claims to the truth of propositions (or of the existential presuppositions of the propositional contents), claims to the rightness of an utterance (with respect to existing normative contexts), and claims to the truthfulness of an expressed intention. With these claims we take on, as it were, a warrant for their redemption, should it be necessary – above all, in that we offer, at least implicitly, reasons for the validity of our speech acts. A hearer knows the content of what is said when he knows what reasons (or what sort of reasons) the speaker would give for the validity of his speech act (under appropriate circumstances). The interpreter (even the social scientific interpreter who deals with linguistically formed data) does not understand symbolically prestructured objects (in the normal case, communicative utterances), if he or she does not also understand the reasons potentially related to their validity claims.

Now the interesting point is that reasons are of a special nature. They can always be expanded into arguments which we then understand only when we *recapitulate* (*nachvollziehen*) them in the light of some standards of rationality. This "recapitulation" requires a reconstructive activity in which we bring into play our own standards of rationality, at least intuitively. From the perspective of a participant, however, one's own rationality standards must always claim general validity; this claim to general validity can be restricted only subsequently, from the perspective of a third person. In short, the interpretative reconstruction of reasons makes it necessary that for us to place "their" standards in relation to "ours," so that in the case of a contradiction we either revise our preconceptions or relativize "their" standards of rationality against "ours."

These reflections do indeed lead to the rather "strong" thesis that we *cannot* understand reasons without at least implicitly evaluating them. McCarthy argues that this conclusion is false, since, even if it is the case that it is necessary to take up a rationally motivated yes or no position on reasons in order to understand them, the interpreter can not only agree or disagree with them but can also practice a kind of abstention; he or she has the option of "leaving to one side" the question of the validity of "their" rationality standards (and hence of the reasons themselves). However, I think that such an abstention is also a rationally motivated position, as much as a "yes" or a "no," and in no way relieves us of the necessity of taking a position. Abstention in this context does not really signify a true declaration of neutrality, but only signals that we are putting off problems for the time being and wish to suspend our interpretative efforts. For example, so long as we are unable to see a perspicuous internal relation between the categorial frameworks of Aristotelian and Newtonian physics, we do not know precisely in what sense Aristotle, in contrast to Newton, wanted to "explain" natural processes. Simply noting the competition between various paradigms comes close to confessing that we do not yet understand the physics and metaphysics of Aristotle as well as we do the basic assumptions about nature in classical mechanics.

The rational character of understanding, which Gadamer always emphasized, becomes especially clear in limit cases, as, for example, in the interpretation of mythical narratives. Undercutting or leaving to one side (or merely shaking one's head while accepting) the totalistic categories of a world view within which the narrative interweaving and (as it appears to *us*) the categorical confusion of surface phenomena lay claim to explanatory power, merely indicate that we are putting off, prematurely breaking off, the interpretive process. This is tantamount to confessing that we do not yet understand the point of mythical modes of thought. We understand them only when we can say why the participants had good reasons for their confidence in this *type* of explanation. But in order to achieve this degree of understanding, we have to establish an internal relation between "their" sort of explanation and the kind we accept as correct. We must be able to reconstruct the successful and unsuccessful learning processes which separate "us" from "them"; both modes of explanation have to be located within the same universe of discourse. As long as this is not achieved, the feeling remains that one does not understand something. It is this perplexity which finds its appropriate expression in suspension.

But it does not follow from this that the sciences which have to establish hermeneutic access to their object domain have to renounce the objectivity of knowledge. I have criticized this hermeneutistic position in various ways.[15] In principle, I do not see any difficulty in achieving some theoretical knowledge even in those domains of reality with which we have contact primarily through norm-conforming or expressive attitudes. My reservations concern only those theoretical positions which ignore the hermeneutic dimension of access to the object domain entirely.[16] If the sentence McCarthy criticizes is to be read as reporting my own view, "that nothing can be learned in the objectivating attitude about inner nature qua subjectivity,"[17] then it may be understood only in the sense of a rejection of *purely* objectivistic approaches to psychology.

McCarthy is further interested in the question whether or not the rationality complexes which have been differentiated in modern Europe and achieved a certain autonomy do not, as it were, also communicate with one another and have their roots in one and the same reason. In my view, this theme can be treated independently of the problem of interpretive understanding. For this purpose, the schema reproduced by McCarthy is not really a fruitful point of departure. Its purpose was only to represent the content of Max Weber's famous *"Zwischenbetrachtung."*[18] Unfortunately, in response to earlier objections I made the mistake of referring to this schema in a systematic way.[19] And McCarthy does the same here. My previous carelessness thus makes it necessary in what follows to distinguish more carefully between my interpretation of Weber and my own views.

V

I want first to isolate those elements of Weber's theory of culture that I appropriated into my own view (1). In so doing, we then encounter McCarthy's concern for the costs of a process of disenchantment that now leaves open the possibility of only a procedural unity of reason cutting across different forms of argumentation (2). McCarthy finally treats the question of the synthesis of the differentiated moments of reason under three quite distinct aspects. He lists three problems that cannot be subsumed under the *same* analytical perspective (that is, the perspective of varying basic attitudes toward the objective, the social, and the subjective worlds) (3).

1. To begin with, let me turn to what I have appropriated from Weber's theory of culture. In Weber's view, the assertion of a differentiation of "value spheres," each with its own inner logic – which was inspired by the Neo-Kantians Emil Lask and Heinrich Rickert – can be plausibly defended in regard to modern Europe on two levels: first, on the level of ideas that can be transmitted in traditions (scientific theories, moral and legal beliefs, as well as artistic productions); but also, second, on the level of cultural action systems, in which corresponding "discourses" and activities are given professionally and institutionally organized form. The differentiation of value spheres corresponds to a decentered understanding of the world which is an important internal condition for the professionalized treatment of cultural traditions separated into questions of truth, justice, and taste. This modern understanding of the world makes possible a hypothetical approach to phenomena and experiences, which are isolated from the complexity of life-world contexts and analyzed under experimentally varied conditions. This is equally true for the states of an objectified nature, for norms and modes of acting, and for the reflective experiences of an "unbound" subjectivity (set free from the practical constraints of everyday life). The well-known distinction of cognitive developmental psychology between structurally defined levels of learning, on the one hand, and the learning of contents on the other, certainly may not be applied in the same way to science, morality, and art. In this respect my formulations were not careful enough.

Compared to the growth of theoretical knowledge, described by McCarthy as accumulation of contents across paradigm shifts, the trends in the development of art (discussed at length above) do not so much signify an accumulation of contents as the progressive constitution of a particular domain of autonomous art and aesthetic experience purified of cognitive and moral admixtures; they also signify expanding explorations that illuminate more and more of this realm of experience. Yet this concentric expansion is not accompanied by the familiar effects of a devaluation of formerly held insights typical for cumulative learning processes. Moral and legal theories occupy a middle position. Here, too, we can observe the constitution of a domain of autonomous morality and moral universalism that distills a class of rationally solvable problems from the complexity of the contexts of ethical life under the single aspect of justice. Learning processes in this sphere are similar to a theoretical progress achieved within the limits of a single paradigm. Thus, in the modern age the explication and justification of moral intuitions make a certain "progress": this progress is not exhausted in ever new reinterpretations of the same moral principle.

However, the thesis that capitalist modernization can be grasped as a selective actualization of the rationality potential contained in modern structures of consciousness requires the counterfactual supposition of a non-selective model of societal rationalization.[20] In this connection I have suggested that for the value spheres of science, morality, and art in modern Europe "we should be able to demonstrate plausible correspondences with typical forms of argumentation, each of which is specialized in accord with a universal validity claim."[21] Thus, the burden of proof is put on the theory of argumentation; leaving aside explicative discourse and therapeutic critique, it has to distinguish and clarify the systematic content of three different forms of argumentation: namely, empirical-theoretical discourse, moral discourse, and aesthetic critique.[22] It was due to the context of Weber's diagnosis of the times that I did not introduce the three rationality complexes via argumentation theory but by way of a schema that was supposed to represent the characteristics of a decentered understanding of the world. Indeed, the modern understanding of the world structurally opens up the possibility of taking objectivating, norm-conforming or expressive attitudes towards three different worlds (objective, social or subjective – in short, to states of affairs, norms, or subjective experiences); it also allows us to vary these attitudes in relation to elements of one and the same world. If we keep to the schema (Fig. 10, p. 238), but leave aside its application to Weber's diagnosis of the times, and pursue instead a systematic line of thought, the three forms of argumentation corresponding to the modern complexes of rationality can, *to begin with*, be correlated with the formal pragmatic relations along the diagonal (1.1, 2.2, 3.3).

2. Based on reflections in the theory of meaning, I take as my starting point that facts, norms, and subjective experiences have their *originary* locus in "their" corresponding worlds (objective, social, or subjective), and, *in the first instance*, are accessible, or identifiable, only from the perspective of an actor who takes a corresponding attitude (be it objectivating, norm-conforming, or expressive). It is with this linear ordering that the first of the three questions McCarthy treats at the end of his article arises.

How is it that we can talk in an objectivating attitude about something in the subjective or social world, that is, about those elements that we *first* experience as something subjective or which we *first* encounter as something normative? In theoretical discourse (scientific discourse, for example) we can only incorporate these elements if we thematize subjective experiences and norms as states of affairs after having transformed them into components of the objective world. In everyday communication we certainly succeed, without much trouble, in transforming expressive utterances (or first-person sentences) into equivalent statements in the third person, or in accurately reporting the content of normative utterances or imperatives from the third-person point of view. On the level of scientific discourse, however, there is a tendency to delimit the object domains of, for example, psychology or sociology, by neglecting their hermeneutic dimensions, in such a way that the components of the subjective or social world are naturalistically assimilated to physical entities or to observable behavior. In each case they are made into components of the objective world, inherently accessible only in the objectivating attitude; that is, they are forced into the basic conceptual framework of physicalism or behaviorism. As opposed to this naturalistic reduction, the point here is only to defend non-objectivistic approaches in psychology and the social sciences.

Mutatis mutandis, the same questions arise for moral-practical discourse, and, indirectly, for aesthetic criticism. These forms of argumentation are also inherently related to components of one specific world, the social or the subjective. Here too, elements of the other two worlds must be brought into play in such a way as to avoid the dangers of, respectively, *moralism* and *aestheticism*, just as previously the danger of *objectivism* had to be avoided. We can thus observe that science, morality, and art have not only been differentiated *from each other*; they also communicate *with each other*. But within the boundaries of each expert culture, the different moments of reason come into contact with one another in such a way as to avoid violating the inner logic of the dominant form of argumentation specialized either in truth, normative correctness, or aesthetic harmony. This is one concern of the last chapter of *The Theory of Communicative Action*.[23]

At this point the motivation behind McCarthy's criticism becomes clear: an interest in the question of how the moments of reason retain their unity within differentiation and of how this unity can be adequately expressed in philosophical analysis. Unfortunately, my schematic presentation of Weber's diagnosis of the times leads McCarthy to conflate three quite distinct questions under a single aspect. As just shown, the formal-pragmatic relations play a role in the analysis of those interactions between the cognitive, moral, and expressive moments of reason. But the other two questions really have nothing to do with this problem: first, the question of how the knowledge produced in expert cultures can be mediated with everyday practices (which I touched upon above in relation to the constellation "art" and "life"); and second, the question of whether we can provide an equivalent for the meaning of traditional world-views – for their function of "*Sinngebung*."

3. With the emergence of autonomous art and science, problems of mediation arise – such as the relation of art and life, or of theory and practice. Since Hegel a corresponding problem has emerged in terms of the relation of morality and ethical life (*Sittlichkeit*). This problem has less to do with an expressive attitude toward the social world than with the fact that the insights of a postconventional morality would remain without any impact on real life unless morality is anchored in concrete forms of ethical life. The deontological ethics developed in the Kantian tradition do indeed offer a solution to the problem of justification; they show

how to choose between controversial norms of action with good reasons (in light of what might be willed by all). But they do not offer any solution for two resultant problems: first, that of the *application* of justified norms which are general and abstracted from any content; and second, that of the *efficacy* of pure moral insights that have been gained under the condition of abstracting from available motivations. Autonomous morality owes its gain in rationality to the transformation of questions of the good life into problems of justice. As a consequence of this deontological abstraction, it can only provide answers to questions lacking specific contexts. This necessary disregard for the complexity of concrete forms of life, in which moral moments are always interlaced with evaluative, cognitive, and expressive moments, calls for specific compensations that make good the deficits with regard to the application and realization of moral insights. I am not able to go further into this question here.[24]

The discussions of morality and ethical life, theory and practice, art and life, all center around the idea of a non-reified everyday communicative practice, a form of life with structures of an undistorted intersubjectivity. Such a possibility must today be wrung from the professional, specialized, self-sufficient culture of experts and from the systems-imperatives of state and economy which destructively invade the ecological basis of life and the communicative infrastructure of our life-world. This same intuition is expressed in Marx's utopian perspective on the realization of philosophy: to the extent that the reason expressed in Hegel's philosophy can be embodied in the forms of life of an emancipated society, philosophy somehow becomes pointless. For Marx, philosophy realized is philosophy *aufgehoben*. The theory of communicative action gives this idea another reading: the unity of reason cannot be reestablished on the level of cultural traditions in terms of a substantive world view, but only on this side of the expert cultures, in a non-reified, communicative practice of everyday life. Indeed, in a certain way the unity of reason is *a tergo* always already realized in communicative action – namely, in such a way that we have an intuitive knowledge of it. A philosophy that wants to bring this intuition to a conceptual level must retrieve the scattered traces of reason in communicative practices themselves, no matter how muted they may be. However, it cannot simply repeat the attempt, long since discredited, to project some theoretical picture of the world as a whole.

I think I have learned from the tradition of Hegelian-Marxism, from the history of critical social theory from Marx to Benjamin,

Bloch, Marcuse, and Adorno that any attempt to embed the perspective of reconciliation in a philosophy of history of nature, however indirectly it is done, must pay the price of dedifferentiating forms of knowledge behind whose categorial distinctions we can no longer retreat in good conscience. All this is not really an argument, but more an expression of skepticism in the face of so many failed attempts to have one's cake and eat it too: to retain both Kant's insights and, at the same time, to return to the "home" (*Behausung*) from which these same insights have driven us. But, perhaps, McCarthy or others will some day succeed in formulating the continuities between human history and natural history so carefully that they are weak enough to be plausible and yet strong enough to permit us to recognize man's place in the cosmos (Scheler), at least in broad outlines.

VI

The philosophical purpose behind Joel Whitebook's attempt to oppose to "linguistic idealism" the truth of the materialist tradition from Feuerbach through Marx and Freud to the later Frankfurt School accords with McCarthy's arguments against banning all substantive moments from the concept of a procedural rationality. The theoreticians of Western Marxism were relentless in their search for some Archimedean point between Kant and Hegel, from which they might retrieve the materialist tradition without surrendering the justificatory achievements of formalist thought on the one hand, or the meaning-giving capacity of holistic thought on the other. These philosophers were in agreement on the goal; they differed as to how to attain it, since they could not avoid paying some price of it, excising part of Kant, or Hegel, or Marx. McCarthy and Whitebook chastise me either for cutting too much from Hegel and totalizing forms of thought (McCarthy), or too much from Marx and materialism (Whitebook). In their common diagnosis of too much Kantianism, both agree with Rorty, who is disturbed less by its formalism than by its supposed foundationalism.

Whitebook's analysis sheds light on the reception of Freudian id psychology by Horkheimer, Marcuse, and Adorno, as well as on their critique of ego psychology and the famous thesis of the "end of the individual." Whitebook himself retains a more or less orthodox interpretation of Freud; from a clinical perspective, he regards the contributions of ego psychology rather as supplements to the classical Freud. However, I see the achievement of Heinz Hart-mann and his allies to lie in having demonstrated the need to revise metapyschology; the revision itself should come rather from cognitive developmental psychology. Piaget's approach can supplement assumptions about the psychodynamic development of the child with hypotheses about the development of cognitive structures, so as to give us a handle on, and make empirically testable, the implicitly normative content of such concepts as "ego strength," "conscious conflict resolution," and "the rational control of drives." I have proposed a communication-theoretical interpretation of approaches deriving from Piaget and Freud. To my mind, this proposal has a number of advantages (1) It creates a common ground between Freud's therapeutic and metapsychological writings, by connecting the structural model of id, ego, and superego with the experiences gained in the communication between patient and analyst.[25] (2) This version conceptualizes clinical intuitions about deviant and successful processes of ego development by making defense mechanisms comprehensible as innerpsychic communication disturbances and by relating the extremes of overly defined/deficient ego boundaries (isolation/diffusion) to the pragmatic presuppositions of intact intersubjectivity and undistorted communication.[26] (3) Reading psychoanalysis in terms of communication theory also explains the central importance and individuating effect of the Oedipal conflict which remains decisive for the development of the structure of personality. Structurally described levels of interaction serve here as a conceptual bridge connecting developmental logic and developmental dynamics.[27] (4) Finally, this reading offers a categorial framework in which metapsychology can be connected up with the basic concepts of research on socialization and the family.[28] In Parson's version, the vocabulary of a theory of drives formulated in terms of energy loses its currency here.

As I see it, nothing of significance is lost in this reading. The hydraulic model and its reliance on a mechanics of instinctual energy has only a metaphorical character, even for Freud himself. In any case, one cannot have both the analytic instrument of a depth-hermeneutics and a theory of drives formulated in quasi-physicalist concepts. The Freudo-Marxism of the earlier Frankfurt School could conceptually integrate psychology and sociology only through the mechanism of internalization; but, as Whitebook shows, this results in a false antagonism between the domain of the organism, which is described in biological terms, and the domain of the social apparatus, which invades the individual from the outside.

It certainly makes more sense to attempt to integrate both disciplines from the beginning within the *same* conceptual framework. Such a framework would permit us to understand the development of personality as socialization, and to understand sociation as individualization.

If one is clear about the purely *methodological character of this decision*, one need not fear the consequences Whitebook has in mind. It is only from the point of view of a reifying theory of drives that the extralinguistic referent of the structure of and autonomy of "inner nature" gets lost along with the vocabulary of instinct and drive energy, cathexis, displacement, etc. But the essential difference actually consists only in replacing "drive energies" with "interpreted needs" and describing "instinctual vissicitudes" from the perspective of identity formation and processes of interaction. In this communication-theoretical reading, inner nature is in no way vaporized into culturalistic haze.[29] It does not determine in advance that the substratum of inner nature has to fit harmoniously into linguistic structures, and even be utterly absorbed into them. But such a categorial framework does decide in favor of the perspective of a life-world intersubjectively shared by participants. One does give up biological or physicalistic third-person descriptions of the organic substratum. This change in the perspective of description does not entail the elimination of inner nature as an extralinguistic referent.

Whitebook is led astray by some of my remarks that belong to another context. They were made apropos the question of whether a theory of natural evolution could be projected from such an internal perspective. Naturally, I am enough of a materialist to take as my starting point that Kant is right only to the extent that his statements are compatible with Darwin. I have never had any doubts about the primacy of natural history over the history of the human species. Nevertheless, it is better not to try to resolve all problems with the same theory, or even with theories of the same type. The neo-Darwinian theory of evolution has a different status and form that Newtonian physics on the one hand, and Romantic theories of nature on the other: the three theories are not concerned with the same "nature." "Instinctual nature" as dealt with in ethology and in psychoanalysis is just as distinct. It seems to me that the single most important question here is whether that "inner nature," whose fateful entwinement in life histories is the object of psychoanalysis, can be better explained through interactional concepts or through concepts with more strongly physicalistic or biological connotations. The value of a theory is surely a matter of empirical fruitfulness and not a matter of the speculative content of its fundamental concepts.[30]

It is, however, quite legitimate to ask how it is that I can hold on to those materialist motifs which Freudo-Marxism drew upon in theory of drives. Whitebook suspects that a theory of society which no longer takes over intact the Freudian theory of drives necessarily truncates an important normative dimension, namely that of happiness. At the same time, he also sees an excess of utopianism built into "linguistic idealism." The "concern for happiness" seems necessarily to become secondary to the "passion for justice" in a theory that gets involved with genetic structuralism and directs its interest to general structures of rationality, both in the development of the individual and in social evolution. I shall limit myself here to the moral and legal dimension, since both Whitebook and McCarthy, each in his own way, renew the critique of ethical formalism (and both with reference to the same passage in my essay on Benjamin).

First of all, I have to point out that I have revised my earlier interpretation[31] of the post-conventional stage of moral judgment.[32] Even if the approach of a discourse ethic favored by Apel and myself should be accepted in philosophical discussions, it would only have achieved an adequate description of the *conditions* of principled moral judgments as such. Previously, I was not sufficiently clear about the fact that such a competence for judgment does *not* eo ipso presuppose a flexible ego identity, even if it no longer accepts as given the interpretation of needs (as does Kantian ethics), but rather (as in discourse ethics) opens them to an uncoerced intersubjective process of will formation. The cognitive capacity to justify moral actions and norms has to be supplemented if it is to become effective in the context of ethical life. Only a capacity for judgment (informed by practical reason) makes possible an application of abstract and general norms that is appropriate to particular situations; only motivational resources and structures of inner control make possible actions which are in accord with moral insight. Without the capacity for judgment and motivation, the psychological conditions for translating morality into ethical life are missing; without the corresponding patterns of socialization and institutions, i.e., without "fitting" forms of life to embodied moral principles, the social conditions for their concrete existence are missing. This is the substance of Hegel's critique of Kant's theory of morality, a critique that has always been recognized in the critical theory of society. Autonomy in Kant's sense, with the strict separation of duty and inclination and without the awareness of the ego's communicative access to its own inner nature, also signifies unfreedom; Adorno developed the implications of this in the third part of his *Negative Dialectics*. In psychological terms, this means that inner nature is not transformed into the perspective of reconciliation merely through the capacity of moral judgment (as it is reconstructed in terms of a discourse ethics). Rather, such a perspective is attained only through the structures of an ego-identity making possible "a freedom that limits itself in the intention of reconciling, if not of identifying, worthiness with happiness."[33]

In the theory of society the relation of morality and ethical life can be found in the contrast between general structures of the life-world capable of being rationalized, on the one hand, and the plurality of existing life-worlds in their specific, concrete historical totalities, on the other. Particular forms of life and life histories form a context that remains in the background and is experienced by us only as an horizon; this context cannot be objectivated in toto. Certainly, different life-worlds may be compared under different abstract points of view; but only a few such aspects are so general that they can be detached from the cultural patterns of a specific life-world. This is true, for instance, of problem-solving capacities that can be measured against the standard of universal validity claims (like propositional truth and normative rightness) and that can accumulate in the development of the forces of production, in the growth of theoretical knowledge, as well as in the stages of moral judgment. However, happiness, unlike justice or knowledge, is not a concept that relates only to one of these dimensions and to general structures of the life-world. It is related to particular constellations of lived practices, value orientations, traditions, and competences as a whole. Its object is always a historically unique configuration. We do indeed have more or less definite feelings about the success of modes of life and – with less deception – about their failure. But enormous difficulties stand in the way of conceptualizing these *clinical* intuitions about the "good life" in a universally binding way, as we can do with morality – though this was once the aim of classical ethics. One has to be satisfied with recognizing *necessary* conditions for such a life.

Many of those who have been raised in a Protestant milieu tend toward the presumption that the balance of happiness, overall and in the long run, cannot be drastically altered. But even this goal would not be achieved if every generation did not set *other* goals for themselves and undertake anew utopian efforts to change the balance of happiness. Perhaps it is a remnant of theodicy to assume that every form of life inherently possesses the same chance to find its happiness. Such speculations are surely idealistic in the bad sense given the overwhelming experience of individual unhappiness and collective suffering, and view of social catastrophes that are so terrible because, for all their quasi-naturalness, they do not arise from natural necessity. Over and over again, the necessary conditions for a "good life" are carelessly and arbitrarily violated. It is from this experience that the tradition of thought that unites Marx and Freud draws its inspiration. I am in full agreement with Whitebook in my desire not to give up *this* form of materialism.

In conclusion, I do not want to pass over in silence the fact that McCarthy and Whitebook touch upon a basic philosophical problem, which, if I am correct, still awaits an adequate resolution this side of Hegelian logic: How is it possible to weaken the claims of statements about totalities so that they might be joined together with the stronger statements about general structures?

Translated by James Bohman

Notes

INTRODUCTION

1. George Lichtheim, "From Historicism to Marxist Humanism," in *From Marx to Hegel* (New York, 1971), p. 175.
2. Jürgen Habermas, "The German Idealism of the Jewish Philosophers," in *Philosophical-Political Profiles* (Cambridge, MA, 1983), p. 41.
3. Jürgen Habermas, "The Dialectics of Rationalization: An Interview with Jürgen Habermas," *Telos, 49* (Fall, 1981), p. 7. This is a translation of *Dialektik der Rationalisierung. Jürgen Habermas im Gespräch mit Axel Honneth, Eberhard Knödler-Bonte und Arno Widmann, Äesthetik und Kommunikation, 45/46* (1981).
4. "The Dialectics of Rationalization," p. 6.
5. Ibid., p. 7.
6. Jürgen Habermas, *Knowledge and Human Interests* (Boston, 1971), p. vii.
7. Max Weber, *The Protestant Ethic and the Spirit of Capitalism*, trans. by T. Parsons (New York, 1958), p. 182.
8. *Knowledge and Human Interests*, p. 308.
9. Ibid., p. 307.
10. Ibid., p. 310.
11. Jürgen Habermas's *Theorie des kommunikativen Handelns* was first published in German in two volumes (Frankfurt, 1981). Volume 1 has since been translated into English and published as *The Theory of Communicative Action I: Reason and the Rationalization of Society* (Boston, 1984). Volume 2 is due to be published in English in the near future. Reference is made to both the German and English editions in this volume.
12. Jürgen Habermas, "What is Universal Pragmatics?" in *Communication and the Evolution of Society* (Boston, 1974), p. 3.
13. Jürgen Habermas, "Historical Materialism and the Development of Normative Structures," in *Communication and the Evolution of Society* (Boston, 1979), p. 97.
14. Jürgen Habermas, "A Reply to my Critics," in *Habermas: Critical Debates*, ed. John B. Thompson and David Held (London, 1982), p. 221
15. Jürgen Habermas, "Historical Materialism," p. 117.
16. Ibid., pp. 119–120.
17. "A Reply to my Critics," loc. cit., p. 227.
18. Jürgen Habermas, "The Dialectics of Rationalization," p. 29.
19. Ibid., p. 15.

PART 1

1. Reason, Utopia, and the Dialectic of Enlightenment

1. Jürgen Habermas, *Theorie des kommunikativen Handelns*, 2 vols (Frankfurt, 1981). (The following translations are mine.)

2. Psychic Thermidor and the Rebirth of Rebellious Subjectivity

1. This talk was given on March 14, 1980, on the occasion of a "Symposium on the Thought of Herbert Marcuse," hosted by the Philosophy Department of the University of California at San Diego. The symposium was organized to honor the memory of Herbert Marcuse who been a professor of philosophy at the University of California, San Diego. No attempt has been made to alter the informal tone of this talk.

3. Neoconservative Culture Criticism

1. H. Rühle et al., eds, *Der Neokonservatismus in den Vereinigten Staaten* (St. Augustin, 1982).
2. Peter Steinfels, *The Neo-Conservatives* (New York, 1979), p. 55.
3. P. Graf v. Kielmannsegg, *Demokratieprinzip und Regierbarkeit* (Stuttgart, 1977), p. 122.
4. Steinfels. p. 65.
5. Joachim Heidorn, *Legitimität und Regierbarkeit* (Bd., 1982), p. 249.
6. Daniel Bell, *The Cultural Contradictions of Capitalism* (New York, 1976).
7. Daniel Bell, "The New Class: A Muddled Concept," in *The Winding Passage* (Cambridge, MA, 1980), pp. 163 ff.
8. H. Klages and P. Kmiecak, eds, *Wertwandel und gesellschaftlicher Wandel* (Frankfurt, 1979), pp. 179–365.
9. Bell, *Cultural Contradictions*, p. 282.
10. Ernst Forsthoff, ed., *Rechtsstaatlichkeit und Sozialstaatlichkeit* (Darmstadt, 1968).
11. Ernst Forsthoff, *Der Staat in der Industriegesellschaft* (Munich, 1971).
12. Arnold Gehlen, *Der Mensch* (Berlin, 1940).
13. Arnold Gehlen, *Urmensch und Spätkultur* (Frankfurt, Bonn, 1956), and by the same author, *Die Seele in technischen Zeitalter* (Hamburg, 1957).
14. Arnold Gehlen, "Über kulturelle Kristallisation," in his *Studien zur Anthropologie und Soziologie* (Neuwied, 1963), p. 321.
15. See the speech by Kohl in the West German Bundestag on September 9, 1982.
16. Arnold Gehlen, *Moral und Hypermoral* (Frankfurt, 1969), and the articles in *Einblicke* (Frankfurt, 1978), pp. 253–530.
17. Dietz Bering, *Die Intellektuellen* (Stuttgart, 1978).
18. Richard Löwenthal, *Gesellschaftswandel und Kulturkritik* (Ffm., 1979), p. 38.

19. G. Rohrmoser, "Ideologische Ursachen des Terrorismus," 1, *Ideologien und Strategien* (Köln, 1981), pp. 273 ff.
20. H. Jäger, G. Schmidtchen, and L. Süllwold, "Analysen zum Terrorismus," 2, *Lebenslaufanalysen* (Köln, 1981).
21. H. Lübbe, "Wissenschaft nach der Aufklärung," in his *Philosophie nach der Aufklärung* (Düsseldorf, 1980), pp. 45 ff.
22. Hans Sedlmayer, "Ästhetischer Anarchismus in Romantik und Moderne," in *Scheidewege, 8* (1978), p. 195.
23. H. Schelsky, *Systemüberwindung, Demokratisierung, Gewaltungteilung* (München, 1978), p. 58.
24. Hermann Lübbe, *Zwischen Trend und Tradition* (Zurich, 1981), p. 17.
25. G. Rohrmoser, *Zäsur* (Stuttgart, 1980), p. 27.
26. Bell, "The Return of the Sacred," in *The Winding Passage*, supra Note 7, pp. 324 ff.
27. Max Horkheimer, *Kritik der instrumentellen Vernunft* (Frankfurt, 1974), p. 41.

4. Reason Without Revolution?

1. Jürgen Habermas, *Theorie des kommunikativen Handelns*, 2 vols (Frankfurt, 1981).
2. Ibid., vol. 1, p. 28.
3. Ibid., vol. 2, p. 179.
4. Ibid., pp. 500–1.

PART 2

1. Habermas and Modernism

1. Shierry Weber, "Aesthetic Experience and Self-Reflection as Emancipatory Processes: Two Complementary Aspects of Critical Theory," in John O'Neill, ed., *On Critical Theory* (New York, 1976).
2. Ibid., p. 79.
3. Ibid., p. 81.
4. For a discussion of this issue in Marx and Critical Theory, see Jeremy J. Shapiro, "The Slime of History: Embeddedness in Nature and Critical Theory," in O'Neill.
5. Marcuse, *The Aesthetic Dimension: Toward a Critique of Marxist Aesthetics* (Boston, 1978); Adorno, *Aesthetische Theorie* (Frankfurt, 1970).
6. Weber, p. 80.
7. See, for example, the essays in John B. Thompson and David Held, eds., *Habermas: Critical Debates* (Cambridge, Mass., 1982), which contain only the most fleeting references to this aspect of his work.
8. Habermas, *Theory and Practice*, trans. John Viertel (London, 1974).
9. Habermas, "Consciousness-Raising or Redemptive Criticism; The Contemporaneity of Walter Benjamin," *New German Critique*, 17 (Spring, 1979); *Legitimation Crisis*, trans. Thomas McCarthy (Boston, 1975).

10. Habermas, *Legitimation Crisis*, p. 78. Much of the same paragraph appears in the Benjamin essay, p. 42.

11. Although this is not the place to launch a full-scale discussion of the relationship between artistic claims to autonomy and the auratic nature of art, it should be noted that rather than simply lengthening the distance between art and life, and thus strengthening the former's auratic quality, the increased focus on art's self-referentiality that grew out of the autonomy claim actually helped to shorten it. This paradoxical effect followed from the demystification of artistic illusion, that "baring of the device" so often emphasized by the Russian formalists, which accompanied the undermining of realist or romantic aesthetics. In fact, the later argument of certain Marxist aestheticians, including Benjamin in his famous essay "The Author as Producer," that art was another form of production like all the rest, derived in part from this prior demystification. Thus the extreme "art for art's sake" position led unexpectedly to its apparent opposite, the reintegration of art and life. The only way to reestablish the distance between the two and contend that autonomous art need not turn into its negation was to distinguish as rigorously as did Adorno between artistic productive techniques and their non-artistic counterparts. Benjamin's refusal to do so was at the heart of their dispute.

12. Habermas, *Legitimation Crisis*, p. 85. For Benjamin's appreciation of Surrealism, see his 1929 essay "Surrealism" in *Reflections: Essays, Aphorisms, Autobiographical Writings*, ed. with intro., Peter Demetz, trans. Edmund Jephcott (New York, 1978). There are other possible candidates for the same function, most notably the *Neue Sachlichkeit*. See the argument in John Willett, *Art and Politics in the Weimar Period: The New Sobriety 1917–1933* (New York, 1978).

13. Habermas, *Legitimation Crisis*, p. 86.

14. Ibid.

15. Bell's article "The Cultural Contradictions of Capitalism" had already been published in *Public Interest* (Fall, 1970) and was cited by Habermas. The book of the same name followed in 1976).

16. Habermas is careful to note that "redemption" for Benjamin never means "the empathy and identification with the past which historicism adopted from Romanticism" (p. 38).

17. In *The Aesthetic Dimension*, published after Marcuse had read Habermas's *Legitimation Crisis* and possibly the Benjamin article, he reversed his position and did consider these implications. See the discussion on p. 50 f. which draws explicitly on Habermas.

18. Habermas, "Consciousness-Raising or Redemptive Criticism," p. 43.

19. Ibid., p. 44.

20. Ibid. For a discussion of the shift in Benjamin's position, see Susan Buck-Morss, *The Origin of Negative Dialectics: Theodor W. Adorno, Walter Benjamin and the Frankfurt Institute* (New York, 1977), p. 160 f.

21. Habermas, "Consciousness-Raising or Redemptive Criticism," p. 46.

22. Philip Brewster and Carl Howard Buchner, "Language and Criticism:

Jürgen Habermas on Walter Benjamin," *New German Critique, 17* (Spring, 1979).

23. Habermas, *Theory and Practice*, p. 241.
24. Habermas, "Consciousness-Raising or Redemptive Criticism," p. 47. The major essays in which Benjamin developed his mimetic theory of language were "On the Mimetic Faculty," in *Reflections* and "Doctrine of the Similar," *New German Critique, 17* (Spring, 1979).
25. Ibid., p. 48.
26. Habermas, "Consciousness-Raising or Redemptive Criticism," p. 48–49.
27. Ibid., p. 57.
28. Ibid., p. 50.
29. Ibid., p. 51.
30. See, for example, his essay "History and Evolution," *Telos, 39* (Spring, 1979).
31. Habermas, "Consciousness-Raising or Redemptive Criticism," p. 58. The full implications of this goal are spelled out in *Communication and the Evolution of Society*, trans. Thomas McCarthy (Boston, 1979) and *Theorie des kommunikativen Handelns*, 2 vols (Frankfurt, 1981).
32. Habermas, "Consciousness-Raising or Redemptive Criticism," p. 58.
33. Ibid., p. 59.
34. Habermas, "Modernity versus Postmodernity," *New German Critique, 22* (Winter, 1981); see Note 31.
35. Habermas, "Modernity versus Postmodernity," p. 8.
36. Ibid., p. 9.
37. Ibid., p. 10–11.
38. Ibid., p. 11.
39. Peter Weiss, *Aesthetik des Widerstands* (Frankfurt, 1975).
40. Brewster and Buchner, p. 23.
41. Anson Rabinbach, "Introduction to Walter Benjamin's 'Doctrine of the Similar'," *New German Critique, 17* (Spring, 1979), p. 64.
42. Richard Wolin, *Walter Benjamin: An Aesthetic of Redemption* (New York, 1982), p. 246.
43. Benjamin, "Probleme der Sprachsoziologie: Ein Sammelreferat," *Zeitschrift für Sozialforschung*, IV, 3 (1935), p. 368.
44. Benjamin, "On the Mimetic Faculty," p. 335.
45. Lyotard, "Reponse à la question: qu'est-ce que le postmoderne?," *Critique*, 419 (April, 1982), p. 358.
46. For Adorno's similar appreciation of the links between the sublime and modern art, see *Aesthetische Theorie*, p. 292.
47. Huyssen, "The Search for Tradition: Avant-garde and Postmodernism in the 1970's," *New German Critique, 22* (Winter, 1981), p. 38.
48. Ibid., p. 36.
49. Bürger, "Avant-garde and Contemporary Aesthetics: A Reply to Jürgen Habermas," *New German Critique, 22* (Winter, 1981).
50. Ibid., p. 20.
51. Ibid., p. 21.
52. Ibid., p. 22.

53. Bürger, *Theorie der Avantgarde* (Frankfurt, 1974).

54. Other deconstructionists who attack Habermas for his alleged belief in a rational utopia of perfect harmony include Dominick LaCapra, "Habermas and the Grounding of Critical Theory," *History and Theory, 16* (1977); and Michael Ryan, *Marxism and Deconstruction: A Critical Articulation* (Baltimore, 1982). McCarthy and Ottmann, in contrast, criticize him for accepting an inevitable hostility between humans and nature. Although they do not suggest the perfect reconciliation that, say, Ernst Bloch would have wanted, they still advocate more of a harmonious unity than Habermas feels is possible. See their contributions to Thompson and Held.

55. Habermas, "A Reply to my Critics," in Thompson and Held, p. 235.

56. Ibid., p. 249.

57. Ibid.

58. Habermas, "Modernity versus Postmodernity," p. 8.

59. Adorno, *Aesthetische Theorie*, p. 86 f.

60. Wolin argues that "language is *rationalized mimesis.* In language the element of correspondence or similarity is wrested away from its primordial state of undifferentiated immediacy (submersion in nature) and raised to the status of *expression*" (p. 243). But why this transformation can be called rational is not very clear. Benjamin, in fact, was well aware of the Romantic roots of his onomatopoeic theory of language. See his remarks on Herder in "Probleme der Sprachsoziologie," p. 250. How such a Romantically derived theory can be harnessed for the Enlightenment intentions of Habermas is difficult to grasp. Habermas's conclusion that Benjamin's attempt to marry his mystically derived linguistic theory with his Marxism was a failure can perhaps be extended to Habermas's own attempt to do something similar.

61. Habermas, *Theorie des kommunikativen Handelns*, vol. 1, p. 512.

62. Gablik, *Progress in Art* (New York, 1977).

2. Reason and Happiness

1. In *Negations*, trans. Jeremy Shapiro (Boston, 1968), pp. 159–200.

2. "The Ego and the Id," *The Standard Edition of the Complete Psychological Works of Sigmund Freud*, vol. XIX, trans. and ed. James Strachey (London, 1975), p. 25.

3. See ibid., chap. V and Freud, "Inhibitions, Symptoms and Anxiety," *SE*, vol. XX (London, 1975), pp. 95–96.

4. Heinz Hartmann, *Ego Psychology and the Problem of Adaptation*, trans. David Rappaport (New York, 1973), pp. 25–26.

5. David Rappaport, "A Historical Survey of Psychoanalytic Ego Psychology," *The Collected Papers of David Rappaport*, ed. Merton Gill (New York, 1967), p. 753.

6. "Moral Development and Ego Identity," *Communication and the Evolution of Society*, ed. Thomas McCarthy (Boston, 1979), p. 71.

7. Quoted in ibid., pp. 72–73.

8. Max Horkheimer and Theodor Adorno, *Dialectic of Enlightenment*, trans. John Cumming (New York, 1972), p. 33.
9. Freud, "The Ego and the Id," p. 40.
10. Horkheimer and Adorno, *Dialectic of Enlightenment*, p. 54.
11. See Margaret Mahler, Fred Pine, and Anni Bergmann, *The Psychological Birth of the Human Infant* (London, 1975).
12. "Sociology and Psychology," *New Left Review, 47* (1968), p. 95.
13. "The End of Internalization," *Telos, 32* (1977), p. 42.
14. See, for example, Andreas Huyssen, "Avant-garde and Contemporary Aesthetics," *New German Critique, 22* (1981), p. 38.
15. Jean Piaget, *The Moral Judgment of the Child*, trans. Marjorie Gabin (New York, 1965), pp. 369–370.
16. Peter Blos, *The Adolescent Passage* (New York, 1979), pp. 141 ff.
17. *The Self and the Object World* (New York, 1977), p. 127.
18. Jürgen Habermas, *Legitimation Crisis*, trans. Thomas McCarthy (Boston, 1975), pp. 90 ff.
19. "The Problem of Nature in Habermas," *Telos, 40* (1979), pp. 41–69.
20. Jürgen Habermas, "Technology and Science as 'Ideology'," in *Toward a Rational Society*, trans. Jeremy Shapiro (Boston, 1970), p. 99. There seems, however, to have been a subtle shift in Habermas's position. Whereas earlier he argued that the norms of bourgeois society could provide the basis for critique, more recently he has been arguing that "bourgeois consciousness has become cynical" and that "bourgeois ideals have gone into retirement." If this is so, where are the norms for critique to be located? Apparently, in the personality structures of individuals who have been socialized in a non-conventional fashion. This seems to be an awfully heavy load for the personality structure to carry. See Habermas, "Historical Materialism and the Development of Normative Structures," *Communication and the Evolution of Society*, p. 97.
21. Habermas, "Moral Development and Ego Identity," p. 90.
22. Ibid., p. 93.
23. Jürgen Habermas, "A Postscript to Knowledge and Human Interest," *Philosophy of the Social Sciences, 3* (1975), p. 170.
24. Marie Jahoda, *Freud and the Dilemmas of Psychology* (New York, 1977), p. 34. Richard Sterba reports Freud as saying, "Methodologists remind me of people who clean their glasses so thoroughly that they never have time to look through them." *Reminiscences of a Viennese Psychoanalyst* (Detroit, 1982), p. 120.
25. See Thomas McCarthy, *The Critical Theory of Jürgen Habermas* (Cambridge, MA, 1978: Cambridge, UK, 1984), pp. 121 ff.
26. See Jürgen Habermas, *Knowledge and Human Interests*, trans. Jeremy Shapiro (Boston, 1971), p. 41.
27. Sigmund Freud, *"Instincts and their Vicissitudes,"* SE, vol. XIV, p. 123.
28. Ibid., pp. 121–122.
29. Habermas, *Knowledge and Human Interests*, p. 241.

30. Jürgen Habermas, "Consciousness-Raising or Redemptive Criticism," *New German Critique, 17* (1979), p. 58.
31. Ibid.
32. Habermas, *Legitimation Crisis*, p. 79.
33. Habermas, "Consciousness-Raising or Redemptive Criticism," p. 58.

3. Habermas and Lyotard on Postmodernity

 1. Jean-Francois Lyotard, *The Postmodern Condition: A Report on Knowledge*, trans. Geoff Bennington and Brian Massumi (Minneapolis, 1984), p. xxiii.
 2. Ibid., pp. xxiv–xxv.
 3. Ibid., p. 60.
 4. Jürgen Habermas, "The Entwinement of Myth and Enlightenment: Re-reading *Dialectic of Enlightenment*," *New German Critique, 26* (1982), p. 28.
 5. Ibid., p. 29.
 6. Ibid., p. 18.
 7. Lyotard, pp. 65–66.
 8. Ibid., p. 60.
 9. Mary Hesse, *Revolutions and Reconstructions in the Philosophy of Science* (Bloomington , 1980), p. 173.
10. Lyotard, p. 8.
11. Ibid., p. 27.
12. Ibid., p. 23.
13. See, for example, Thomas McCarthy, "Rationality and Relativism: Habermas's 'Overcoming' of Hermeneutics," in *Habermas: Critical Debates*, John B. Thompson and David Held, eds (London, 1982).
14. Raymond Geuss, *The Idea of a Critical Theory: Habermas and the Frankfurt School* (Cambridge, 1982), p. 94.
15. Ibid., p. 83.
16. Jürgen Habermas, *Paris Lectures*, III, p. 3. In the spring of 1983, Habermas gave four lectures in Paris on the theme of modernity. These lectures will form part of a book on modernity to be published in 1985. References are to a typescript translation of the lectures by Thomas McCarthy and will be referred to as lectures I, II, III, and IV.
17. Ibid., I, p. 17.
18. Habermas, "Entwinement," p. 18.
19. Habermas, *Paris Lectures*, I, p. 17.
20. Ibid., p. 18.
21. Hans Blumenberg, *The Legitimacy of the Modern Age*, trans. Robert M. Wallace (Cambridge, MA, 1983), p. 184.
22. Habermas, *Paris Lectures*, I, 18.
23. Ibid., III, p. 30.
24. Ibid., p. 15.
25. Ibid., II, p. 28.
26. Habermas, "Entwinement," p. 29.
27. See Iris Murdoch, "Against Dryness," reprinted (from *Encounter*,

1961) in Stanley Hauerwas and Alasdair MacIntyre, eds, *Revisions* (Notre Dame, Indiana, 1983).

28. John Dewey, *Reconstruction in Philosophy* (Boston, 1957), p. 164.
29. Lyotard, p. 72.
30. Ibid., p. 79.
31. I pursue this contrast in a discussion of Derrida called "Deconstruction and Circumvention," in *Critical Inquiry*, 11, 1984.
32. I wrote this essay while enjoying the hospitality of the Center for Advanced Study in the Behaviorial Sciences, and while being supported in part by National Science Foundation Grant No. BNS 820-6304. I am grateful to both institutions, and also to Prof. Martin Jay of the University of California at Berkeley who made several helpful comments on the first version of the essay.

4. Reflections on Rationalization

1. *Theorie des kommunikativen Handelns*, 2 vols (Frankfurt, 1981). Volume 1 has appeared in English translation as *The Theory of Communicative Action, I: Reason and the Rationalization of Society* (Boston, 1984). Numbers appearing in parentheses in the text will refer to the English translation.
2. Appealing to Weber, Habermas views "autonomous art" as a manifestation of cultural rationalization. The conscious grasp of aesthetic values means that the "inner logic" of art can develop independently (160). But he seems also to endorse Adorno's view that this type of rationalization extends to the techniques of realizing values and not to the values themselves (161). In any case, "the cultivation of experiences in dealing with inner nature, the methodical-expressive interpretation of a subjectivity freed from the everyday conventions of knowledge and action" (161) does not appear to be continuous and cumulative in the sense that the cultivation of technically useful knowledge is.
3. See, for example, the discussion of justifying norms in *Legitimation Crisis* (Boston, 1975), pp. 102–117, and in "Legitimation Problems in the Modern State," in *Communication and the Evolution of Society* (Boston, 1979), pp. 183 ff.
4. "What Is Universal Pragmatics?" in *Communication and the Evolution of Society*, esp. pp. 65 ff.
5. Ibid., pp. 66–67.
6. Compare the earlier indications of a constitution-theoretic approach to reality in *Knowledge and Human Interests* (Boston, 1971), and in the "Postscript to *Knowledge and Human Interests*," *Philosophy of the Social Sciences, 3* (1975), 157–189; see also the Christian Gauss lectures delivered at Princeton University in 1971 and now published as "Vorlesungen zu einer sprachtheoretischen Grundlegung der Soziologie," in *Vorstudien und Ergänzungen zur Theorie des kommunikativen Handelns* (Frankfurt, 1984), pp. 11–126.
7. "Meanings, whether embodied in actions, institutions, products of

labor, words, networks of cooperation or documents, can be made accessible only from the inside. Symbolically prestructured reality forms a universe that is hermetically sealed to the view of observers incapable of communicating; that is, it would have to remain incomprehensible to them. The lifeworld is open only to subjects who make use of their competence to speak and act. They gain access to it by participating, at least virtually, in the communications of members and thus becoming at least potential members themselves" (112).

8. See the critique advanced by Herbert Schnädelbach in his review of *Theorie des kommunikativen Handelns* entitled "Transformation der kritischen Theorie."

9. Habermas himself provides a socio-psychological foothold for this ability in the "Einführung" to *Die Entwickung des Ichs*, R. Döbert, J. Habermas, G. Nunner-Winkler, eds. (Cologne, 1977). In his view, a key element in the development of structures of social interaction is the introduction of the perspective of the observer into the domain of interaction. Thus in learning to play social roles.

   . . . the reciprocity of perspectives that is bound to the communication roles of "I" and "thou" can itself be made an object. Each of the participants in interaction can not only take up the role of the other, but can also know from the standpoint of a third person how his own perspective is reciprocally connected with that of the other. The concept of a norm of action that entitles all members of a social group to certain expectations of behavior is first formed when interactive egocentrism has been dismantled to such an extent that the child objectivates reciprocal structures of expectation from the standpoint of a group member not actually involved. The communication role of "alter" is split into the role of the "alter ego" a participating counterpart – and that of the "neuter" who is involved in the interaction only as an observer. (21)

On this account, role behavior presupposes the differentiation and integration of two attitudes: the performative attitude of the subject and the neutral attitude of the observer with the ability to objectivate structures of expectation from a third-person standpoint. The growing child acquires the competence not only for role behavior but for strategic action as well, that is, the ability to view the social norms and values, which he or she now comprehends as such, as boundary conditions for the pursuit of his or her own interests.

Similarly, in adolescence release from the sociocentrism of traditional role behavior turns on the ability to place validity claims in question, to suspend recognition of them, to treat them as hypothetical. At this stage we find

   . . . on the one hand, a complex form of strategic action in which the actor is guided by hypotheses . . . and on the other hand, argumentative speech in which validity claims that have become problematic are problematized . . . as soon as domains of action arise that are no longer regulated exclusively by tradition – as is regularly the case in modern societies – there are matters for conflict that cannot be mastered within the framework of normal role behavior. Apparently one can leave this framework to engage in strategic action (in the sense of behavior based on rational choice) or to attempt to clarify problematic validity claims argumentatively, if once again a fundamentally new attitude is introduced into the domain of interaction, viz. the tentative attitude we adopt toward hypotheses, in which validity claims are suspended. (23–24)

Again, the structures underlying the perception of action situations at this level can be specified either normatively or strategically. When normative claims are subjected to argumentative examination in discourse, the performative attitude is retained at a reflective level. In reflective-strategic action, by contrast, normative claims, which are understood as such, are not dealt with "frontally," in the performative attitude, but in the third-person attitude of a strategic actor.

In his "Reply to Critics" in J. Thompson, D. Held, eds, *Habermas: Critical Debates* (London, 1982), Habermas singles out the ability to adopt a third-person attitude as a presupposition of empirical psychology. Whereas the moral subject and the moral philosopher adopt the performative attitude – of one making moral judgments and, at the reflective level, of one taking part in practical discourse – the developmental psychologist "explains learning processes from the third-person perspective of an observer, such that empirical assumptions are oriented exclusively to the claim to propositional truth" (258). It is just this ability to adopt a non-performative attitude toward normative reality, to comprehend it while bracketing questions of its validity – to which one might appeal in grounding the possibility of social inquiry free from *value judgments*, if not from value relations (*Wertbeziehungen*).

10. See footnote 25 on p. 420 of *The Theory of Communicative Action*.
11. This position bears obvious similarities to Kant's idea of the "two standpoints" in the third section of the *Groundwork*. It does not, however, provide a satisfactory answer to the question we raised above concerning the (conceptual) possibility of adopting different attitudes toward the same *formally* defined world. When social relations are objectified as facts, do they then become elements of the objective world? Or do they remain elements of the social world, viewed now objectively? Habermas is not consistent in his references to the different worlds; for though they are defined and referred to as *formal* world concepts, it seems to me that he repeatedly falls back into the material mode of referring to them as object domains in the usual sense. Moreover, even if we bracket the question of whether objectivating social science is a rationalization of relations to the objective world or to society, we are left with other unanswered questions. Where do the historical-hermeneutic forms of social inquiry fit into the schema? They would seem to involve a performative attitude toward society; but there is no indication of social inquiry of any kind in square ? ?

Where does critical social theory itself belong? Even more troublesome in this regard is what to do with the lifeworld. As defined, it cannot belong to any of the three worlds; and yet it is referred to as the object domain of the social sciences, for instance on p. 108.

12. See the discussion of the relation between these two claims on pp. 312 ff.

13. See Note 9 above.

14. "Walter Benjamin: Consciousness-Raising or Rescuing Critique?" in *Philosophical-Political Profiles* (Cambridge, MA, 1983), p. 156.

15. "Reply to my Critics" in *Habermas: Critical Debates*, pp. 243–244.

16. Ibid., p. 245.

17. Habermas's own reflections along this line in *Knowledge and Human Interests* give rise to a number of aporias, as I have argued in *The Critical Theory of Jürgen Habermas* (Cambridge, MA, 1978: Cambridge, UK, 1984), pp. 91 ff. These spring in part, I think, from the predominantly epistemological orientation of his discussion of "nature-in-itself." If we keep in mind that Habermas's "quasi-transcendental turn" includes the sciences of nature as well, then the superordinate point of view ought to be the moral-practical, for "the cognitive processes to which social life is indissolubly linked function not only as a means to the reproduction of life; in equal measure they themselves determine the definitions of this life. What may appear as naked survival is always in its roots a historical phenomenon. For it is subject to the criteria of what a society intends as the good life" (*Knowledge and Human Interests*, pp. 312–313). Since the "good life" has to be thought of as a marriage of the right and the good, of virtue and happiness, this points in the direction of Kant's attempt to unite the realms of nature and purpose.

18. "Reply to Critics," p. 249.

19. There is a parallel problem in his classification of moral practical relations to nature as not susceptible of rationalization, on the grounds that this could not be carried out "at the same level that Kant attained in his moralization of social relations" (ibid.). Using this approach, one could deny the status of rationalizations to social science and social technology on the grounds that they do not attain the same level as the natural sciences and their associated technologies.

20. *Knowledge and Human Interests*, p. 284.

5. *Questions and Counterquestions*

1. Richard Rorty, *Philosophy and the Mirror of Nature* (Princeton, 1979), p. 390.

2. R. J. Bernstein, *Beyond Objectivism and Relativism* (Philadelphia, 1983).

3. H. Schnädelbach, in *Kommunikation und Reflexion*, ed. W. Kuhlmann and D. Böhler (Frankfurt, 1983), p. 361.

4. J. Habermas, "Die Philosophie als Platzhalter und Interpret," in *Moralbewusstsein und kommunikatives Handeln* (Frankfurt, 1983), pp. 9 ff.

5. Habermas, *Theorie des kommunikativen Handelns*, vol. 2 (Frankfurt, 1981), pp. 586 ff.

6. I have never used the term "neoconservative" in this connection. I did once, in passing, compare the critique of reason in Foucault and Derrida to the "*Young Conservatives*" of the Weimar Republic. Usually Hans Freyer, Arnold Gehlen, Martin Heidegger, Ernst Jünger, and Carl Schmidt are numbered among this group. They all take from Nietzsche the radical gesture of a break with modernity and a revolutionary renewal of pre-modern energies, most often reaching back to archaic times. Like any comparison, it has its weaknesses, but in the German context it does illuminate intellectual affinities that, notwithstanding the politically contrary positions, stem from the authority of Nietzsche. (See my "Modernity Versus Post-Modernity," *New German Critique, 22* (1981), 3–22.)

7. P. Bürger, *Theory of the Avant Garde* (Minneapolis, 1983); also his "Institution Kunst," *Vermittlung, Rezeption, Funktion* (Frankfurt, 1979; and his *Kritik der idealistischen Ästhetik* (Frankfurt, 1983).

8. J. Habermas, *The Theory of Communicative Action* (Boston, 1984), vol. I, pp. 157 ff.

9. Ibid., pp. 40 ff., and the references given there.

10. P. Bürger, *Kritik*, pp. 104 ff.

11. See also P. Bürger, "Das Altern der Moderne," in *Adorno Konferenz 1983*, ed. J. Habermas and L. von Friedeburg (Frankfurt, 1983), pp. 177 ff.

12. Habermas, "Modernity," pp. 12 ff.

13. See A. Wellmer, "Wahrheit, Schein, Versöhnung," in *Adorno-Konferenz*, pp. 138 ff.

14. Ibid., p. 165.

15. Habermas, *The Theory of Communicative Action*, vol. 1, pp. 120 ff. and 130 ff. Also, "Interpretative Social Science and Hermeneuticism," *Social Science as Moral Inquiry*, ed. N. Hann, R. Bellah, P. Rabinow, W. Sullivan (Berkeley, 1983), pp. 251–270.

16. Habermas, *Zur Logik der Sozialwissenschaften* (Frankfurt, 1982).

17. Habermas, *The Theory of Communicative Action*, vol. I, p. 237.

18. Ibid., p. 238.

19. Habermas, *Vorstudien und Ergänzungen zur Theorie des kommunikativen Handelns* (Frankfurt, 1982).

20. On this "rather risky model," see *The Theory of Communicative Action*, vol. I, pp. 239 ff.

21. Ibid.

22. See my "Excursus" on argumentation theory, ibid., pp. 18–42.

23. "In each of these spheres, the process of differentiation is accompanied by a countermovement which always re-incorporates the other two, at first excluded validity aspects under the primacy of the dominant one. In this way, non-objectivist approaches to the human sciences also bring into play the perspectives of moral and aesthetic critique, while not endangering the primacy of the question of truth; only in this way

is an encompassing theory of society possible. The discussion of an ethics of responsibility and the more pronounced consideration of utilitarian motives bring the perspectives of the calculation of consequences and the interpretation of needs into play in universalistic ethics, perspectives which lie within the cognitive and expressive validity domains; in this way, materialistic ideas can also be given their due, without endangering the autonomy of the moral perspective. Finally, post-avant garde art is characterized by the simultaneous presence of realistic and engaged intentions, along with the authentic continuation of classical modernity, which distilled out the internal meaning of the aesthetic sphere. With realistic and engaged art, once again the cognitive and moral-practical moments enter into art, at the level of the wealth of form set free by the avant garde." Habermas, *Theorie des kommunikativen Handelns*, vol. II, pp. 585–586.

24. See Habermas, "Über Moralität und Sittlichkeit: was macht eine Lebensform rational?" in *Rationalität*, ed. H. Schnädelbach (Frankfurt, 1984), pp. 218 ff.

25. This was in any case my intention in the Freud chapter of *Knowledge and Human Interests*. I do not find any basis in Freud for the strict separation between a clinically justified theory of neurosis and a metapsychological superstructure that Adolf Grünbaum proposes in "Freud's Theory: The Perspective of a Philosopher of Science," *Proceedings and Addresses of the American Philosophical Association, 57* (1983), 57, no. 6. This separation makes the specific roots of Freudian theory in the experiences of the analytic dialogue unrecognizable. Such an operation may be useful for the argumentative purpose of assimilating Freudian theory to the standard model of unified science, only to reject it then for failing to measure up to its standards. At the same time, it expresses the simple decision not to consider the hermeneutic character of this science.

26. Habermas, "Der Universalitätsanspruch der Hermeneutik," in *Zur Logik der Sozialwissenschaften*, pp. 331 ff.; also "Überlegungen zur Kommunikationspathologie," in *Vorstudien*, pp. 226 ff.

27. Habermas, *Moralbewusstsein*, pp. 152–168.

28. R. Döbert, J. Habermas, and G. Nunner-Winkler, *Entwicklung des Ichs* (Köln, 1977), pp. 9 ff.

29. K. Horn expresses similar reservations in "Geheime kulturalistische Tendenzen der modernen psychoanalytischen Orthodoxie," in *Psychoanlyse als Wissenschaft* (Frankfurt, 1971), pp. 93 ff.

30. With respect to the empirical questions, I would like to point out that my reflections on the change in symptoms typical of our times and on the significance of the adolescence crisis are quite similar to those of Whitebook. See my *Theorie des kommunikativen Handelns*, vol. 2, pp. 567–571.

31. Habermas, "Moral Development and Ego Identity," in *Communication and the Evolution of Society* (Boston, 1979), pp. 78 ff.

32. Habermas, "A Reply to My Critics," in *Habermas: Critical Debates*,

ed. J. B. Thompson and D. Held (London, 1982), pp. 258 ff. Also see the essays in my *Moralbewusstsein und kommunikatives Handeln*.

33. Habermas, "Moral Development and Ego Identity," p. 94.

Notes on Contributors

Richard J. Bernstein is professor of philosophy at Haverford College. He is the author of *Praxis and Action, The Restructuring of Social and Political Theory*, and *Beyond Objectivism and Relativism*. He was editor of *Praxis International*, 1981–84.

Anthony Giddens is Reader in Sociology at the University of Cambridge. He has written extensively on problems in social theory and the philosophy of social science. His most recent book is *The Constitution of Society*. He is an editor of Polity Press.

Jürgen Habermas is professor of philosophy at the University of Frankfurt. He was co-director of the Max Planck Institute in Starnberg. A major book dealing with theories of modernity and postmodernity will be published in 1985.

Martin Jay is professor of history at the University of California, Berkeley. He is the author of *The Dialectical Imagination*. His most recent books include *Marxism and Totality: The Adventures of a Concept from Lukács to Habermas* and *Adorno*.

Thomas McCarthy is associate professor of philosophy at Boston University. He is the English translator of several books by Jürgen Habermas and the author of *The Critical Theory of Jürgen Habermas*. He is the general editor of the series, "Studies in Contemporary German Social Thought" published by MIT Press.

Richard Rorty is professor of humanities at the University of Virginia. He is the author of *The Linguistic Turn, Philosophy and the Mirror of Nature*, and *Consequences of Pragmatism*. He is currently writing a book on Martin Heidegger.

Albrecht Wellmer is professor of philosophy at the University of Konstanz. He is the author of *The Critical Theory of Society*. A collection of his essays dealing with the dialectic of modernity and postmodernity will be published by Suhrkamp Verlag in 1985.

Joel Whitebook is an associate editor of *Telos*. He has taught philosophy at the New School for Social Research and has written extensively about Critical Theory. He is a psychoanalytic candidate at the New York Freudian Society.

Bibliographical Note

There are two excellent bibliographies of works by and on Habermas. See the "Select Bibliography" in *Habermas: Critical Debates*, edited by John B. Thompson and David Held (London: Macmillan, 1982). See also Rene Götzen and Frederick van Gelder, "Jürgen Habermas: The Complete Oeuvre. A Bibliography of Primary Literature, Translations and Reviews," *Human Studies*, 2 (1979). This bibliography is reprinted in the paperback edition of Thomas McCarthy, *The Critical Theory of Jürgen Habermas* (Cambridge, MA: MIT Press, 1978; Cambridge: Polity Press, 1984).

Index

and cultural differentiation
166–73
and morality 214
and reason 12, 17
transcendental philosophy 16,
17, 211
knowledge 170–1, 173, 193
in Habermas 4, 8–11, 13–14,
16, 96, 98, 112–14, 177–83,
189–90, 207–9
and hermeneutics 9, 205
and narrative 167–8
objectivity of 205
"pre-theoretical" 16
scientific 8–9, 163, 181–2, 215
see also interests, cognitive
Knowledge and Human Interests 4,
8–15, 17, 96, 161, 190n17
Kohl, Helmut 81, 88n15
Kohlberg, Lawrence 3, 16, 117,
131, 153–4, 159
Kolakowski, Leszek 193
Kosík, Karl 72
Kristol, Irving 79
Kuhn, Thomas 163

language:
in Benjamin 130–1, 133–4
in Habermas 51, 96, 99, 116–17,
129–31, 133–4, 154–7, 187
in Mead 105
in Parsons 108
Lask, Emil 206
law:
bourgeois 35–6, 40, 51–2, 65
in Critical Theory 50
in Habermas 55, 62–3, 102
universalization of 40, 84
in Weber 40, 42, 43, 54, 108
"Legitimation Crisis" 126–7
Lenin, V. I. 38, 167
Lévi-Strauss, C. 117–18
Lichtheim, George 1, 3
life-world (*Lebenswelt*) 22–4,
26–7, 62, 89, 93, 101–2,
105–6, 120, 158–9, 202, 215
idealized 57–61

integration of 28, 55, 107–8,
132, 135–7, 139
"internal colonization" 55,
108–9, 110–11, 121, 133
rationalization of 54–8, 60
"linguistic turn" of Habermas 14,
17–18, 116, 155, 157
Lipset, Seymour Martin 79
Lowenthal, Leo 27, 69, 71, 125
Lowenthal, Richard 84, 88
Lübbe, Hermann 92
Luhmann, Niklas 30, 95, 106, 131
Lukács, Georg 2, 6, 103, 105–6
and modernity 39, 41
rationalization 22, 97
Lukes, Steven 52
Lyotard, Jean-François 30, 134–6,
138
on postmodernity 161, 174–5
on science and narrative 162–5,
170–5

McCarthy, Thomas 10, 28–9, 136,
164, 176–91, 198, 200, 203–9,
211, 214, 216
Mallarmé, S. 134
Marcuse, Herbert 2, 29, 62, 67–77,
130, 199, 211
affirmative feature 67–70, 73
and Freud 27, 140–2, 144–5,
157, 159, 211
and happiness 152–3
and Heidegger 70–1
and modernity 67
negative dialectics 44, 45, 70
and *Praxis* group 31
see also aesthetic experience
Marković, Mihailo 32
Marx, Karl 7–8, 14, 58, 64, 108–10,
125, 160, 161, 169, 173, 210
and Frankfurt School 140
influence on Habermas 2, 3, 11,
26, 57, 100, 120–1, 211, 216
and Marcuse 72
on reason 13, 22, 50–1
theory of capitalism 35–9, 44,
45, 52, 107–10